Man as a Social Being
and the Mission of Conscience

Karl König M.D. (Vienna)

MAN AS A SOCIAL BEING
AND THE MISSION OF CONSCIENCE

The Threefold Structure of the Social Organism
Five Lectures, 2nd–30th March 1964

The Threefold Social Order
Single Lecture, 9th August 1964

On Community Building
Three Lectures, 20th–29th September 1964

Man as a Social Being and the Mission of Conscience
Five lectures, 13th December 1964–6th January 1965

Re-awakening and Resurrection
Four Lectures, 11th–19th April 1965

The Social Organism is Threefold
Essay, undated

KARL KÖNIG

Translated by Rev. Baruch Urieli
Edited by Nicholas Poole

Camphill Press

1st Edition 1990

Published by Camphill Press
on behalf of
The Association of Camphill Communities

British Library Cataloguing in Publication Data

König, Karl *1902–1966*
Man as a social being.
1. Christian social ethics
I. Title
241

ISBN 0 904145 36 0
ISBN 0 904145 37 9 pbk

The publication of this volume
has been generously assisted by
a grant from Delrow College

Typeset by Camphill Press, Botton Village
Printed by Studio Print, Guisborough

Contents

The Threefold Structure of the Social Organism

The Threefold Social Order

On Community Building

Man as a Social Being and the Mission of Conscience

Re-awakening and Resurrection

The Social Organism is Threefold

Introduction

In September 1962, in the Camphill Schools near Aberdeen, Dr. Karl König opened the first hall of the Camphill Movement, a movement which has since grown to become a world-wide organisation. It was the crowning of twenty-three years of work in Britain in the service of the child in need of special care. This hall, which was called the Hall of Memory and Conscience, represented Dr. König's battle for the recognition of the true stature of man hidden in every child and adult, whatever his or her limitation or handicap may be.

Not long after this event Karl König decided to hand over his responsibilities in Britain to younger members of the Camphill Movement and to spend what were to be the last, very few years of his life in one of the Camphill centres in Germany. In doing so he brought a very special gift to the culture of middle Europe: his profound insight concerning man as a social being, as a *zoon politikon*. Seventeen of the thirty-two lectures which Karl König delivered in Camphill in Germany during this period are concerned with or related to man as a social being. These seventeen lectures are published in this volume.

Karl König's concern with the social aspect of the human being arose out of his conviction that healing can be brought to the so-called handicapped child and adult only in a setting that is truly human, i.e. that is truly social. As he states in the lecture of 22 March 1964: 'Man can only be *man* if he is together with his fellow men: if he is alone he is not man. We are born out of our fellow man; fed and taught by our fellow men; loved and hated by our fellow men.' Of course, this is an extreme statement but it highlights how, like the great social reformers of the eighteenth and nineteenth centuries before him, Karl König was keenly aware of the importance of the social setting. However, in König's work the inner dimension that is now added to the outer one is especially underlined.

In the first five of these lectures Karl König speaks about the ideals of a threefold structure of the social organism. Drawing on his intimate knowledge of the teachings of Rudolf Steiner on this subject, he traces back their historic origins, elaborates on them and gradually leads the listener or reader to an understanding of social structures and social phenomena in the past and in the present. In the second cycle of lectures, given about half a year later in the autumn of 1964, he turns to two historic buildings—a castle and a congress centre—and, using these two structures as exemplars, enters into the secrets of community building. Three months later follow the five lectures given during Advent and Christmastide. These are entirely introspective. The processes of the inner relation of man to man are described in the light of the Advent and Christmas experiences of man. Gradually the growing voice of conscience is recognised in them, a voice which is to develop from its still, small beginnings into a challenge; a call that is to be the compass for the future development of man.

Finally, these are followed three months later during Holy Week and Easter 1965 by the four lectures entitled *Reawakening and Resurrection*. Here we are shown that the being of man comprises not only the earth and all that is on it, but reaches to the uttermost part of the earth, embracing even the spheres of life which surround it. But just as in the previous set of lectures we were led to understand that Christ is the core of the processes which take place from human Ego to human Ego, so we are now made aware that the Risen One is also the core of the pulse-beat and breath with which man encompasses the depths of the earth and the spheres of life surrounding it. Man can only be a social being in as much as he is a Christian being; a Christ-endowed being. In this way Karl König presented to his friends in Germany what amounts to a spiritual and moral legacy. Less than a year later he crossed the threshold.

Added to the eighteen lectures of this volume is a short,

undated essay on the social organism discovered in the literary estate of Karl König. It is probably of much earlier origin than these lectures and the uncrystallised presentation of the last nine paragraphs indicate that the essay was never fully completed. Nevertheless, in its challenging statements it contains a number of valuable images which—if worked upon *meditatively*—can greatly deepen our understanding of the social being of man. If, for example, the family is described as the unit of the life of rights, such a statement can certainly not be taken at face value. Only if it is recognised that a family is a grouping of destiny that is ordered into ranks of standing (c.f. Karl König's book *Brothers and Sisters*), does a comparison with the life of rights become tenable. The same holds good for the statement that the congregation is the unit of economic life. This can only be accepted if we realise that a congregation gathers around an altar in order to fulfil worthily the Divine Service in the togetherness of man, just as a workforce gathers around a work bench in order to create a new work of art or craft. The images of family or religious congregation can immensely deepen the concepts of legal or economic life.

Karl König's insights into the social stature of man have been fundamental for the development of the Camphill Movement. May these insights now go out into the wide world and help to build community wherever it is needed.

Rev. Baruch Urieli.

The Threefold Structure of the Social Organism

Five Lectures

Föhrenbühl and Brachenreuthe, 2nd–30th March 1964.

First Lecture

Föhrenbühl, 2nd March 1964

It is my intention in these lectures to work on the threefold structure of the social organism. I thought that today I would only give an introduction so as to provide the historical background to Rudolf Steiner's work on this subject. Without doing this we could not easily gain a true understanding of the idea of a social organism in a threefold form.

We know, of course, that this idea was developed during the First World War. In 1916 Rudolf Steiner conceived his first thoughts on this subject and then, in 1917 and 1918, he endeavoured to formulate them as short memoranda which were then handed to leading personalities ruling at that time. These included the Crown Prince of Baden, who became Chancellor of the German Empire in the last year of the war; Foreign Minister Kuhlmann, and the Austrian Emperor. But the memoranda made hardly any impact, and unfortunately we have to concede that all this effort towards a threefold structure of the social organism bore no results whatsoever. Seen superficially, as a movement it failed. We must confess this openly because it would falsify history if we said that in this realm Rudolf Steiner achieved any outer success at all. His followers, our anthroposophical friends, through their own lack of understanding were unable to represent these ideas in such a way that they could be truly understood. This is no accusation: none of us would have done any better. Although the tendencies of the age called for an idea such as that of a threefold social structure, they did not allow it to become reality and so it had to be gradually buried from 1920 or 1921 onward. Rudolf Steiner suffered greatly through the fact that things developed in this way. Be that as it may, the idea of a threefold social structure is closely connected with the second decade of the century, our twentieth century, in which it was born.

It is also not without significance that we occupy ourselves with it today, because exactly half a century has now passed since the beginning of the First World War, an event that dissolved and in fact destroyed those social orders which had become established in Europe and America since the beginning of modern times. It was one of the greatest historic events in the entire development of mankind, and although half a century has passed since then we cannot yet fully appreciate this because we still live immersed in its after-effects. Through the First World War the social structure which had evolved since the fourteenth, fifteenth and sixteenth centuries was destroyed.

What social structure was this? It was in fact the first attempt towards a social constitution for the fifth post-Atlantean epoch; a first European attempt to order states in such a way that the freedom of the individual, of the single personality, was given a new opportunity to unfold. If we look at ancient Rome and the decay of its great empire, or at the decline of the great Egyptian or Persian empires—and we could go further and further back—it would be superficial to say that we can see how similar things have happened before. This is not the case. What is happening around us today is so utterly new, historically, that one can hardly compare it with any former events. This has been recognised by a number of present day historians, and if you have the time to study a book such as *Freedom and Domination*[1] by the recently deceased Rüstow, you will realise that here is a man who has come to the realisation that our present time cannot be regarded as a mere repetition of any preceding epoch, but is something completely new. This evolving of a new order was severely shaken by the chaos of the First World War, and was then utterly destroyed in the events that followed it and which led to the Second World War. Indeed, the social renewal which Rudolf Steiner strove for in the twenties of this century has not succeeded. Therefore today we stand amid a heap of ruins of former social orders from which, stone by stone, the 'house' of the coming social order will have to be rebuilt.

We can now ask what really happened in the years since the fifteenth, sixteenth and seventeenth centuries? What kind of constitution developed over this time? We can, of course, describe the development of modern times in a number of ways, saying for example that these times are essentially nothing else than the beginning of the era of scientific thinking. The great Galileo (whose 400th birthday it was two weeks ago), along with the great scientific thinkers of the sixteenth and seventeenth centuries, among them Copernicus and Kepler, started the revolution in human thinking and the new cognition of nature which are based on experience and experiment. This is one aspect.

However, we could also say that modern times—and here I mean all that is contained in recent centuries—are characterised by the fact that the Reformation spread widely, struggling to overcome the old, traditional religious forms of the Christian faith by taking as its reference the single individual who tries to regulate his personal relation to the supersensible world or to God. This is also a fully justified characterisation of the beginning of modern times, in which we have both the development of natural scientific thinking, based on sensory experience, observation and experiment, and also the Reformation.

A further essential point concerns the age of discovery. From Europe—notably England, Holland, Portugal and Spain—seafarers set out to discover the roundness of the earth; to make the far continents accessible and to widen their view of the world which, in the geographical sense, had until then been narrow. People broke out of their medieval dwellings in towns and villages because they wanted to know what really was in the North and South, in the East and West. In fact, people had known this in earlier times, but now they wanted to experience it with their senses; they wanted the experience of discovering unknown countries, and so they undertook their great voyages. This is also a characteristic of the beginning of modern times.

Finally, the process of the mechanisation of life began, a process which is still continuing and in which we all live today. It is a process characterised by the rising importance of machinery and technology; of mechanisation expressed in the ordering of both the practical, industrial life, as well as of spiritual life by means of the magnificent scientific discoveries which have been made. This has, of course, changed the life of the states and their institutions fundamentally.

What has it all led to? It has given rise to what we call the centralised state. A centralised state did not exist at all in the ninth, tenth, eleventh and twelfth centuries, it could only develop from the beginning of modern times. The term centralised state means a political structure which comprises and governs most of the spheres of social life.

From what I have just mentioned you can see that this has developed from that historical moment when the voyages of discovery were made. For when the newly discovered continents were opened up they could not be left alone, and consequently Spain, Portugal, England, Holland and finally—straggling behind as always—Germany, each built up a colonial empire. This meant that streams of people went out to these newly discovered continents, settled there as Spaniards, Portuguese, English, Dutch and Germans, thereby annexing these countries to their homelands so that they became regions of exploitation for the respective governments. In this way England acquired an empire, Spain a short-lived empire and Holland a great empire. Thus the state began to take upon itself the exploitation of economic life. It became not only the protector but also the usufructuary of the markets which developed in South Africa, America, or wherever. India became a part of Great Britain, Indo-China a part of France, and Indonesia a part of Holland. The state became the bearer of the economy.

At the same time something else developed which is hardly noticed today but which, twenty or thirty years ago, was still an essential aspect of the life of the state: a state church developed. Churches, and hence also the religious life, became part of the state. This had its roots in the Reformation. The main point here is not whether the Reformation developed like the English Reformation under Henry VIII, or like the German Reformation; what matters is that the church was fundamentally reformed so that the individual could find his own relationship to the supersensible, and consequently the religious life became subordinate to the state. You know that in the sixteenth and seventeenth centuries the principle *cuius regio, eius religio* ruled, which means 'in whose region I live, his religion must I embrace'. If I had lived in Saxony I would have had to be a Protestant; if I had lived in Austria, a Catholic—or I would have been forced to emigrate. Mind you, those were not yet the dark times of the Thirty Years War! However, if we are honest things became even worse in the twentieth century.

I should still add the following. I said that the religious life became an affair of the state and that the economic life was also regulated by the state. But the state itself was determined by the principle of Roman Law contained within its fundamental structure. This was the heritage of the fourth post-Atlantean epoch, and the centralised state was the social organization by which the separate spheres of human life were mixed together, united and forged into a single unit. Within this structure it was of course quite possible for men to pursue their destinies. As a social structure it was also fully appropriate until a certain moment which fell at the turning point of the eighteenth and nineteenth century, approximately between 1760 and 1820. This was the time of the Industrial Revolution, the French Revolution and the Napoleonic Wars. It was an historic juncture of similar importance then as was the First World War in our own century. From that time onward the centralised state could only be preserved by force.

I do not want to go into all the historical details, but one thing ought to be mentioned. Through the Industrial Revolution something dreadful, but nonetheless necessary, entered the thinking and the will of men, and this was the production of goods in bulk. For example, people stopped producing only as many shoes as there were feet to wear them. The idea suddenly spread that in order to have progress prices must be brought down so that everyone can afford to wear shoes; everyone can possess tables and chairs; everyone can have suits—and not only two or three, but twenty suits! This became possible through the fact that by means of technical inventions these articles could be produced in bulk.

This gave rise to another factor which we should recognise clearly, namely that labour was no longer simply labour but, to speak in Marxist terms, had become a commodity. Man could sell his working power. Can you understand what I mean? The activity of the muscles, the will to work, became saleable. Labour was sold to those people whose capital gave them the power to introduce so many machines that they were able to degrade the proletarian to the level of a slave. We should never forget that the middle of the last century was the worst time in this respect. Children were made to work in factories from the age of five onwards, and parents were forced to have twelve, fourteen, even sixteen children so as to send them as quickly as possible into the factories in order that the few pennies which the children earned in a twelve or fourteen hour working day could be used for food and drink. Only towards the end of the last century were laws regulating child labour really put into practice in England, Scotland, Germany and Holland. The nineteenth century was indeed the century in which labour was so degraded that it became a commodity.

At the same time something else happened that had a similarly destructive effect on social life, and this was that capital took hold of landed property. People believed, as they still do today, that the best investment was to possess land. The consequence of this was that agriculture was deprived of the land and became a servant, a slave of capital. This meant—and these two things are closely connected with each other—that human labour was degraded to the level of a commodity, and that land, the real estate which is part and parcel of Mother Earth, became an investment. All this was indeed decisive for the social life of the nineteenth century. It was the foundation on which the centralised states were built.

We shall continue to dwell on this in the coming lecture, but now I would like to point out a fact which alone made it possible for the madness of National Socialism, the most despicable activity of this century, to gain a footing in this country.* Having first degraded labour into a commodity, the Ruhr industrialists

* The reader is reminded that Dr. König is speaking in Germany.

then united with the estate owners in the east of this country and thus prepared the horse, so to speak, on which barbarism could force its way into Middle Europe. This has to be said, if only once, and it does not matter if many or few hear it. But the results of what had been prepared in the nineteenth century, namely that land became capital and labour became a commodity, had to be wiped out. For those of you who remember (although hardly any of you here will be able to) it is still possible to recollect the first warning trumpet which sounded in the spring of 1912 when the *Titanic* sank, and with her the representatives of those layers of society which had brought about what I have just described. This clarion call was hardly heard, and then came 28th June 1914. I still remember that day clearly. It was a day of radiant sunshine, a Sunday, and the people of Vienna were out for walks. I was with my father beside the Danube and suddenly it seemed as if life had stopped. I hardly understood when I was told that the Crown Prince, Franz Ferdinand of Austria, had been assassinated in Sarajewo. But in that event we sensed what the British Foreign Minister expressed on August 1st of that same year with the words 'The lights over Europe are going out'. Since then the lights over Europe have not been relit, they have remained dark. In that First World War twelve million people were killed and thirty million became cripples. Mankind allowed this to happen; it then encouraged a Second World War and is now speedily slithering into a third.

Then followed the disastrous Treaty of Versailles in 1918. Through their stupidity and autocratic principles the ruling circles of that time, notably Clemenceau (the 'father' of De Gaulle), Lloyd George and Woodrow Wilson—perhaps in the present context one could even call them criminals—the opportunity to rebuild Europe was arbitrarily stamped out. The idiocy which is seen in France today has its forerunners in Poincare and Clemenceau, and what is happening in Great Britain now is very similar to what Lloyd George committed then. But what did Woodrow Wilson intend? He wanted one thing only. He recognised that the centralised state had come to an end and that something else would have to emerge in its stead, and so he took up the

Napoleonic idea of the national state. Of course, for nationalities to form states is the worst thing imaginable! However, Woodrow Wilson took this idea very seriously but the others cheated him both openly and behind his back. Do you know how this was done at Versailles? Clemenceau and Lloyd George feared a re-unification of the German peoples of Austria and of Middle Europe, so they imposed on Woodrow Wilson a plan in which they proposed to conclude a treaty with Austria in order to protect the freedom of that country in relation to Germany—which was something Woodrow Wilson could understand. During the treaties they cheated him in similar ways wherever they could. They were convinced, of course, that their existing states were ideal, but that if they allowed others to emerge then they would lose their own power; they might lose their colonies and so would lose their spheres of influence. Therefore they concluded treaties in the most underhand, deceitful way in order to prevent any such national states really coming into being. Nevertheless, national states did form, as in Poland, Yugoslavia, Czechoslovakia, Hungary. But what had once been Austria was dismembered and destroyed: what could have become Middle Europe was stamped out.

However, something further should be added. In this chaos the consciousness of the proletariat awoke and with it arose a longing for social reform. It was believed that these reforms (which we shall consider in the next lecture) could be brought about by offering the workmen a spiritual life which was materialistic and agnostic. The proletariat accepted this and we can see the results today. Workmen have become a class of satisfied, well-to-do *petit bourgeoisie* who no doubt talk about the proletarian revolution from time to time, but for them it has become an empty phrase.

It was into this state of affairs that Rudolf Steiner introduced the idea of a threefold structure for the social organism, an idea which took into account the individual as well as the state in order to form those structures which should rightly develop in our time. Rudolf Steiner rejected the national state completely! He also rejected the centralised state, the one coming from the past and the other demanded by a false view of the future. Between these two he placed something which can be described in the following way. The state must be limited to the realm of the legal life, which means that the state's task is to order the legal inter-relationships of its citizens. The state must neither interfere with the economy, nor with religion and the spiritual life. The state is the organisation through which the citizen is held legally in his place. In the next few centuries it will become clear that the citizen rightly enjoys the protection of the state, for the judiciary and the police all belong to the sphere of the state. But economy will be freed from the realm of the state, and also labour and landed property will be freed from the realm of economy. Economy is nothing else but the production, distribution and sale of goods. (Goods can be produced by agriculture, or any other process.) To produce, dispatch and sell goods is an activity that does not belong to the realm of the state; it should be administered quite independently of the state and in a parliamentary way by those who produce, dispatch and sell goods. However, labour, or rather the legal aspect of labour, does belong to the state since labour is not a commodity. (We shall come back to this next time.) Also land, real estate, does not belong in the sphere of economy. However, the *laws* concerning landed property are part of the state, just as are the laws governing labour, but a commodity and everything that leads to the production, distribution and sale of commodities belongs in the realm of economy.

Then there is the sphere of the free spiritual life in which belong the realms of education, of creed, of research and of art—and also, of course, capital. Capital is part of the realm of the free spiritual life, because its only justification lies in its serving the objectives of the free spiritual life. Capital is not a possession: capital is the means by which the free spiritual life is made possible.

You see, instead of a centralised structure a threefold order would be created. Parts of it do develop, but unfortunately with epileptic cramps, as for example, an organisation such as the Common Market which attempts to develop associations within the economic life. But as soon as an idiot like De Gaulle comes along who wants to turn it into a political organisation, the politicians are all taken in and immediately try to form a centralised, political Europe! We have to see the reality in these things. By this I mean that the heap of ruins on which we stand today does offer some starting points for social growth, but these are hardly understood and therefore they perish again and again.

This is as far as I wanted to go today. Perhaps it gives you a bit of background and will also call forth an interest to study the book, *The Threefold Social Order.*[2]

Second Lecture

Brachenreuthe, 8th March 1964

Today we will continue our contemplation of the threefold structure of the social organism. You will perhaps remember how we tried first of all to sketch the historical background of the events which, at the end of the First World War and the beginning of the twenties, lead to the idea of the threefold structure of the social organism being put into the world by Rudolf Steiner for the first time. However, despite the fact that he spoke about it to thousands of people, the idea of a threefold structure was only understood by a few. Among those who did not understand it and who at that time held leading positions in society, the idea was either ridiculed or rejected and as a result further developments followed which I shall try to characterise a little today. I shall try at first to describe, as a kind of backcloth, whence present day social institutions and experiments have developed.

You will recall how in the last lecture we tried to understand the historical formation of centralised states, namely those European—and later American—institutions through which the state became the carrier of all three spheres of the social organism; of the economic, the legal and the spiritual life. That these three spheres exist need not be explained, for this is understood of itself. Anyone who concerns himself, however little, with man as a social being, will know how this becomes clear from the phenomena: that if one is a social being then one lives in the spheres of the economic, the legal and the spiritual life. This cannot be denied, just as one cannot sensibly ask whether we have eyes, ears and limbs. We need not prove this. In exactly the same way the three spheres of social life need not be proven, for they are simply the limbs, the parts of the human social organisation. These three spheres were unified historically in the centralised state–which still exists to a large extent today. The European centralised state began to direct the economic life; to rule out of the legal life, and to deeply influence the spiritual life.

However, something else has developed, particularly in this century, through the unfortunate policy of Woodrow Wilson and the misguided policies that followed at the end of the Second World War, so that all we meet today in the spiritual life, the political life, and the economic life are the catastrophies which resulted from the gradual formation of national states.

What is happening today in China, Asia, and in Europe under the protection both of the United Nations and of the great power blocks of the East and West, amounts to one of the most devastating political experiments which mankind has ever made. For the failure of colonialism is its failure to educate those people who had been exploited and suppressed for centuries by the centralised states (which are themselves ruled by economics). The failure of such states to set free their utterly exploited and uneducated children–and the error of filling them with the poison of nationalism–has led to the continual eruptions which destroy the entire political life of the world, and will certainly lead to further explosions. One can only be astonished that people applaud, out of a completely idiotic idealism, when a Congo or a Nigeria–or any other such state–is given, as we say, national freedom. This is not the fault of these states themselves; rather it is the fault of those who, over the last three or four centuries, have failed to see, understand and strive for what should be justly due to these so called 'natives'.

There are two things here and we have to discern clearly that they are polar opposites if we are not to just babble a repetition of the idea of the threefold structure of the social organism, or to merely repeat the kind of newspaper gossip by which we are continually misled today. On the one hand there is the attempt to proclaim centralised states; on the other hand the attempt to proclaim national states. We have already spoken about the centralised states and we have seen that they have their origin in the Anglo-Saxon state. The centralised state evolved in earlier centuries in such a way that the economic life became the dominant influence, forcing the legal life and the spiritual life more and more under its domination. This can still be experienced today quite clearly in England, Scotland, America, Holland, Scandinavia and so on. Everything that falls within the sphere of influence of the Anglo-Saxon peoples tries to maintain the old Utopian idea of the centralised state under the control of the economic life. So we must ask where is the origin of national states to be found? Just as the centralised state originated in the Anglo-Saxon countries, so the national state had its origin in one European country only, and that was in France. As early as the fourteenth century the idea of nationalism arose under Philip le Bel. (It was Philip who enticed the Pope to Avignon in France and held him there as a prisoner, and who also stamped out the great international organization of the Knights Templar.) This idea then developed under the various rulers of France. I cannot now go into the details of French history, but if you were to really study it according to the phenomena you would recognise that it is nothing but a national state coming into being, a state which came to a remarkable flowering under Louis XIV and which then attempted to transform the whole of Europe into national states under Napoleon I.

If you study Napoleon's campaigns and conquests, you will discover that he intended to split Europe into many very small, diverse national states and then to set one of his relatives as ruler over each of them. It was nothing but a kind of family business which was intended to destroy Europe and bring the idea of French nationalism to full sovereignty. What we see today under De Gaulle is indeed only a repeated attempt to put the idea of nationalist France as the 'sun of all peoples' into the skies. Will you please note that it is nothing else than the latest, but already somewhat ridiculous, attempt to establish French nationalism.

However, it is important to understand what developed partly in England and partly in France. You see, Joan of Arc's mission was to drive the English out of France and so end the Hundred Years' War by restricting England to its islands and giving back to France its continental domain. As a result the development of the centralised state, bound up as it is with imperialism and the spreading of the whole economic life, was achieved. On the other hand, the idea of the national state was connected with France. Both these directions of development had to emerge because both were necessary. This happened simultaneously with the dawning of the age of the Consciousness-soul at the beginning of the fifteenth century. Here one can see—at least I can see—how two entirely different but necessary impulses of the social structure of states have developed. They permeated Europe until at the end of the eighteenth and the beginning of the nineteenth century something new arose which tried to penetrate the structures of both the centralised and the national state and, by means of revolutions, to radically change them.

This was so new and unexpected that it was completely unforseen by those who lived a secure, carefree life. A migration of people suddenly began in Europe, yet it was not a horizontal but a vertical migration, for those who belonged to the lower classes pressed upwards. Those who until that time had been ordinary workers—servants, serfs, agricultural labourers and so on—began to drift into the towns and became the industrial proletariat. This occurred first and foremost in England and thereby brought about what is called the Industrial Revolution. Spinning machines were invented which for the first time could handle cotton, and consequently an *industrial* economic life first arose in England. In France however, all this took place in a quite different fashion. It occurred in such a way that the poor, the oppressed, the servants and the agricultural labourers revolted against their masters; against the upper classes. This was an entirely different revolution from the Industrial Revolution in England and therefore it would be quite wrong to equate the two and simply say: Well, it took place here in one way and there in another. The Industrial Revolution took place in the economic life, but the French Revolution—in which for the first time the slogan 'Liberty, Equality, Fraternity' was used—happened solely in the legal life. We must be able to see this clearly in order to do justice to both revolutions. In Middle Europe at that time (Germany did not yet exist as a socio-political entity) a kind of renaissance in the spiritual life was taking place; poetry and philosophy suddenly took on new life.

Therefore we can see that in England the revolution took place in the economic life; in France it occurred in the legal life, while in the German regions of Middle Europe it took place in the spiritual life. These are three events which, although connected with each other, are entirely different in themselves and different from each other; for in England the masses demanded fraternity; in France they wanted equality, and in Germany they asked for freedom. I have described this because it is the historic background to what was proclaimed at the beginning of the twentieth century as the idea of the threefold structure of the social organism. You can see that these processes are historic, preparing for what took place a hundred years later.

However, these three starting points at the turning of the eighteenth and nineteenth century were later wiped out. In England growing colonialism took hold of the Industrial Revolution, grasping a certain share of the profits made by exploiting the colonies. In France the French Revolution was destroyed by Napoleonism, which was a form of nationalism, while in Germany the idealism that strove for freedom was swallowed up by the charming Biedermaier and quite new conditions set in. Bourgeois conditions prevailed which no longer had anything to do with liberty, equality and fraternity. But what I called the vertical migration of people from below upwards could not be stopped, in spite of Biedermaier, colonialism or Napolean's nationalism, because something began to develop, straining and stretching like an awakening giant, which the leading circles could not understand.

What was it that developed? Those who have not lived through the events of the beginning of this century, and so have not experienced what was called social revolution at that time, can hardly understand what it meant when the workers rose up in hundreds of thousands and demanded their rights; when a common will suddenly spread internationally, overcoming all political barriers. The ideals which lived in those people at that time, even though in a vague way, were indeed a first hope for new social conditions. If one had oneself marched in those ranks then one knew the ferment that whirled—one cannot say 'lived'—inside people then. We do not encounter this any more today, for slackness is the characteristic feature of the present generation, and in any case it is no longer necessary. The worker's movement has been overcome by degrading workers into a *petit bourgeoisie*. By virtue of the fact that they possess a bigger or a smaller car it is no longer necessary for them to transform the social life! One can see why men like Robert Owen, Lasalle, Marx, Engels and others were convinced that a new social order would have to be built as a consequence of the decline of liberalism in the middle of the last century, and of the failure, the slackening of the middle classes. But at the very moment when this realisation began to dawn, when the vertical revolution began to stretch like an awakening giant, events occurred which we can see if we really study history.

The idea of evolution was seized upon by Darwinism. That great and mighty idea of evolution which awoke in thinkers like Herder, Goethe, Karl Ernst von Behr and others, was suddenly reduced to being a 'struggle for existence'. At the same time something else happened. The Industrial Revolution spawned collective labour which began not in twos and threes but in hundreds and thousands. For the first time a collectivity developed in the economic life which had not happened since Egyptian times. Collective labour was then appropriated by capitalism, just as the idea of evolution was seized upon by Darwinism. What was only a theoretical idea in Darwinian thought was put into practical effect by capitalism. Capitalism made the struggle for existence a reality, and what else could the workers or their prophets do but themselves take up the war cry and create the destructive slogan of the 'class war'? New camps suddenly opposed each other: capitalists and proletarians; class war instead of liberty, equality and fraternity. Consequently the end of both the national and the centralised state was inevitable—there was no way out—and therefore the First World War erupted. That war wiped out all previously existing social structures. Then, at the end of it, the idea of a threefold structure of the social organism was born. However, instead of taking up this idea men continued in the old ways of thinking and outdated emotions and so plunged back into old errors by creating new national centralised states or, if you like, centralised national states. That is the history, the social history, which took place between the two world wars, between 1918 and 1938.

What I shall now say some of you may perhaps not understand. Through the infuence of the West, starting from England—and also to some extent from America—Bolshevism developed in Russia. This means that the idea of the centralised state was realised over in the East in an exaggerated form. Then, starting in France, the idea of National Socialism and Fascism was put into reality in a crass form. In this way the two national centralised states arose. This could lead to nothing else but the total corruption of all social conditions and therefore the Second World War had to break out. It could not be otherwise, because these were no social solutions, only social madness.

In a sense the Second World War is still continuing today. In fact we live in the middle of war. Although we have enough to eat, and although we can build houses, we nevertheless live in a cold war and the dreadful thing is that this cold war is the only way of preventing the hot war which continually knocks at the door. Do not think that we can still speak of a stable social structure today: we cannot because it no longer exists. What we have are transitional social institutions which everybody knows are unlikely to function for long. That anything like states exist at all is also a Utopian concept. Of course, in Africa there are national states, but do you really believe that the German Republic, whether it be the West or the East, is a state, or that England or France are states? No, they are parts of power blocks which no longer know how they should behave towards each other. But underneath them—and I am describing this in a way that we can grasp what really matters here—the first seeds of the idea of the threefold structure of the social organism are growing in the most diverse places. Like a magic herb which can hardly be found, it appears here and there. It is trodden down again and again and yet it exists.

Now the question remains, from where did the idea of the threefold structure of the social organism arise? Did Rudolf Steiner simply discover it suddenly and then, after having known it for thirty years, write it down in 1916 in a secondary chapter of his book *Riddles of the Soul*?[1] Or did it already try to express itself earlier sometime, somewhere? We can say with certainty that just as the mighty idea of the evolution of organisms awoke in mankind at the turning point of the eighteenth to the nineteenth century, first of all in Herder, and later in Geoffrey de St. Hilaire, Lammarck, Goethe and others, hardly having been foreseen and having never before been publicly known or even divined, so also in the same way the idea of a threefold principle in social life appeared at the turning point of the nineteenth to the twentieth century as something entirely new. But we can also say with certainty that although Rudolf Steiner was the first to bring it to a real synthesis, threefoldness had often broken through in earlier centuries. For example, the alchemists and the Rosicrucians of the fifteenth and sixteenth centuries spoke about the fact that there is a threefold process in nature—that of salt, mercury and sulphur. By this they did not mean the substances salt, mercury and sulphur, but the processes. By salt they meant the salt-process, the structure-forming process; by mercury the balancing process; by sulphur the process of burning and combustion. That was the very first growing point of the threefold structure which was then taken up by Paracelsus, for example, and introduced into the medical world not only in the preparation of medicaments but also in the realm of illness. He spoke about illnesses of salt, of sulphur and of mercury, and he described the illnesses according to their salt, mercury or sulphur function. Here something new broke through. Centuries later a German philosopher and psychologist who is completely unknown today spoke about the fact that within the Son of Man three processes take place: the processes of thinking, feeling and willing. This man was called Tetans. (Rudolf Steiner referred to him, otherwise we would know nothing about him today.)

So we can say that the threefold idea emerged firstly in the processes of nature, (salt, mercury, sulphur), then in the soul of man, (thinking, feeling, willing), and then a little later in the social life, (liberty, equality, fraternity). These are growing points of the concept of a threefold structure of the social organism which began to take shape in Europe in recent centuries. It would be wrong to say that Rudolf Steiner began this; rather he described it once more in an all-embracing way by virtue of the fact that he looked upon man as an organic whole. And because he strove to describe the phenomena he was able to give a first comprehensive description of man as a threefold being. He described him as being 'joined together' out of three different spheres; that of a sensory-nerve system, a rhythmic system and a metabolic-limb system, although joined in such a way that these three are not parts independent of each other, but are links working together. The sensory-nerve system is centred in the head, giving form and shape, and receiving impressions in a mirror-like fashion; the metabolic-limb system works and transforms in us; and between them, bringing about the equilibrium between above and below, the breath and heart-beat in the rhythmic system. So there is the sensory-nerve system, the rhythmic system and the metabolic-limb system. The moment we begin to realise this, we also know that the salt processes work in the sensory-nerve system, forming, shaping, salt-producing, bone-forming; the mercury processes work in the rhythmic system creating equilibrium, dissolving and forming, forming and dissolving, and the sulphur processes work in the metabolic-limb system, combusting and setting alight with fire. At the same time we recognise that the sensory-nerve system is the carrier of our thinking, the rhythmic system is the bearer of our feeling and the metabolic-limb system carries our willing. In this way the threefold idea becomes a key to open world secrets. In the head resides our day-consciousness, in the rhythmic system our dream-consciousness and in the metabolic system our sleep-consciousness. You see, waking, dreaming, sleeping; thinking, feeling, willing; salt, mercury and sulphur. And so we have:

Thinking—day-consciousness—salt
Feeling—dream consciousness—mercury
Willing—sleep-consciousness—sulphur

If we really want to understand the order of the social life, we have to gradually learn to look at this threefoldness as a united whole. This is impossible without trying to renew the idea of threefoldness, because a renewal of social existence will only be able to break through out of the spiritual life; it will definitely not arise out of the economic or the legal life.

If we look at the world of plants and really observe a root, a leaf or a flower, we will find that here too is a threefoldness. In the root we find the processes of salification at work. In the leaves, in the interplay between light and shadow, between the taking in and the giving out of carbon dioxide and oxygen we see the breathing rhythm, the mercurial element at work. In the flowers it is the dispersing, the disintegrating but also fructifying element which is at work. We may begin to appreciate that the head of man corresponds to the root of the plant, while the flower corresponds to man's metabolism, and that therefore upper, middle and lower are not the same in the plant as in man, for the plant grows upwards out of the salt process, enters the mercury process and unfolds above into the flowering process which is a metabolic, a sulphur process.

Just as the plant is formed in threefoldness, so the social spheres are similarly ordered. However, we can not simply say that man's metabolic-limb system corresponds to the economic life merely because we eat and work there. That would be far too superficial. A deeper understanding can only be reached if we recognise that the real similarity between the economic life and the roots of the plant lies in the fact that both take in given actual conditions. The soil provides the organic matter for the farmer; from the mines come the minerals and the metals for the craftsman. Man builds machines for production, but the foundation for any production is the earth itself, and from it stems all economic life. From this basis the legal life develops upwards in a mercurial way and the flowers and fruit of the spiritual life unfold. This is not just an image but also a seed for understanding the three spheres of the social co-existence of man which are still so little understood.

Of course, we can also add that man as an individual stands with his metabolic-limb system in this 'root-head' of the economic life, for the many people who work together are anchored in the 'root-head' of the economic life. Rhythmic man breathes within the legal life of his own state, and just as he works in the economic life, so man pronounces himself in the legal life, and therefore we use the expression 'to pronounce judgement'. We cannot do otherwise, for only where the same language is spoken can a uniform judgement develop. It is nonsensical indeed to believe that the law is the same everywhere: the law is definitely not the same everywhere. It is governed solely according to the circumstances of those who speak the same language. What appears to be justice to us is injustice for others because the law is not international, as economy is. Economy embraces the whole globe; the realm of law belongs to the individual folk groups. In the flower of this plant appears the head of man, creative and thinking.

There now appears before us the phenomena of standing and walking, speaking and thinking—which no animal can acquire—and it is this that makes man into a social being. Man is unique in that in the course of the first three years of life he learns firstly to walk, and this is transformed into work whereby he orders himself into the economic life; then secondly he learns to speak and thereby can become an equal citizen when he is ripe for it; and finally he learns to think and thereby can take part in the freedom of the spiritual life. If we begin to see this, if we take in such images and meditate upon them imaginatively and imagine them meditatively, then fundamental recognitions form themselves which become seeds for a future threefold structure of the social organism.

Third Lecture

Föhrenbühl, 22nd March 1964

Tonight we shall attempt to reflect further on the threefold human and social organism, and perhaps at the outset I may briefly recapitulate the first two lectures. First of all we considered some historical aspects, looking back at the centuries that have passed since the beginning of the age of the Consciousness-soul. Then within this historical context we observed the formation of certain types of state; the centralised state, the national state etc. in order to gain a background image for what could be called the proclamation of the threefold social life through Rudolf Steiner. Finally we asked where the idea of threefoldness originated, which source of man's spiritual life it gradually developed from, and again we had to point to the age of the Consciousness-soul. I described how the idea of salt, mercury and sulphur arose within the Rosicrucian-alchemical spiritual life, and that in some philosophical systems the threefoldness of the soul life was described as thinking, feeling and willing, while the threefoldness of liberty, equality, and fraternity was proclaimed in what led up to the French Revolution. We saw the idea of threefoldness gradually developing out of these first origins in nature, in the human soul, and in the social co-existence of man. Then, in 1916, 1917 and 1918, the true concept of threefoldness in man connected with that of threefoldness in the social organism was formulated by Rudolf Steiner. In fact, we could say that this mighty idea of social threefoldness was quietly born during the storms of the First World War.

Calling to mind the existence of what is termed the sensory-nerve system--of which we often speak but without really understanding even its first, elementary significance—we could see that it is connected with concepts and thinking, while the rhythmic system is connected with feeling and sensation, and that willing is revealed in the metabolic-limb system. These are ideas, imaginations, truths which demand far more than the empty words we generally use when speaking about them. In connection with this threefold articulation of man according to body and soul, and as a continuation of it, Rudolf Steiner developed the idea of the threefold structure of the social organism.

Now I shall say something which may perhaps not be pleasant for many of you, but it is necessary nonetheless. It applies not only to all of us here, but to every human being today. The truth is that it is hardly possible for us to grasp or really understand what the social element is in which every human being is embedded. Let us try to be honest with ourselves and ask what we really imagine when we speak about the economic life, the legal life or the free spiritual life. What do we imagine? If we are utterly honest we have to admit that we imagine nothing whatsoever! They are just words; words we use to cover up, to camouflage or mask something which cannot yet be grasped at all. Excuse me for being so blunt, especially those among you who are older! Naturally, what I say applies also to me, just as well as to everyone else, but I know that I do not know anything, and I would like to help you to realise that you also know nothing! Please understand what I am alluding to, for this is very bound up with anthroposophy. Where do we find the spiritual life, legal life and economic life? How can we begin to grasp them, even if we write—but especially if we speak—about them with extraordinary cleverness? So our aim tonight will be to ask ourselves: What does it mean for man to live within a society?

I should mention that Aristotle expressed this somewhat unpleasantly. I never liked his assertion that man is a *zoon politikon*, which means a social, a political beast or animal. It is unpleasant, but he is right nevertheless! Man—and here I have to say in all sincerity that we should not forget to include ourselves—is only man by living among men, and by devoting himself to other men. Man could not be truly man without his fellow men. But we forget this all too easily, especially if we are anthroposophists, because we believe that freedom consists in the fact that we exist, but we only exist by virtue of the fact that we exist with others, and that others exist with us. I do not mean this at all philosophically; I mean it quite realistically because if we wish to gain an understanding of the threefold social organism, we have to start to grasp that man really is a *zoon politikon* and that only through this fact can he be a human being. I cannot be man without my fellow men. This can be shown, of course, by such dreadful exceptions as solitary confinement or insanity, in which we are debarred from communication with our fellow men. There is also the practice of anchoritism which I consider to be just as dreadful because it dehumanises the hermit who practises it. It may lead him to God, or even make him god-like, but it cannot make him human. Man can only be man if he is together with his fellow men: if he is alone he is not man. We are born out of our fellow man; fed and taught by our fellow men; loved and hated by our fellow men. This is a reality of human life and we must begin to realise it in order to learn to understand that man does not consist only of a physical body, ether body, astral body and Ego—of body, soul and spirit—but also of what he and his fellow men are. As the whole of humanity on earth, as the nation in which we live, as the family into which we are born, as the karmic group we join between birth and death—all this together makes man a human being and without it we are not men. To gradually gain this recognition is the first step towards an understanding of being man on earth among our fellow men.

The next step is to ask: What is the reason, and how is it possible, for man to become a *zoon politikon*? Animals are not political beasts. They can live in herds or form associations, but these are purely functional, utilitarian associations. An ant hill or termite mound is simply a functional association. The purpose of herds is to facilitate propagation and so make life possible, but this has nothing to do with community or the way in which community develops as political, social life among men. Therefore the comparison of an ant 'state' with a human state is an aberration of thinking, although it is often mentioned. It is sheer nonsense to compare a group of cells with a political state! It is simply stupid because it compares things which cannot be compared. If we ask seriously why man is the focus, the centre for his fellow men—and every man is a centre for others, as they are for him, so that he is at the same time centre and periphery—then there is only one answer. This is that after birth the small child acquires the abilities of walking, speaking and thinking in the first three years of its existence. This makes it possible for him to become a man among men. Consider this: no animal learns to walk upright, to speak or to think—only man can do so. For man these three years are in a sense set aside. Man does not learn to walk, speak and think merely in order to be able to say 'I' to himself at the end of the third year; rather he learns to walk, speak and think in order to fulfil the psychosomatic conditions of becoming a man among men. Man rises into the vertical and thereby lays the foundation that enables the most varied individuals to meet each other. Then he learns to speak—which he does only with the help of other men—and with speech he develops the ability to communicate with other upright-walking, upright-standing beings through the medium of language. Finally he learns to think, and thereby he can not only communicate, but he can also convey to others what he experiences as an individual. If you put this image before you, you will recognise that it is the power of uprightness with which the child learns to stand and walk, and it is this power which makes it possible for us to form a human society of individuals. That we speak makes it possible for established individuals to communicate with each other, and thinking makes it possible for this communicating to become an imparting from I to I. These are the prerequisities for the formation of a human society. And it all happens in the first three years of life.

Now, this means that the first three years of life are those which prepare the child to become a member of humanity. Man is born out of the isolation in which he existed in the maternal womb, because there he was nothing else but an isolated, developing being; a being given up to cosmic powers; a being spun into its own karma. This however, is a germ which unfolds and grows into walking, into speaking and communicating, and into thinking and imparting, thereby developing the prerequisities for a social life. (I am trying to express this as clearly as possible.) We also know that something else develops out of walking, speaking and thinking. The sense of word develops out of walking and thereby speaking comes into being; the sense of thought develops out of speaking and thereby thinking emerges, while the sense of Ego develops out of thinking and thereby the knowledge, the immediate, sensory experience arises that the other person is an individual. You see, walking, speaking and thinking are the prerequisites for a social organism. The sense of word, the sense of thought, the sense of Ego; these three make communication possible in the social organism. An animal can neither walk, which is to say walk upright, nor can it speak or think. Today this is very well known, even in scientific circles. What is not known however, is that the next step, namely the acquisition of the sense of word, the sense of thought and the sense of Ego, the three highest senses of man, is not achieved in order that we may live as individuals, as isolated Egos, within the earthly world but in order that we can communicate with our fellow men, and thereby the social organism develops. Not until we experience more and more clearly within ourselves the knowledge of the three higher senses—the study of which is the condition for all community, all social community—will everything that I tried to present at the beginning reveal itself. We should not use empty words that have nothing behind them: we should begin to fill our words with real life.

Let us now ask what it is in human society that gives us the senses of word, thought and Ego. I have often described the way in which these three higher senses function, and I must assume that some of you know it well. However, in this connection we have to present it once more in utter clarity. Everyone should ask himself the following: What do I experience in my fellow men, in being together with my fellow men, through the sense of word? I experience that my fellow man speaks, be it by words or by gestures. I experience by means of the sense of word that the other person speaks, which means that I know immediately without having to reflect upon it—because it is a sensory experience—that the other person is a speaking being. Thereby something extraordinary happens. By the power of uprightness a sense awakens within me which tells me if my fellow man speaks or is dumb; that he is a bearer of speech or not. By means of the sense of word I experience that my fellow man is a speaking being. These are extremely important differentiations, because they begin to point to the anatomy of the social life.

By means of the sense of thought I do not experience that my fellow man speaks, but I experience *what* he says, which means that I understand the words. I do not understand by means of the sense of word, for that only lets me know that the other person is also a speaking man and that he is endowed with the wonder of speech. But the sense of thought immediately reveals to me *what* the other says. That some of you grasp what I mean here is the work of the sense of thought. Is this distinction clear? This is the backbone, muscle and nerve of all social life. I live in the social realm with others by recognising that the other person speaks, and by understanding—sometimes—what he says to me. The latter is actually much more difficult.

What happens by means of the sense of Ego? The sense of Ego enables me to perceive the revelation of the other Ego. This is something entirely different. You see, the sense of Ego exists not only so that I may know that you are there, or that I am satisfied with knowing it: the sense of Ego does much more. Now if I were to ask each of you—I won't do so, never fear—to recite a line such as 'The moon shines brightly tonight' and you began to listen to it with your sense of Ego (from which nobody can escape), then you would discover how the Ego of the other person reveals itself in the diction and tone, in the phraseology, in the rhythm and melody of speaking. One can only understand this with the sense of Ego. These infinitely delicate variations, which can only be understood by that great artist the sense of Ego, are what the other Ego reveals to us. Now we may have already noticed that only through this 'ladder' are we given the prerequisites for establishing a social community which is not simply a tribal community based only on blood ties. We notice that human society is established by means of our three higher senses on the foundation of thinking, speaking and walking.

Now I shall digress a little in order to let you peep behind the curtain of creation—it won't be for long and we shall immediately draw it again thereafter! Where does all this come from? It comes from a single source which metamorphoses itself, and this source is hearing and the ear. Out of hearing arises the sense of word, the sense of thought and the sense of Ego because in the ear the power of uprightness starts to work, speech makes use of hearing, and thinking and hearing work together. Thus the ear is the social sense organ. Again and again I have drawn attention to Rudolf Steiner's assertion that before man was, the ear was. The ear was present at the very beginning and then later, out of the ear, man emerged. So we can now say—and don't worry, I shall soon close the curtain again—that the ear, the true ear and true hearing, encompasses the entirety of all mankind. This is not so for the eye, because the moment man went through the Fall his eyes were opened; and just as the eye isolates, so the ear communes. We cannot avoid hearing, but we can close our eyes. With the ear we are connected to our surroundings, our environment, and to humanity. The ear opens us to all that happens around us. The eye does not do this; it only sees what covers the truth. Through the eye we look at, we behold the wonder world of *maya* (illusion)—and indeed nobody should miss this. However, that which lies behind it, that which is our fellow man, is revealed to us through the ear. The ear is the original organ of man as a social being. One cannot express this in a clearer way.

If we have made this step successfully, we can now go a bit further. We can ask: Where does the sense of word work? Where does the sense of thought work? Where does the sense of Ego work? This is another threefoldness. The sense of word works in the sensory-nerve system, and by so doing it gives us the perception that the other person speaks. The sense of thought works in the middle system and through it we learn to comprehend what our fellow men say to us. The sense of Ego has its field of activity in the limb system, and partly also in the metabolic system. Thus we have a sense of word, a sense of thought and a sense of Ego. Please try to follow me, little by little!

Let us pose the question once again: what do we perceive by means of the sense of word? We perceive language as language. This means that just as I see man as man, so I understand by means of the sense of word that language is language, otherwise I would not know that it *is* a language. The sense of thought allows me to grasp within the language the information which it conveys. This means that we comprehend not just language as language, but language as information. The sense of Ego, as I have already said, reveals to me the language of the other Ego. Thus there are three realms of language, which is the sphere that builds the bridges, weaves the threads, fords the streams and levels the paths which lead from man to man.

It is language, not speaking, which actually circulates through the entire social organism, through man and among men. One could almost say that just as the blood pulsates through the human organism, so language pulsates through the social organism. No man could live without the flow of blood, and no social organism could exist without the flow of language.

Now, just as the blood changes continually, so also does language. The language of nations, of peoples and of small groups is constantly changing from year to year. If you go through Überlingen today with a discerning ear in order to hear how the Überlingian speaks, and then return again next year, you will notice that the language has changed. It has not remained the same; it has altered—perhaps not by very much—but still it has altered. Of course, today we are so coarse, so boorish and so narrow-minded that we do not notice at all that the organism of a language is in continual metamorphosis. I can remember during the war how I listened out of interest from time to time—although not very often—to announcers on the German radio broadcasts, and I noticed that I hardly understood the German language any longer. It had become something entirely different and I had to gradually get used to it again. But because we are always in the middle of this process we do not notice the change. It is really very different to hear the German language today from what it was ten or twenty years ago. But this does not depend on those who speak; it depends on the language itself.

Finally, let us enliven these things in order to notice that we are not isolated human beings but are embedded within the currents of social existence, just as we are embedded in the currents of the etheric, astral, cosmic powers. Social existence is not an abstract web of thoughts spun by a professor of economy; it is one of the greatest realities in which men live, and it is maintained and enlivened by the pulse of language.

The sense of word reveals language as language. It reveals to me that the other person is my brother because he also speaks. Because we share speech we are brothers, and just as we both speak so we also both work—be it with our hands, with our brain or our language. The speaking man is also the working man, and as working man he produces, he forms, he builds, he manufactures. We do this as a man among men: we plough, sow, spin, throw pots, saw, hammer or whatever. All this is the revelation of language as language. Perhaps now we may begin to understand that the economic life belongs to the sphere of words. The economic life, in which I work and in which I speak, is the sphere of production. In it we stand next to each other, man next to man, brother next to brother in uprightness, and we grow into this sphere as walking men. This is the sphere of the economic life.

However, where language becomes understanding, where the influence of the sense of thought begins to work, I no longer stand upright next to my neighbour, but I speak to him and for social life to function he must begin to understand me. This is something entirely different: it is now a mutual relationship—I speak and the other person understands what I say. We do not stand next to but opposite each other; one opposite many, or many in pairs, it is all the same. This is the sphere of the legal life. In it we pronounce judgement. It is the sphere of speaking where men commune with one another and understand what they say to each other. Finally, where language becomes the revelation of the other Ego, where we take hold of the sense of Ego, we establish the sphere of the free spiritual life.

In this way we have advanced a good bit further, for we now know—or at least we begin to know—that in the sense of word the economic life develops more and more. We could also say with full justification that out of the economic life which we share as men, out of the brotherliness of being together, and out of the uprightness of being together, our sense of word arises. We can also continue and say that in that sphere in which the legal life has to be established everywhere, namely where people speak to one another so that they understand each other—in other words where the sense of thought is present—there we live with others in the sphere of thought. You see here how realities begin to arise, because this is not artificially thought out. You see how out of the mighty ear of all humanity, the working man and the economic life suddenly develops; the mutually understanding man and the legal life, and the man who reveals his being to his fellow man by means of language and the free spiritual life. This is what matters, namely that we know now that it is these three highest senses which make us a *zoon politikon*. Man is not isolated, and the reason for this is that he is the bearer of the sense of word, the sense of thought and the sense of Ego. Now this begins to come alive, because it is connected to the being of man.

Consider why the human brain is formed in such a way that it carries the senses of word, thought and Ego. These senses are imprinted into the brain. It does not grow so much bigger in man because he is so much cleverer than the animal. That is nonsense: animals are much cleverer than man! Man's wisdom bears no comparison to that of the animals. Spiders and their webs, wasps and their nests, bees and their hives are all filled with outstanding wisdom, compared with which we are fools. The reason that we have such a large brain is due to the fact that thereby we may become a man among men.

You will remember that Rudolf Steiner told us that these three abilities of the small child—uprightness, speaking and thinking—can only come about by virtue of the fact that the power of Christ begins to work in every single child during its first three years. Then it withdaws again. This means that we receive the foundation of our social existence out of the Christ-powers which form walking, speaking and thinking, through which we become social men, and that the senses of word, thought and Ego develop in connection with it as an emanation of what can be called the

Holy Ghost. You see, this streams into the entire social sphere wherein we are embedded and in which we live. Once upon a time, many thousands of years ago, man was able to look into the spirit-worlds and perceive the heavens clairvoyantly, but this ability was lost during the course of the Atlantean period and human language was formed and developed in its stead. Language developed because clairvoyance was lost, and if you read, for instance, the essay entitled *Our Atlantic Fore-fathers*[1] by Rudolf Steiner you will learn how the rise of language led to the formation of states in Atlantis. You see, society developed out of language, but it developed—and let us take this as an image—because the heavens withdrew their wisdom. What came to an end then appeared later as social life in the form of the circulation of language.

The social structure of mankind becomes more and more 'visible' from century to century, and now the time has come when it must divide into what is sense of word, what is sense of thought, and what is sense of Ego. In other words it must divide into economic life, into legal life and into spiritual life, and every one of these three realms must be filled with the new spirit—with the healing spirit; with the Holy Ghost. What matters is that we gradually learn to understand that peace, peace among men, can arise only when insight is gained into the new spirituality which fills today's society and the social life of man.

This is as far as I wanted to go tonight. I believe that this is a suitable preparation for the coming Passion Week and on Easter Sunday, a week today, we shall continue our deliberations.

Fourth Lecture

Föhrenbühl, 29th March 1964

During the past weeks here we have tried to gain a measure of insight into what Rudolf Steiner described and proclaimed as the threefold social organism some decades ago—more than four decades ago, in fact. We first approached these ideas from an historical point of view. Then last Sunday we gained a fundamental insight—or so it seems to me—into the connection between man and the social organism, because we realised how right Aristotle was when he called man a *zoon politikon*. I was even compelled to say that man is only man if he lives and works in community with others, and that alone he cannot reach his humanity. If, for instance, he grows up in isolation he is denied the means of becoming a speaking being who can express himself through language. He is therefore unable to develop thinking and no doubt loses, after some time, the power of uprightness which he might have gained before.

While formulating things in this way I pointed out the fundamental significance of something which we were already able to comprehend last time, namely that, contrary to animals, the human being becomes man just in those first three years of life when he gains uprightness, when he begins to speak and when he unfolds his thinking out of language. This is of such essential importance that I strongly believe we shall have to inscribe it ever more deeply into our hearts—that the walking, upright-standing man is rooted in the economic life; that the speaking man lives in the legal life, and that the thinking man is the being who establishes the free spiritual life in community with others.

This was the first step we made, and it was followed immediately by a second, namely that the three spheres of society—the economic life in which everything is manufactured, processed or produced; the legal life in which men meet each other as equals; the spiritual life in which everyone can freely and spiritually create, but yet can co-operate with his fellow men—that these three spheres are neither dependent solely on the individual nor do they grow only out of the social interactions between men, but in fact develop out of those qualities in the human being which Rudolf Steiner calls the three highest senses. Perhaps you will now understand what I mean by saying that man is complete only if he is socially active; only when he begins to realise that the senses of word, thought and Ego continue outwards into society—the sense of word by forming the sphere of the economic life; the sense of thought by forming the sphere of the legal life, and the sense of Ego by forming the sphere of the free spiritual life. I would like to give one or two examples to make clear what I mean.

What we have just tried to describe concerning man is hinted at in some of the animals as an image, albeit in a materialised, hardened or narrowed way. When fishes build their nests in the water, for instance, or birds construct their nests or beavers their dens, this is not something which happens outside the animal realm. It is the case that the formative forces of a bird can stream outwards at certain times of the year and form not only wings and beak, but also fashion a nest in conformity with its species, its shape and being. A nest of sand, clay, leaves or soil—whether round, cornered, oblong, or whatever shape it might be—is part of the bird, the swimming fish, or the ingenuity of the beaver. It belongs to the animal organism rather than to the social organism, for it is an externalising of the formative forces which envelop a little more than the body.

Something similar takes place—although perhaps we would have to say the same process, but on a higher level and in a different sphere—where the sense of word, which grasps language as language, forms out the economic life; where the sense of thought, which grasps the content of the spoken word, permeates the legal life, and where the sense of Ego which appreciates a fellow man directly as an Ego, forms the spiritual life. This is what we reached in our discussions last Sunday.

Perhaps we have therefore started to acquire the fundamental conviction, without which we cannot even begin to grasp what the social organism is, namely that a state, a people, a community, a village or a town is not merely the sum total of all the people living there but that it is a higher organism. It does not consist of flesh and blood, however, but is created and formed by soul and spiritual powers. Wherever the same language is spoken an organisation also develops in which the various dialects can be likened to the different organs, and every one of these dialects develops distinct forms of gesture. For it is not the case that man only imitates his fellow men, but formative powers, etheric forces are at work which bring about the recognition of language not only as language, but also as content. The more we begin to look at this as a soul-spiritual organisation, the more will the economic organisation, the sphere of rights and the spiritual life as described by Rudolf Steiner become alive.

However, all this was not present from the beginning. It has taken many thousands of years for such soul-spirit forms of social life to develop. It was language, always language, which created the starting point for such forms. Let us look back for a moment to the beginning of Atlantean times when the body was of a very different make-up from what it is today, and when language was still alive and flexible. Apart from the sounds man could hardly pronounce a word, and the ruling historic powers only very gradually implanted language into the developing soul so that the various original Atlantean tribes gradually began to speak. At the same time the first group-formations developed, not simply as a parallel event but arising from the same cause. Tribes did not develop only on the foundation of blood-ties, but the speaking man began to communicate with his brother. Those who spoke and understood the same language formed a group. In such a group there was always one who spoke best, and at the same time also had the best memory. He became the leader *because* of his memory and his ability to speak. Later it was the case that, by means of language, memories and experiences were handed down to the children and the grandchildren, and so families based on a common language were formed. Thereby not only did a community develop, but it was handed on from generation to generation by means of language. This was no more than the beginning of the future legal life. Some individuals had a sort of spiritual life, but it took place fully in the lap of the spiritual world. The earth, not man, was the economic life, because the earth itself formed and created. This was the situation at the beginning of the development of mankind, at the time when men united more and more in groups.

With the onset of the post-Atlantean age things changed slowly, very slowly and steadily, for the majority of men were not yet at all conscious of the social life. A few individuals were the rulers, such as the king, his commander-in-chief, and the priests. Surprisingly perhaps, it was the priests who led the economic life, for they indicated when the sowing should be done, when the harvest should be gathered, and the way in which way this or that musical instrument should be made. The generals dispensed justice, and the kings and the bards gave the myths whereby the innermost spiritual needs of the people were fed. The social spheres did not yet exist. Yet the future bearers, the seeds of a conscious social life were already there. Naturally, there were warriors and they belonged to the legal life. There were also land men, cattle breeders, craftsmen and so on, and they were integrated into the economic life, and there were a few scattered artists, bards and master builders who belonged to the spiritual life. But this was still an entirely natural order, into which was woven the power of uprightness with the sense of word, speech with the sense of thought, and the sense of Ego.

When did man wake up consciously for the first time in regard to social life? This only happened in the Graeco-Roman cultural epoch, in the so called fourth post-Atlantean epoch which began in about 747 BC. Many of the Greeks and the Romans awoke to the realisation that man is a social being. At that time the longing for a new social order arose, a longing which also tries to break through today but by way of revolution. It brought the experiments of the *res publica*, and the experiments of the town-states like Athens, Sparta and Thebes, whose people felt called upon to take part in the affairs of their town or country, and were enlisted to fight in its military campaigns.

Then Cato committed suicide because the political forms which Caesar created differed from the ones he thought right. Imagine what this awakening meant! It happened because just at that time something quite new had taken place in the evolution of mankind.

Before the Mystery of Golgotha, during the fifth, sixth and seventh centuries before Christ, something entirely new occurred. Jaspers, a great modern thinker, pointed out this fundamental turning point in the history of mankind and called it a 'node of history'. He even wrote a book about it.[1] Twenty-five years earlier Rudolf Steiner had already pointed it out and described how, suddenly, mighty heralds of entirely new religions appeared in the Far East and the Middle East: Confucius, Laotse, Buddha, Pythagoras, the Greek philosophers and dramatists. He showed how new qualities awoke within the human soul; how the first early Greek philosophers like Anaximander (610–546 BC), Heraclitus (540–475 BC) and many others only began to think by virtue of the fact that something had woken up in man which until then had been foreign to his nature—he began to wonder. Thales wondered about the world which opened up before him. Rudolf Steiner described how this wonder, this profound amazement arose. In these people a conscious recognition suddenly dawned that in the forms and phenomena of nature they met something which they knew, but which they were unable to place. Read the dialogues of Plato and you will notice how the foundation of all the discussions is always one of questioning amazement: What is man? What is beauty? What is love? What is nature, the sky, the stars, the trees, the world, the soul qualities of man? The earlier spiritual insight which had vanished had now become wondering reflection.

If you examine the religions which developed at that time as to their innermost truths you will find that the core of the teachings and views of Laotse, Confucius, and especially of Buddha, is the teaching of compassion and love. This hardly existed before, but now man began to suffer with his fellow men; to know about his fellow human beings; to care and live for them, until finally—and one can almost pinpoint the year it happened—the voice of human conscience awoke. What the early Greek dramatists still presented as the Erinnyes later became the voice of conscience within. Three qualities awoke in man: amazement, out of which philosophy developed; compassion and love, out of which a new religion arose; and conscience, through which something developed within man which began to harness his natural drives and desires. This is the mighty step which took place soon after the beginning of the fourth post-Atlantean epoch; the step which prepared the central event of earth-evolution: the Mystery of Golgotha. And this preparation took place *within* man in such a way that conscience, compassion and love, and wonder began to awaken within him.

This is easily said, but the questions remain: What is conscience? Why was it that compassion and love developed at that time? What is this amazement and wonder which arrests racing thoughts in the thinking man, which reins in the runaway horse of thought bringing it to a halt, just as when the disciples arrived at the grave on Easter Sunday morning it brought them to a halt? These are no simple questions or problems. Yet today we can advance a step further in our understanding, or so I believe, especially if we begin to divine that here again man takes steps towards becoming man as a member of mankind; towards becoming a social being. These are steps taken through wonder at all that is around him, through love towards all that is with him, and through conscience for all that is within him. Man begins to overcome his drives, his negativity, and his asocial nature in order not to harm his fellow men. This, like everything that happens in the development of mankind, is also a step of inner deepening. Man does not become man by reaching outer perfection, as the animal does by having the best muzzle, the best teeth, the best limbs, the most agile body etc., but by turning his formative forces inwards: not by perfecting his organs but by diverting this power, elevating and transforming it. The child is not engaged in bringing the formation of its bones, muscles and organs to perfection as every animal does, because before perfection is reached these powers are freed and become forces of thinking, of speaking, and of deciding. In the same way a process of turning inwards takes place here also. Yet we still have to ask: What is turned inward when conscience develops, when wonder arises, and when compassion and love awaken?

The three forces which bring about walking, speaking and thinking are transformed, metamorphosed, and appear as soul forces. The power of uprightness by which the child achieves his upright stature in the first year of life turns inward, and out of it conscience is formed. In this way a new power of uprightness arises by means of which drives and passions, desires and emotions can straighten and order themselves. If we were to describe this physiologically, we would have to say that the organ of conscience is the heart, in so far as it is a spatial structure, the axis of which goes from front to back; from left to right; from above to below, retaining the centre. It is not the heart itself, but the heart as a spatial structure which is the organ of the inward power of uprightness which began to work in all men from approximately the fourth and fifth centuries BC onwards.

It is similar with compassion and love. The child learns to speak through having received the mighty faculty of imitation, for man is an imitating being soon after he is born. Just as the transformed power of uprightness becomes conscience, so the transformed power of imitation becomes the power of compassion and love. One can divine that this is connected with language, connected with the sphere which was given to man out of the Logos and that the core of the Logos—the power of love—began to awaken. Here again the heart is the organ for this faculty; not as a spatial structure, but through its power of devotion. For it is not true that the heart propels the blood. Rather, the heart constantly gives itself up to the blood in order to guide and harmonise it by continually sacrificing itself to the flow. This power of devotion of the heart makes it possible that on earth compassion and love can awaken in the soul of man.

And the power of wonder? I have already said that wonder arises so that thinking is not continually given up to perception and observation; so that it is not constantly submerged in all that is presented to it as experience, but so that it stops, becomes quiet, looks around and then stands in awe of everything that is revealed to it as 'world'. Here again the heart is the organ, for as we have learned from Rudolf Steiner the heart is an organ of consciousness, an organ for our waking consciousness, and as such it is the organ of wonder.

Thus enclosed within the heart like a secret is its spatial structure, its faculty of devotion and its power of consciousness. Out of these three characteristics and together with them conscience, compassion and love, and wonder were unfolded in those centuries before the Mystery of Golgotha and gave man an entirely new position in life. He awakened as the Roman citizen; as the Greek in his *polis*. This was in fact an entirely new experience and if we follow this just one step further we arrive at the Mystery of Golgotha. We can divine, perhaps even know, that the awakening of man to these three new faculties was a necessary preparation which gave him the consciousness to be able to say: I am only a man if I am among men. Alone I am nothing; alone I cannot be a man.

Then the Mystery of Golgotha came to pass, and it did so in a threefold way: on Maundy Thursday, on Good Friday and on Easter Saturday which then streamed on into the mystery of the Resurrection on Easter Sunday. What really took place on Maundy Thursday? You see, when Christ sat with the disciples at the Last Supper and broke bread and shared it with them, and when He blessed the wine and thereby gave Himself to the disciples, and when He took the towel and knelt in front of each one to wash his feet then, through His deed, His sacrifice, Christ permeated the awakening conscience which entered the circle and which through the disciples could work further into the whole of mankind. On Maundy Thursday conscience was christianised. Because the voice of conscience was silent in Judas, he was cast out of the community into the dark night of loneliness and solitude. Through this event what will gradually appear later as the economic life was christianised in the image of bread and wine. At that moment Christ said: 'He that eateth bread with me, hath lifted up his heel against me'. He will become the Lord of the earth on which we all tread. This earth is both the foundation of all production and also the body of Christ; it is the wounded and bleeding head which we tread on when we walk, and consequently we know the truth of the words 'He that eateth bread with me, hath lifted up his heel against me'. But in this event resounded the clatter of thirty pieces of silver. This still echoes today because whoever sells or is forced to sell his labour, his working-power, for money immediately becomes a follower of Judas again. Here christianised conscience began to appear and to work in the realm of fraternity; in the realm of economy.

Then follows Good Friday. Christ was accused, put on trial, judged, sentenced to be executed and the sentence carried out. His sacrifice worked on, permeating the christianised sphere of rights with compassion and love. Annas, Caiaphas and Pilate were cast out because they experienced neither love nor compassion. Pilate's question 'What is truth?' was completely beside the point, for at that moment it was not truth that was at stake but *recognition* borne of compassion and love. Pilate, the Roman citizen, lacked this recognition, as did the Pharisees and Saducees, and therefore the trial took place which has the cross as its image.

Then came Easter Saturday. All work had stopped. The trial had also come to an end because the Sabbath had arrived. Now the image is the grave. The dawn of the mystery of the Resurrection began to light up the earth and enter into single individuals such as Nicodemus and Joseph of Arimathea. They began to wonder, to arrest their thinking. Even one or two of the Jews were startled as to what might happen on that day because everything had become so still. The disciples were together in the Upper Room but they also did not understand what had happened. They lacked the necessary wonder. However, in such men as the Pharisee Nicodemus and the Essene Joseph of Arimathea there arose a similar wonder as in the Greek philosophers, only it had become christianised and had as its centre the grave out of which no voice, no stirring, no sound could be heard.

Thus the economic life, the legal life and the spiritual life were christianised in these three days through the devotion of Christ, the sacrifice of Christ and through the light of the Resurrection which began to shine and which tried to awaken wonder in human thinking. What does this mean? Why am I telling you all this? In a special lecture held on 8th May 1912, Rudolf Steiner vouchsafed us something which is of the utmost importance for the future of mankind. He entrusted to us the knowledge that since the Mystery of Golgotha the bodily nature of Christ is being woven out of what arises in man as wonder, as compassion and love, and as conscience. Rudolf Steiner expressed it as follows:

> People in whom the great revelations and truths of the spiritual worlds can evoke wonder, nourish this feeling of wonder, in the course of time this creates a force . . . which attracts the Christ Spirit. Christ draws His astral body . . . from all those feelings which have lived in single human souls as wonder. Whenever the soul is moved to share in the joy and suffering of others . . . Christ unites Himself with the human soul through compassion and love. Compassion and love are the forces from which Christ forms His etheric body until the end of earth evolution.
>
> With man's conscience Christ is most intimately connected. From the impulses which spring from the conscience of individual human souls Christ draws His physical body.[2]

The christianised power of uprightness inwardly transformed into conscience, and carried through the sphere of production, will at the end of earth-evolution be the physical form of the Christ Spirit. The transformed faculty of imitation, filled with the power of the Logos and becoming compassion and love, will weave and spread through the legal life, and create the etheric form of the Christ Spirit. The wonder of the thinking man in the spiritual life, where thought itself is halted will form the astral body of the Christ Spirit. Therefore we may be allowed to say: Yes, if we are able to christianise these social spheres in which we men become Man, then in them we will weave the new earth, the new Jerusalem. Rudolf Steiner speaks about this immediately after the above passage. He says:

> The reality of an utterance in the Bible becomes very clear when we know that the etheric body of Christ is formed from men's feelings of compassion and love: "Inasmuch as ye have done it unto one of the least of these my brethren, ye have done it unto Me".

Read in the twenty-fifth chapter of the Gospel of St. Matthew how as judge of the world Christ parts the sheep from the goats in the Last Judgment and says to the sheep: 'For I was an hungered and ye gave me meat; I was thirsty and ye gave me drink; naked and ye clothed me'. This is indeed what we can do as men, if we let Christianity speak within us, for then in our social working with and among men we weave the garment of Christ. That is the core of it all.

I would like to add that what Rudolf Steiner gave us as the Foundation Stone Meditation should help us to develop brotherliness, equality and freedom in conscience, in love and in wonder. For to 'Practise Spirit-recollection' is the conscience of Maundy Thursday; to 'Practise Spirit-mindfulness' is the awakening of compassion and love on Good Friday, and to 'Practise Spirit-vision' is the wonder, the amazement which takes place on Easter Saturday. Then there arises the image of the New Earth, of the Risen One, of whom is said:

> O light Divine!
> O Sun of Christ!
> Warm Thou our hearts,
> Enlighten Thou our heads,
> That good may become
> What from our hearts we would found
> And from our heads direct
> With single purpose.[3]

This is man among men, and only thus can he become Man. Being permeated by Christ, being led by Christ, he becomes a man in whom can grow the voice of conscience, the light of love, and the sheen of wonder.

Fifth Lecture

Föhrenbühl, 30th March 1964

In many places throughout the world, perhaps even in hundreds of places, people will gather in the course of this day in order to commemorate 30th March 1925.* Probably on all continents, in North and South America, across all of Europe, in Australia, South Africa, perhaps even here and there in Asia, people remember Monday 30th March 1925, either as a few individuals or in larger or smaller groups. To picture this vividly gives one an image of how far anthroposophical spiritual science has implanted itself ever deeper into the experience of mankind today. I believe it is important to frequently try to imagine where, how and in which way spiritual science has become alive and active. Of course, taking into account present day population figures, it has only been taken up by very few, and yet today there are many individuals who have done so. I am reminded of the growth of Christianity which also spread from an improbable few to such an extent that today everyone on earth, or nearly everyone, knows, divines or experiences what is meant when the word 'Christianity' is mentioned. It is similar in the case of anthroposophical spiritual science, for we must be clear that the spreading of this spiritual seed which was given by Rudolf Steiner develops further in spite of all the opposing powers both inner and outer; despite the enemies of anthroposophy and even despite its representatives! I do not wish to condemn by using such words, but I want to point out the phenomenon which we can recognise in ourselves (and I say this to close friends here), namely that despite whatever we do imperfectly, whatever we omit to do,

* Anniversary of the death of Rudolf Steiner.

whenever we are unable to jump over our own shadow so to speak, spiritual science nevertheless grows in spite of our imperfections and our unsuccessful deeds. People come together and discuss these things and thus seeds are planted into human hearts and begin to germinate. Some wither away, some continue to grow, some flower, a few bear fruit and seed out again; so this growth continues step by step, like the working of a leaven which has become active within mankind today.

We should earnestly take to heart the knowledge that, despite all the failures, spiritual science continues to spread its roots, its branches and flowers, and all become active. However, we should pay particular attention to one thing and that is the recognition of opposing powers within us and around us which try to prevent the spread of spiritual science. These powers are not particular associations of people, although in certain associations they are especially active. These forces of retardation will be active in us, in every single one of us, unless we turn our attention to them again and again and try to recognise them for what are.

Rudolf Steiner frequently pointed this out, and time and again we failed to see it and were deceived by the many temptations with which our age is beset. If we wish to characterise these opposing powers in some way, we could say that they reveal themselves in a threefold garment. One aspect is Jahveism,* and by Jahveism I mean that which once led the Jewish people as the monotheistic godhead and which, with full justification in its time, implanted into the Jews the belief that they were the chosen people. This lives on today. It would however, be wrong to imagine that it is found only in the Jewish people because it lives in all peoples, but first and foremost in the German peoples who are still deeply attached to Jahveism and to a belief in being a chosen people. It is present in Americanism; it has flourished in France; it lives in Protestantism and in Catholicism. It lives wherever a belief is so fanatically convinced of its own mission that it tries to embrace the whole world; in other words it thrives where the monotheistic deity, having the character of a Father-God, works and tries to veil

---

* Dr. König uses the older term Jahve instead of Jehovah for the God of the Hebrews.

the being of Christ, the Son, and thereby also the being of the Holy Ghost.

Along with Jahveism, centralism is one of the worst enemies of spiritual science. Wherever centralisation tries to spread, or where a small group wants to gain central control over greater contexts; where the responsibility to decide is taken from people, or where all things are forced to flow together towards a centre, be it a parish, an industrial concern or a state; in other words wherever centralisation raises its head—and today it is in almost every society—the influence of spiritual science as a seed or working power is made impossible.

The third opposing power is nationalism. Nationalism has begun to thrive again in communities of men, be it whole peoples or states. Wherever nationalism appears it will work in cooperation with centralism and Jahveism and these three are the powers which oppose spiritual science.

But these are not only faults in others, they are also to be found in every one of us. Man has centralist, nationalist and Jahveist tendencies, and day after day we have to try to work against these tendencies within and around ourselves; to escape centralism, to dispense with Jahveism, to curse nationalism. The fact that hundreds of people have nationalist, centralist and Jahveist tendencies in spite of spiritual science does not show that we, or any one of us, are better than the others, but it does show what lives in every human being as an opposing power to true spiritual cognition in our time. This can also be seen as the beast in us and in our time; for instance, as one of those beasts described in the Book of Revelation and in many other places. Wherever something is of itself convinced that it should have central, national, Jahveist power (and aren't we all secretly convinced of this in many corners of our life?) we should know that there the enemy within is us. This is the enemy in us that opposes the true mission of anthroposophy, the spiritual science of Rudolf Steiner.

But what do we mean when we say the true mission of spiritual science? This can only really be explained in one way, namely that the true mission of spiritual science is to permeate all that exists with the new Christ impulse. Whoever tries to shut his eyes to this, or to deny it, falls prey to centralism and to Jahveism, for Rudolf Steiner stressed many times that spiritual science strives to become one with, to unite with, the mission of Christianity. This however, cannot remain idle talk or empty words but must be put into effect. Spiritual science only becomes reality, it only develops—and fortunately it *does* develop—where the Christ impulse becomes active in the work. We can easily cite the example of anthroposophical medicine which is beginning to take effect here and there. However, an anthroposophical doctor is not merely someone who knows how to use the seven metals, or when to prescribe Infludo and Cardiodoron and when not to, for everybody can do this. An anthroposophical doctor only becomes such when he tries to transform his medical thinking through the Christ impulse so that silver and gold, frankincense and myrrh begin to live within him, and become active when he talks and acts with his patients. Similarly, eurythmy is not yet a new art, but will only really become an art when the eurythmist gradually gains the faculty of knowing that it is the Christ impulse which begins to work in it. Without this impulse all the religions, be they Christian or non-Christian, will also die out despite the conclaves and huge missionary meetings in which tens of thousands of people gather. These initiatives are wonderful, and right, yet if the new element of the Christ impulse does not begin to awaken; if the laboratory table does not become an altar for scientific experiment; if in the realm of philosophy there does not awaken that same Pauline thinking which begins to unfold in, for instance, *The Philosophy of Freedom*[1], and if in agriculture Christian prayer is not directed in devotion towards the ground of the earth, then spiritual science will remain sterile in man. I have tried to show that it has not remained sterile by pointing out the fact that today we can imagine the many hundreds of places all over the earth where this anniversary is remembered.

When we ponder about Rudolf Steiner, whether about his life, his death or his work, we have to recognise what he wanted to implant as Christ impulses into human social life, for this is what worked through him. This impulse can sometimes appear within the family, in communities of men, or in individuals, but wherever it may be we must recognise it for what it is. In a lecture held on 11th February 1919, which I have often quoted and to which I shall refer again later, Rudolf Steiner said:

> He [Christ] Himself said—I have often quoted it: 'I am with you always, even unto the end of the world.' This means: Christ did not speak only during His time on earth; His utterance continues, and we must continue to listen for it. We should not wish merely to read the Gospels (though certainly they ought to be read over and over again); we should listen to the living revelation that springs from His continued presence among us. In this epoch He declares to us: 'Make new your ways of thinking' (as His forerunner, John the Baptist, said: 'Change your thinking'), 'so that they may reveal to you man's threefold nature which demands also that your social environment on earth shall have a threefold membering.'[2]

The Christ impulse demands to be shaped, to be put into effect even as far as into the historical-social realm. In this lecture Rudolf Steiner shows two ways in which men can serve the Christ impulse today. He describes a path in the realm of thinking, and a path in the realm of willing. It is one of the lectures, hundreds of which he held in the year 1919, proclaiming the new order of social life, and showing the phenomenon that mankind approaches the threshold in this century. One can even add that today mankind has now reached the threshold and performs a dreadful dance at its edge. Rudolf Steiner reminds us how man can become a servant of the Christ impulse in the realm of thinking and willing. He says:

> This is only possible if we know that the human being living since the Mystery of Golgotha has a certain defect, for which he must compensate by his own activity during his life here on earth.[3]

Rudolf Steiner points out the fact that it is a matter of course for every healthy person to believe in God, and that only a person who is ill, really ill, can deny the words '*Ex Deo Nascimur*'. This no longer suffices today and something else must develop in us, namely the knowledge that we are born in such a way that we are ruled by prejudice. He says this in the following way:

> I am born a prejudiced person, and freedom from prejudice in my thinking is something I have to achieve during life.
>
> And how can I achieve it? The one and only way is this: instead of taking an interest merely in my own way of thinking, and in what *I* consider right, I must develop a selfless interest in every opinion I encounter, however strongly I may hold it to be mistaken. The more a man prides himself on his own dogmatic opinions and is interested only in them, the further he removes himself, at this moment of world evolution, from the Christ. The more he develops a social interest in the opinions of other men, even though he considers them erroneous—the more light he receives into his own thinking from the opinions of others—the more he does to fulfil in his inmost soul a saying of Christ, which today must be interpreted in the sense of the new Christ-language.
>
> Christ said: 'Inasmuch as ye have done it unto one of the least of these My brethren, ye have done it unto Me.' The Christ never ceases to reveal Himself anew to men—even unto the end of earthly time. And thus He speaks today to those willing to listen: 'In whatever the least of your brethren thinks, you must recognise that I am thinking in him; and that I enter into your feeling, whenever you bring another's thought into relation with your own, and whenever you feel a fraternal interest for what is passing in another's soul. Whatever opinion, whatever outlook on life, you discover in the least of your brethren, therein you are seeking Myself.'[4]

This is an extraordinary saying, and if Rudolf Seiner says such a thing, then we can be sure that he himself listens to the heart of the Christ and hears him speaking, calling to men: 'Through the least thought of your fellow men which you accept; through the interest which you develop for the least thought of your fellow men, you accept and receive Me in your fellow man.' If only we could be ever mindful of this, so that instead of hastily passing judgement we would listen to what the other has to say, even if he seems to be very stupid. What matters is that we listen, even though we need by no means agree. We can have our own opinion, but we need not represent it in a centralist, nationalist or Jahveist way. Rather we can listen, hear, appreciate and know that in my fellow man Christ thinks at least as strongly as in myself. Rudolf Steiner continues:

> If I do not look on myself alone as the source of everything I think, but recognise myself, right down into the depths of my soul, as a member of the human community—then, my dear friends, one way to the Christ lies open. This is the way which must today be characterised as the *way to the Christ through thinking*.'[5]

This is one path.

Speaking about the path of willing, Rudolf Steiner describes how the practice in today's education all too often results in destroying the enthusiasm of young people or—as indeed many of us have experienced—to whip it up in a particular direction. However, it does not depend only on this innate enthusiasm (which Rudolf Steiner calls 'youthful' enthusiasm) for this youthful enthusiasm has to be replaced by something new. He says:

> Something further is required—idealism must spring from inner development, from *self-education*. Besides the innate idealism of youth, we must see to it that in human society something else is achieved—precisely an *achieved idealism*: not merely the idealism that springs from the instincts and enthusiasm of youth, but one that is nurtured, gained by one's own initiative, and will not fade

> away with the passing of youth. This is something which opens the way to the Christ, because—once more—it is something acquired during life between birth and death.
>
> Feel the great difference between instinctive idealism and achieved idealism! Feel the great difference between youthful enthusiasm and the enthusiasm which springs from taking hold of the life of the spirit and can be ever and again kindled anew, because we have made it part of our soul, independent of the course of our bodily existence—then you will grasp this second idealism, which is not merely the idealism implanted in us by nature. This is the way to Christ through *willing*, as distinct from the way through thinking.[6]

This is in fact one of the many aspects which Rudolf Steiner gave us for the attainment of the true mission of spiritual science. The true mission of spiritual science is identical with a renewed Christianity. This cannot be explained away because if it could spiritual science itself would be explained away. The consciousness must arise in us that here on earth we are not confined between birth and death, but that the life of every human being is illumined by his pre-earthly existence and also that into every human being the sun-radiance of his post-mortal existence penetrates. We do not reach perfection between birth and death but each one is a spiritual being surrounded by hundreds and thousands of other spiritual beings. This consciousness, or at least this promise or presentiment, of an awakening to a spiritual existence penetrates us and is the result of the renewed Christ impulse. However, what for Rudolf Steiner at the end of the 1890's was the 'standing in most earnest celebration of recognition' wherein the Christ impulse revealed itself to him; only this—whether we acknowledge it or not—led to the birth of spiritual science. Spiritual science is alive; it lives in the light-wings of the Risen One. In the same lecture Rudolf Steiner says:

> Can I justify this that I am doing or thinking, not merely with reference to the immediate circumstances of my life and environment, but in the light of my responsibility

> towards the supersensible spiritual world? Can I justify it in the light of my knowledge that everything I do here on earth will be inscribed into an akashic record of everlasting significance, wherein its influence will work on and on? Oh, it comes powerfully home to one, this supersensible responsibility towards all things! It strikes one like a solemn warning, when one seeks the two-fold way to Christ—as though a Being stood behind one, looking over one's shoulder and saying repeatedly: 'Thou art not responsible only to the world around thee but also to the Divine-Spiritual, for all thy thoughts and all thy actions.'[7]

This is the Being of spiritual science.

> But this Being who looks over our shoulder, who heightens and refines our sense of responsibility and sets us on a new path—he is the one who first directs us truly to the Christ, Who went through the Mystery of Golgotha. It is of this Christ-way, how it may be found and how it reveals itself through the Being I have just described, that I wanted to speak to you today. For this Christ-way is most intimately connected with the deepest social impulses and tasks of our time.[8]

Let us endeavour to realise ever anew that the true working of spiritual science is identical with the new Christ impulse.

The Threefold Social Order

A Single Lecture

Newton Dee, 9th August 1964.

The Threefold Social Order

Newton Dee, 9th August 1964.

It is a great pleasure to be with you all again after such a long time. I have been asked to tell you something about the threefold social order—about the *idea* of the threefold social order—because you are going to work on this great and important theme. So I should like to give you a kind of historical introduction.

Whenever one opens a newspaper, periodical or illustrated magazine these days, one sees some picture or article referring to what happened fifty years ago. It was at this very time, half a century ago, that the first great World War started. It began both on the continent and in this country, and as the years went by it gradually spread to involve America and even Asia. During those years of fighting ten million human beings were killed, and thirty million were crippled or became invalids. It was a tremendous tragedy. The First World War still seems so recent—at that time most of your parents were still children; perhaps some had not yet even been born—and yet so far away. The soldiers and civilians of that period were different from today, and when we see pictures of them and observe what men, women and children looked like then, we sense that they belong to a time gone by, for when the war came to an end and the so-called 'peace' was finally declared, something entirely new began in the history of mankind.

Many people can still remember what life was like before the First World War, but there is a gulf between what had existed previously and everything that has happened since. Before the outbreak of war peace still reigned; a peace which permeated man and mankind, but afterwards there was no longer any real peace; even today we do not really live in peace. We have experienced the truth of this during the past week—how war is on the brink of breaking out everywhere—and we should understand that since 1914 there has been no peaceful life for the world at large. Today we have no idea what it was like sixty, seventy or eighty years ago. When the First World War came to a so-called 'end' and the actual fighting in the trenches, on the battlefields, in the air and on the oceans had ceased, there was chaos all over Europe. People did not know what was going to happen, but millions were longing for a new social order. Then revolution broke out—in Germany, Austria, France, Russia and the Balkans—because everywhere, especially on the continent of Europe, something had come to an end. Imperialism was over: every state which had been ruled by a king or an emperor came to an end. But what was to come? Nobody knew.

Into this chaotic situation Rudolf Steiner launched a new *idea* of ordering and arranging the whole social life. In 1919, 1920 and 1921 he began to speak and write about this new social order, which until then had been unknown. But many powers opposed it. Old thoughts and ideas, and deep-rooted traditions, were against him, and although he tried to take them up and mould them to fit these new ideas, they made it impossible to implement such a social experiment, even in a small way. We should learn to understand what these powers were. They brought the old social ordering of the life of the people to an end so that everything still remaining from former times was broken up. However, these special powers were of the greatest importance in establishing twentieth century life.

If we look back to the eighteenth century we can see the beginnings of the Industrial Revolution, which continued throughout the nineteenth century in all civilized countries. Before the Industrial Revolution, two or three people would have worked together to make something, but now great masses of people began to work in factories, using machines and engines to produce goods in large numbers. Before, there would have been a family of weavers, each of them sitting at a loom and doing their work, but now mills came into operation in which threads and material were mass-produced. Before, a cobbler would have made a shoe; now factories sprang up in which shoes were made by the thousand. The same thing happened with clothing, with everything. Hundreds of thousands of people left their villages for the towns to gather around the factories, and so became *workmen*. They lived a terrible life. Despite working twelve or fourteen hours a day they were underpaid, and even children of four or five years old were forced to work in the factories in order to earn a few pennies to help their parents.

In these people a great question arose: Are we not human beings too? Are we not as human as anyone else? They saw how the factory owners who bought their labour could live in freedom and they asked themselves: Should we not also have the right to live in freedom? These people were fighting for social equality and social freedom. Men like Robert Owen in this country, and Marx and Engels on the continent, became their mouthpiece, and this social, labour movement grew increasingly as a revolution from below breaking through the old established habits and traditions. Its aim was to give everyone what so far had only been granted to a few.

At that time there was a strong wish among the working people to become more fully human. However, most of their leaders lacked the insight necessary to understand what being human actually means, and what is needed in addition to food, clothing and a little money in order to remain human. So today, because of these misguided leaders, this social movement no longer exists. A hundred years ago there were workmen who knew what they wanted, and this was still the case when Rudolf Steiner launched the idea of the threefold social order. But today there are only bourgeois people who have enough money, and who no longer care about new social ideas.

The threefold social order could have been taken up in 1919 and 1920. Instead it was disregarded, pushed aside and dismissed. For this reason the Second World War became inevitable, and a third war seems bound to come. The whole twentieth century will be drenched in blood and misery, and this will go on until the idea of the threefold social order gradually develops in small communities, and it will continue until this social ideal spreads over whole countries and continents.

What is this idea? In order to explain it I will start from a quite different standpoint. The Greek philosopher Aristotle, one of the greatest philosophers who ever lived, had a deep insight into the nature of man. He called the human being a *zoon politikon*, a Greek term meaning that man is a social being. In saying this he meant that a man by himself is nothing; that as a single being he has no meaning. Man is only able to live as man if he is together with other people. We will understand this if we remind ourselves that everything we have learned has been acquired not on our own but through being taught by others. We have learned from our parents, our teachers, our masters, and from each other. None of us would even be able to speak if we had not grown up surrounded by other people. If a child were to grow up on a lonely island he would never learn to speak, and if he could not speak he would have no idea how to think. In the first three years of our lives we all make three fundamental steps. In the first year we learn to stand upright and walk; in the second year we begin to speak, and in the third year we formulate our thoughts. Walking, speaking and thinking are the three fundamental steps by which every human being prepares to become what Aristotle called a *zoon politikon*, a social creature.

The fundamentals of the threefold social order are contained in these three steps. In the family, the smallest entity in the social structure, we learn to *stand upright*. To *speak* is something that we have in common with the peoples among whom we are born—whether we are English, Scottish, German, American, French or whatever, we speak the language of the people to which our parents belong. But we *think* in common with all men. Once this is understood we will learn to see that there are three different realms in which man is a social being, and for which there are three preparatory stages. First we are embedded in the family. Later, at the age of seven, we go to school. Then, after puberty—although generally later at eighteen, nineteen or perhaps twenty—we go out into the world to live and work, and to found our own family. These stages constitute the social development of each human being. First we live in the family, then we go to school in order to learn, and after school or university is completed we go out into the world and work.

If we observe ourselves we can see that in reality we live in three different realms or layers of a social order. We live in the realm of *economy* in which we work in order to produce things. But we do not only produce, we also have to buy things which are made for us. We need our food, our houses, our clothes and so on; we need thousands of things without which it would be difficult to live. We need shelter and a warm room in winter, so houses have to be built and fire harnessed; clothes and shoes must be made and food prepared; all of which means work. Through their work the farmer, the shoemaker, the builder and the factory worker all belong in the realm of economy. And even before we *join* this sphere of economy we are nevertheless *part* of it, because we have to eat, to be clothed and to live in houses. But the economic sphere also includes other aspects as well. Certain things are grown in foreign countries which we need here, so thousands of ships are required to bring all kinds of food from overseas; meat, grain, vegetables, butter, eggs and so on. Britain is too small to produce enough food for all the people who live here, so we have to import much of it, usually as raw produce. However, Britain also manufactures goods and machinery which it ships to many other countries. If we could gain an overview of the economic sphere across the whole globe, we would see a tremendously complicated network with thousands of different goods coming and going. And everywhere there would be men and machines, working, producing, building, destroying and so on. All this is part of the economic sphere.

Today people sometimes seem to think that there is *only* an economic sphere. But who is going to decide how many hours each person should work? Who will determine how much payment each will receive for the production of goods, or for the work done? Or if somebody wants to build a house, who will decide where it should be built, or determine the ownership of the ground on which it will stand? If two people are at cross purposes with each other, who is to judge who is right and who is wrong? These are questions which belong in a second sphere: the realm in which *laws* are made and enforced; where *rights* are established. This is really the sphere in which the general connections between groups and individual human beings are determined. There must be a written or unwritten law somewhere which determines what we may and what we may not do; what is and what is not permitted.

These two spheres often seem to be quite sufficient. However, there is also a third, which is the realm of what is called the *spiritual life*. As human beings we do not only work and live under certain laws, but we also educate our children, we go to religious services, and we meet in order to learn, or to enjoy art and music—we meet in order to enhance each other. All this belongs to the third sphere.

I would like to draw your attention to the fact that these three spheres are always within us and around us. The idea of the threefold social order was not intended to *determine* the three spheres, but rather to be the means by which to divide and distinguish them. Now we come to something which I hope you will be able to grasp. Let us go back to the time before the First World War began and look at the different kinds of states that existed in Britain, Germany, Austria, France and elsewhere. In each we would find something which had been built up during recent centuries, from the thirteenth, fourteenth and fifteenth century onwards. We would find, of course, that the administering of the sphere of rights came under the government of the state. But we would also discover that the spiritual sphere had increasingly fallen under state control as well, so that a state religion emerged working hand in hand with the government. Even the economic sphere had gradually come under the jurisdiction of the state so that the economy was also ruled by the government, with the production of goods being controlled in such a way that the state held a kind of monopoly. For example, the government imposed a customs levy on goods imported and exported, and still today there are ministries of finance, of trade and industry, which govern the economic sphere.

Rudolf Steiner said we should gradually learn to *disengage* these three spheres from each other. The state *should* be responsible for the sphere of rights, which means that it should decide what kind of laws are introduced, and it is for the government and judiciary to ensure that people abide by the law. But that is *all* the government should do! The sphere of economy, however, should be kept quite apart from the state and should be entirely independent of its influence. The cry "Workers of the world, unite!" was right and justified in the sphere of economy. Economy should be allowed to work freely all over the globe, which means there should be no trade barriers between states. Instead, there should be import and export, coming and going, of goods. In the process of distribution, and the making and selling of goods, the state really should have nothing to say. In the same way it should have no voice in the sphere of spiritual life. It is completely against humanity that a ministry of education determines what kind of curriculum should be taught in schools. Parents aught to have a free say in the education of their children, and teachers should not be state officials, but should be supported by their villages or their towns. If education were allowed to be an enterprise then a free spiritual life would be able to unfold and gradually develop. The same holds good for medicine, and would also apply if priests were to depend entirely on the free support of their congregations.

This is what Rudolf Steiner tried to make clear to people. However, you will understand that the state and its officials would have lost an enormous amount of money if the economy were freed to work in its own sphere. They could not imagine how an 'unregulated' economy could possibly work. Nor could they imagine what would happen if frontiers were opened for goods to flow in and out from one country to another. They also did not have enough faith to see that it might be possible for schools and education, for art and religion, to live out of their own resources and power. Consequently this new idea was utterly doomed. Instead of the threefold ideal came the terror of nationalism and National Socialism. In Italy, Germany and Russia the state took everything into its own hands, and people were forced to do what their dictators told them to, and were even told what to think—every freedom was lost.

It was a kind of breaking of these fetters that unleashed the

Second World War, and since its 'end' we have remained in a state of continual warfare. Civilization moves in the opposite direction from the way it should, so that all over the world we now only have countries where the state rules; where the government—and in any government only a powerful few—determines what we should do, what we should eat, what we should think, how we should behave, and how we should work. Because of this, preparation is being made for the coming of another disaster. We really must recognise this. What we can do against it is not to *preach* the threefold social order, but in a humble way learn to *understand* it. Then tiny little plants—but beautiful plants nonetheless—will spring up in the realm of the human spirit, and they will gradually grow together, so that in time to come, when those of us here are no longer living, the idea of the threefold commonwealth will gradually take root in the social order of man.

Discussion

Question. Should we not speak of the commonwealth in two words, so that we don't think of the British Commonwealth? The word 'wealth' means 'weal'.

Dr. König. 'Threefold commonwealth' is really an incorrect term. We may understand what is meant, but when we talk to the world at large it will be misunderstood. We should use the term 'threefold social order'.

Question. If the state and the economy were separated, would the workers go on wanting more?

Dr. König. I think not. As soon as they are made responsible for their own economic life, responsible for their own factory or their own production, there will no longer be any individuals who take the money for their own work, but they will determine collectively how much each one needs to have.

Question. Will another war break out?

Dr. König. No one can say for certain. But it looks as if another war is going to come.

Question. The world will have to learn how to live together—the East and the West.

Dr. König. It will take a very long time before that happens. But in the meantime there will be a great deal of chaos.

Question. It is an advantage to live in a community. Although we cannot stop such chaos from occurring, we can really think together about what we are doing or what we have done, and begin to sow a new seed.

Dr. König. Yes, that is exactly what I mean.

Question. In the nineteenth century there was the Industrial Revolution. In the twentieth century we have seen a revolution in the social order, or at least its beginning. What will the twenty-first century bring?

Dr. König. It is my impression that a new social order will begin in the twenty-first century. In the twentieth century there is bound to be chaos and little else. We could not have escaped the chaos even if Rudolf Steiner's idea had been accepted. It will be the task of the twenty-first century to prepare men to understand what it means to be a real human being here on earth.

Question. How will the individual stand in the new social order?

Dr. König. The individual will matter in the free spiritual life: he will be important as an individual. He will stand as a brother in the economic life. It is the continual mixing up of these three spheres that has brought about the present chaos. The Common Market in Europe would have been an excellent idea if it hadn't been taken over by political forces. The moment the economic sphere is made political—the moment economics begins to take into account what kind of government rules a country—it begins to go wrong.

Question. Do you think the threefold social order will put science back on the right lines?

Dr. König. Yes, such things will begin, but you should not think it is going to be paradise. It will be a hard struggle, but it will be a worthwhile struggle. Rudolf Steiner's idea was the following. In the sphere of rights all men are equal. In the sphere of economy men should establish a kind of brotherhood and help each other. In the sphere of spiritual life each individual should be free in what he likes to think, to believe, and so on. Men would help each other in the sphere of economy; they would accept that naturally every man is equal before the law, without discrimination, and they would recognise that in the spiritual life each one is free. If this gradually comes about, then the right thing can arise. But it will take centuries before it achieves its proper order.

On Community Building

Three Lectures

Föhrenbühl, Michaelmas 1964.

First Lecture

Föhrenbühl, 20th September 1964.

Last Sunday I told you a little about our journey to Bohemia and about some of the impressions made on those of us who travelled together. We can definitely say that it was our visit to the Karlstejn castle which impressed us most.

As I have been interested both in the building itself and its history for a long time—perhaps for more than thirty years—I thought that it would be right to describe a little of the significance and position of this castle within the spiritual life of Europe. I propose to do this not simply because I have preoccupied myself with this building, but particularly because Rudolf Steiner referred to it from time to time in private talks. He said, for instance, that the builder of the Karlstejn, Karl IV, was 'the last initiate on an emperor's throne'. During a visit there—I believe it was in 1920—he accompanied Count and Countess Poltzer to the Chapel of the Holy Cross and pointed out that the frescoes along the staircase, which depict scenes from the life of St. Wenceslav and his grandmother St. Ludmilla, are in fact pictures illustrating the same path as that described in the Chymical Wedding.[1] In this way he indicated that this 'last initiate on an emperor's throne' had built and shaped this castle out of spiritual impulses.

For many people who visit this castle, when they enter one or other room or when they walk through this or that particular door, a spiritual recognition suddenly dawns; while others, perhaps hundreds of thousands, walk through the castle for whom it means nothing. Thus this building stands in the very centre, the very heart of Europe, yet it is still as pure and untouched as it was at the beginning. It is almost impossible to understand how the serenity of its structure, the strict beauty of its form, has remained intact, preserved in the state in which it once was. This was our impression, despite the enormous crowds. The guide told us that every year a quarter of a million people are herded through the castle in droves, yet it has lost none of its spiritual charm.

The castle is situated to the south west of Prague. If you approach it from either side you travel along the Beraun valley, ascend to a landscape of hills and forests, and suddenly the castle appears with its central tower and surrounding buildings high up on a rocky limestone outcrop, unapproachable from north, west and east: an enchanted place. You may ask why it is so enchanted: it is bare and square, and yet it is extraordinary.

It is important to consider the historical background against which this architectural structure arose. The foundation stone of the Karlstejn was laid in 1348; more or less exactly in the middle of the fourteenth century. But what is the significance of that century? Well, the Karlstejn is part of a mighty building impulse which sprang particularly from the personality of the emperor Karl IV. At the same time as the Karlstejn was constructed a certain part of Prague, the so-called 'small side', was also built. It was owing to Karl IV that the great artist Peter Parler built St. Veit's Cathedral; that the castle on the Hradshin was enlarged to mighty dimensions, and that Karl's Bridge spanning the Moldau was built in the heart of Prague. All these buildings still exist today, and if you cross Karl's Bridge you can hardly imagine how such a structure, so full of formative strength, was built six hundred years ago. As you walk across it the Hradshin and St. Veit's Catherdral gradually appear in sight.

However, this building development did not take place only in Prague. In Vienna, for instance, St. Stephen's Cathedral was built at the same time, as was Freiburg Minster and Cologne Cathedral. This building impulse had its roots in the Gothic period, yet was no longer in the true Gothic style, for it lead out of the height of the Middle Ages into the strange, extraordinary fourteenth century in which the old forms were broken down so that new ones could be created. These, however, were not in themselves yet perfect but they prepared the way for later forms to emerge.

During that same period Karl IV founded the first German

university in Prague. Very soon afterwards, in 1364, the University of Cracow was founded and then, only a year later, Vienna University; the University of Pecs followed in 1367. As a result the focus of European cultural life, in the sciences, theology and medicine, shifted from the west and south of Europe towards the east. This was also the time that the Order of Teutonic Knights spread eastwards into the Baltic countries, Poland and east Prussia. In contrast, we may recall how earlier, in the thirteenth century, the University of Paris was the centre of all knowledge and learning: Thomas Aquinas, Albertus Magnus and all the other reknowned men of the time taught there. Shortly before that, to the south of Paris, the School of Chartres had been a centre of medieval spiritual life, and there were also many famous universities in Italy. Now suddenly the east began to awaken and we can see that one of the characteristics of the fourteenth century is that central Europe was no longer limited by the boundary of the Rhine, west of which all the essential events had so far occurred. Now Bohemia, Hungary, Poland and the Baltic countries began to awaken. After Karl IV was crowned German king in 1346, and then Roman emperor in 1355, he became the first ruler to move the centre of his empire to eastern Europe. So for the first time Prague became the capital of Europe, and in and around it central institutions sprang up.

At the same time the first preliminaries of what would later be called Humanism and the Reformation developed in various places. Spanning the end of the thirteenth and the beginning of the fourteenth century towers the mighty figure of Dante—and we can hardly mention Dante without at the same time remembering his contemporary Giotto. In them we witness something like a conclusion of the Middle Ages, while at the same time we see the emergence of a modern trend of that time. For immediately after Dante lived Petrarch and Boccaccio, those two great Italian poets and writers who began to develop and present their thoughts and feelings in a more modern spirit. Just to read Boccaccio's *Decameron*, or some of the writings of Petrarch in which for the first time an attempt is made to transform Graeco-Roman culture into a European-Italian culture, is to realise that an important transition has occurred, namely that the ancient, all-embracing thought realm of men like Dante, which until then had been a kind of macrocosmos, has now come to an end. Mankind was beginning to acquire a new outlook.

We know through Rudolf Steiner that around the middle of the thirteenth century, approximately in the year 1250, a mighty incision in the spiritual life of mankind took place; an incision which brought to an end all immediate, direct spiritual perception. In the middle of the thirteenth century the boundary between the physical and spiritual worlds became impenetrable and even such great personalities as Thomas Aquinas no longer had the faculty to gain even the slightest insight into the spiritual world. Instead, what men did was to create a world of thought out of their own power of thinking. There was however, no more spiritual imagination, let alone spiritual inspiration, and so it is really the twilight of an earlier spiritual insight that Dante conveys to us in such magnificent beauty. At that time the last remnants of what had formerly been direct, immediate spirituality in the Middle Ages came to an end. Men were waking up, gaining self-recognition but at the same time losing the last vestiges of spiritual perception which previously they had still divined within themselves.

However, when such an event takes place it imprints a seal, and in the middle of the fourteenth century a terrible seal was impressed into European mankind which marked the end of the Middle Ages. This seal was the plague, which at that time was called the Black Death. I believe that today we cannot even begin to imagine the extent to which the plague ravaged Europe. Spreading from Constantinople in 1347, it made its way from Messina and Venice across the whole of Italy, swept through Switzerland and Southern Germany, through France to Northern Germany and Bohemia, and on into the Baltic countries reaching as far north as Iceland and Greenland. It then crossed the Atlantic to North America where it destroyed the last remnants of the Vikings in the settlements over which they had ruled for centuries. It is estimated that in central Europe alone almost half the entire population was exterminated during these few years. Untold millions perished; whole generations disappeared, parents and children, especially in the towns, but also the rural villages. The attacks recurred in the fifteenth, sixteenth and seventeenth centuries, but definitely not to the same extent as in the fourteenth century.

It is interesting to describe, at least tentatively, the character of this disease. It is an epidemic which is transmitted by rats and fleas. We should examine this because it is the lowest, the most devilish forms of animal existence which become the carriers of this epidemic. The flea picks up the plague bacillus from rats and transfers it to man. Festering boils develop where the fleas bite, but the centre of the plague's attack is the lung, the organ which Rudolf Steiner described as representing the earthly, solid element, and it is this element which is destroyed. You see, it is significant that just at the very time when man became a bearer of earthly, of sensory thoughts, millions were destroyed by this merciless epidemic which had its origin in Tibet. We should discuss this at length one day.

In the fourteenth century, concurrent with the first preparations by Petrarch and Boccaccio for the later humanism of the fifteenth and sixteenth century, the precursors of the Reformation also appear. From the point of view of world history something extremely interesting now emerges, because for the first time the close spiritual relationship between England and Bohemia became visible. The Reformation really began with John Wycliffe. Wycliffe was born in Yorkshire in approximately 1320, and later became a professor of Divinity at Oxford University. (Oxford was already a very famous university when the University of Prague was founded). Wycliffe was one of the first to harbour doubts both in Church Christianity, which by that time had become pompous and rigid, as well as in the priesthood and the supremacy of the Pope. He turned against celibacy and doubted the Transubstantiation in the Sacrament of Communion. He said—and this was one of his main teachings—that the Church should really be an invisible institution. For him the Church was nothing else than (and here I am quoting his own words) 'the invisible community of those who are predestined for blessedness or to a blessed life'. I mention this because it is most important to see how a new spirit, a new way of thinking emerges in the fourteenth century, even as far as into the realm of community. Wherever we look at the end of the Middle Ages we find only institutions; but institutions which are fixed outwardly by rules, habit and statutes. Now someone appears—and it is typical that he is an Englishman—who asserts that the true Church is not the visible one, but the invisible community of those who are predestined to blessedness or to a blessed life. At the same time, due to the awakening thought life, he doubts the Transubstantiation, for from where should he draw knowledge of it in order to know and accept it?

Wycliffe had a pupil called Hieronymus who was born in 1365 and was later known as Hieronymus of Prague because he became a teacher of Divinity at the University of Prague. He studied under Wycliffe in Oxford and later took his teachings over to Bohemia. This is one connection. Now, Hieronymus was a contemporary and friend of the great reformer Jan Hus, who was born in 1373 and who also taught at the University of Prague. Together these three, Wycliffe, Hieronymus of Prague and Jan Hus were really the fourteenth century forunners of the Reformation which took place in the sixteenth. We should not forget that both Hus and Hieronymus were burnt in Constance: Hus in 1415 and Hieronymus in 1416. This was during the time of the Council of Constance, which took place between 1414 and 1417. For us it is important to remember that these two men, who with Karl IV may be called the leaders of the Czecho-Bohemian awakening in the fourteenth century, were burnt here* by the Catholic Church.

Yet, underneath the outer spiritual life of this time, a new stream enters the religious as well as the literary and artistic life, and manifests as a building impulse. This stream is German mysticism. It emanated from the Order of the Dominicans—and only from them—in the thirteenth century, and flourished in the fourteenth. It began with Meister Eckhart who had sat at the feet of both Thomas Aquinas and Albertus Magnus, and who had created for himself a kind of renewed Platonism. He was able to

* Föhrenbühl, where these lectures were held, is situated on the Lake of Constance.

kindle within himself the spark of divine light through inner schooling—inner schooling because spiritual insight was no longer possible—and he calls this light his 'sparklet', by which he means the eternal light which every human soul can kindle within itself. He had pupils, who were also Dominicans, and one of them was Heinrich Seuse who lived either here in Überlingen or in Constance, from 1295 to 1366. Heinrich Seuse was an extraordinarily lovable personality, unbelievably delicate in his spiritual perceptions, but also extremely clear and determined in all he did. He was the first German biographer, and I would advise you to read his autobiography, or that of Karl IV, if you want to become better acquainted with the spirit of this region. However, the greatest of the first three German mystics is undoubtedly Johannes Tauler who lived from 1300 to 1361 and whose mighty activities centred on Alsace, Strasbourg and Basle. These three stars of the Dominican Order whose work streamed outwards as sermons from their innermost souls, were a further influential source for what came to pass in the fourteenth century.

Now, it is known that this mysticism was connected, particularly through Tauler, with the subterranean stream in history that is related to the activity of the 'Friend of God'. This 'Friend of God' was an exalted personality, none other than the great Zarathustra, who appeared again and again throughout history in order to lead mankind. In the cooperation between the great 'Friend of God' and the mighty preacher Tauler something appeared (for those who can recognise it) which worked as the innermost heart during the enigmatic history of that time.

You see, in the twelfth and thirteenth centuries—we could say until about 1220 or 1230—it was still possible for pupils who strove in earnest to find their spiritual teachers. Rudolf Steiner once described[2] in a touching way how these meetings took place. He related how the eye of the teacher could behold the pupil in such a way that immediate spiritual recognition developed, and how the pupil was then led to experience the spirit of his youth and the spirit of his old age, and that in doing so he discovered that in yonder world there is reality, while in this world there is only unreality. But as we have seen, this all came to an end after the turning point of the twelfth to the thirteenth century because that time no longer allowed immediate spiritual meetings. Instead, the following happened. Single individuals who ardently sought for the spirit gathered together and prayed, meditated and searched in common. As a result a very intimate mood began to fill such small circles, which made it possible for spiritual beings to appear to these small groups—although not in a physical sense—and tell them: 'Through your humanity, through your prayer, through your devotion you have called me'. So at the end of the thirteenth and throughout the fourteenth century these small spiritual beginnings developed in this way. By 'small' it is not implied that these were spiritually small, but rather germ-like beginnings which grew into what later became Rosicrucianism.

In this connection I would like to read you a passage from the work of Rudolf Steiner:

> But now in this pursuit of spiritual research we can detect the development of something that is of very great beauty. There are, as we said, the three brethren and the four. The three are only able to attain their goal when the four work with them; the two groups are absolutely interdependent. The three receive the revelations from the spiritual world; the four are able to translate the revelations into ordinary human language. What the three give would be nothing but utterly unintelligible pictures, were the four not able to translate them. And again, the four would have nothing to translate, if the three did not receive their revelations, in picture form, from the spiritual world. This interdependence gave rise to the development within such communities of an inner brotherhood of soul, a brotherhood in knowledge and in spiritual life, which in those days was held in some circles to be among the very highest of human achievements. Such small groups of men did indeed learn to know the true worth of brotherhood. And gradually they came more and more to feel how in the evolution of humanity towards freedom the bond between men and Gods would

> be completely severed were it not kept whole by this kind of brotherhood, where one looks to the other, where one is in very truth dependent on the other.[3]

So there were these small brotherhoods in which from time to time the three 'went out' as it were, received spiritual impulses and brought them back as images. The other four translated these images into signs or language comprehensible for that time, and so were able to use them and convey them to others. We must imagine not just one but several groups. Often they did not know of one another, for one group lived perhaps in a town, while another moved from village to village. Wherever they went they healed, and they spread preparatory impulses for what later became, in the fifteenth and sixteenth centuries, the secret Order of the Rosicrucians. These were the three and the four.

All these phenomena form part of the true recognition of what took place inwardly during the fourteenth century. But what happened outwardly? We shall just mention a few of the highlights. For instance, in 1381 Switzerland became a confederation. The state of the Teutonic Order developed in the East. In addition, the important ruling dynasties and their influence also came to an end with the close of the Middle Ages. There were no more Teutonic, Salian or Hohenstauffen emperors; all this was finished. Instead, one or other member of the various lineages ascended to the throne. For example, Karl IV was from Luxemburg: before him ruled a Bavarian, an Austrian, a member of the Hapsburg family. Thus it was quite uncertain who would rule.

Although Karl IV was small in stature, he was ingenious both in the realm of organising and of building. He instituted something which in my opinion is always completely misunderstood; he created the pragmatic law known historically as the Golden Edict. What was it, and what did it mean? The Golden Edict was a law which set out the regulations governing the election of the German Emperor, which it did in the following curious way. There were seven so-called Electors who had the right to appoint the Emperor. Thus there was no longer a hereditary succession based on the blood line. Instead, the seven were meant to find the most suitable person. Do you see the importance of this? Well, they mostly failed of course, but that was the intention! Who were these seven electors? They were made up of three clerical and four secular persons. Can you now see what Karl IV was driving at? He wanted to create something born of his knowledge derived from those small, inspired circles who were active in the substratum of history. So the Golden Edict demanded three prelates who were meant to receive inspirations and four secular rulers who should translate them and put them into action. The three were the Archbishops of Mayence, Treves and Cologne. The four were the rulers of Saxony, Brandenburg, the Palatinate and Bohemia. The strange thing is—and this is so characteristic of Karl IV—that the three clerics represented the world—Cologne stood for Italy, Mayence for Germany and Treves for Burgundy—while the four secular office bearers were the Lord Cup-bearer, the Lord High Steward, the Lord Marshall and the Lord Chamberlain. Now, of course this did not mean that they served wine and food to the emperor and kept his rooms tidy. They represented the wine and the bread of the Eucharist, the altar and the vestment. In this way the spiritual and the earthly were intertwined in the Golden Edict, and at its core we find the wellspring of the Rosicrucian impulse to which we have already drawn attention.

This underlying Rosicrucian source is the true, hidden background of the building of the Karlstejn. Nowadays historians and others who write about the Karlstejn explain that it was built solidly in order to safeguard the Crown insignia and the important documents of the state securely within its walls. Of course, outwardly they are right, but they are also wrong because Karl IV was an initiate on the emperor's throne and although his aims were premature, nevertheless in reality they tried to express the spiritual efficacy of the emperor as representative of the spirit on earth. The emperor's insignia were kept in the place of holiest Christianity; the documents of state were drawn up and signed in the place of highest activity of faith. This was the intention, the purpose, for which the Karlstejn was built.

Perhaps we may still undertake a brief survey of the building itself. I have already told you how we meet various structures on approaching the Karlstejn. In fact, the highest structure is a square tower which stands alone, connected only by a small wooden passage to a second building which is a little larger, but which lies somewhat lower and is also isolated. This building, too, is connected by a passage and gallery to a much larger building which is laid out like this: *(see diagram below)* These are the three main buildings. The entrance is about here; here is a first gate, here a second gate, and then there is a large courtyard; there is a fourth building here and then we come upon something else which I shall mention in a moment. You will notice that all this has a strange layout: it is a kind of snail which has its mid point in the highest and most central part. The building with the adjoining

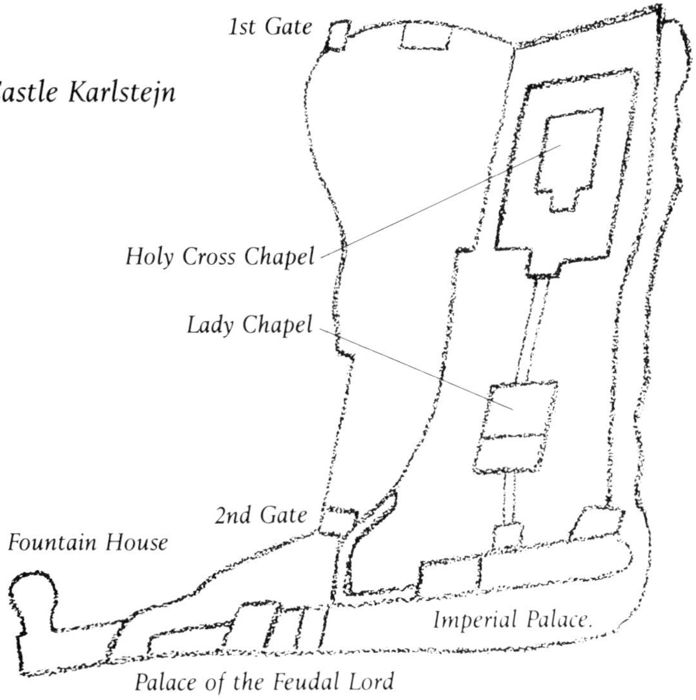

Castle Karlstejn

yard was the palace with the apartments of the feudal lord and has nothing to do with the castle itself. This was a kind of courtyard, and in it is a spring which still flows today, immured as it is deep under the earth. It is all built on rock and you can still see the rocks showing. This larger building here is the Imperial Palace; here are the living rooms and there is a small chapel for the imperial family and its entourage.

Then you walk on a little further and enter a part of the building which consists of two sections. The one is the Lady Chapel which was originally decorated with scenes from the Apocalypse; wonderful representations of the whole Apocalypse of which, unfortunately, only a few remains can be seen today. The small side chapel adjoining the Lady Chapel was built for Karl IV. He would enter it every year on Maundy Thursday staying there in prayer and meditation until Easter Sunday, during which time he did not receive anyone. There was only a small hatch through which the most important documents could be handed in for signing, as well as drink and a little food. Then you go up to the tower in which a long flight of steps leads to the highest chapel, the Chapel of the Holy Cross. On the left side of the stairs are pictures showing the life of St. Wenceslav, while on the right are scenes from the life of his grandmother St. Ludmilla. The pictures of Wenceslav show him sowing and harvesting the corn; threshing the wheat, milling flour and baking the bread. Then follow scenes of pruning and gathering the grapes, pressing and preparing the wine. Then you arrive at the door of the chapel, and above it Karl IV is shown in front of an altar and behind it his three deceased wives. When the door opens you find yourself standing in a large room which is divided in two by a lattice, the larger part being in front of it. The walls are inlaid everywhere with beautiful, precious stones; carnelian, topaz, beryl, etc. The walls above are covered with portraits of saints which were painted by the great Theoderich of Prague: about a hundred and thirty portraits altogether. It is forgotten today that behind many of these portraits a relic connected with that saint was set into the wall. In the smaller part is an altar and above it holy relics from Golgotha were also set into the wall. So you can actually feel yourself surrounded by the sacrifice and suffering of so many important saints. Even today, anyone who so wishes can feel himself similarly surrounded. In the atmosphere of this room something quite extraordinary lives and weaves. The documents relating to the Golden Edict were kept in the chests along the wall, while behind the altar the insignia of the Empire were locked.

So you see, here (*pointing to the Imperial Palace*) was the place of bodily existence; then on entering the Lady Chapel the life of the soul was experienced and finally, ascending to the highest place, the Chapel of the Holy Cross, something of the fire of the Holy Spirit was kindled. In this way one aspect of the Karlstejn can be described. On another occasion we shall discuss this castle in connection with the threefold structure of the social organism, but to do so today would lead us too far.

In conclusion, however, I would like to draw your attention to the following. The fourteenth century which we have tried to understand is framed by two important events: one occurs in 1314 and the other in 1413. In 1314 the last Knights Templar were burnt together with their last Grand Master Jacques de Molay at the instigation of King Philip le Bel of France, one of the most evil figures in history. In this way the Middle Ages were destroyed by fire and sword. Then the first stirrings of the pre-Reformists and pre-Humanists began, and the first beginnings of Rosicrucianism and mysticism also appeared at this time. This leads over to the year 1413 when a new impulse emerges—the age of the Consciousness-soul sets in, in which we still live today. This is the time of the fourteenth century, the time of Karl IV, who was born in 1316 and died in 1378.

In this same year, 1378, Christian Rosenkreutz is reborn. In his journeys he goes to Holland, where he becomes a brother. From there he travels to Damascus, Arabia and Egypt, where he absorbs the last remnants of eastern spirituality. On his return he founds the Order of the Rosicrucians in 1459, uniting the many small springs of those brotherhoods of seven which we described earlier. The Reformation now breaks out. As well as Humanism, printing is invented, and what we know as the modern times gains momentum. It is something very profound that happened, because the inner stream of the continuity of the Spirit was preserved. But the decision as to whether this would be possible or not fell in the fourteenth century to the one who helped both to turn it outward, and yet on the other hand helped to preserve it inwardly; to Karl IV. The Karlstejn is the monument to these events. This can still be experienced today if we have an open heart for a meeting with this building; the influence of Rosicrucianism can still be divined. When we walk through the gates we can somehow feel that Christian Rosenkreutz himself passed through them.

This is what I wanted to describe today and I hope we will be able to come back to it on the 28th September in the spirit of Michaelmas.

Second Lecture

Föhrenbuühl, 28th September 1964.

Today forty years have passed since Rudolf Steiner addressed a large circle of people for the last time. It was on the 28th September 1924[1] that he gave an address, after weeks of concentrated work and lecturing, being in severe pain and seriously ill. He said on that occasion that the approaching mood of Michaelmas—and these are his words—'which shall radiate out from this day also into the day of tomorrow and the days following' gave him the urge to speak once more. Many of us have made it a custom to read this address every Michaelmas and perhaps more often throughout the year. We might have experienced that on approaching this address its words cause a particular mood to arise. All that Rudolf Steiner says in it is permeated by a mood of sorrow, of farewell. Those who were present at that time confirm this, independently of each other. It is indeed the same farewell which can be experienced in nature at this time of year; the farewell which arouses a gentle sorrow in the soul, a sorrow connected with the experience of early autumn.

However, from within the sorrow that resounds in Rudolf Steiner's words there arises something like the hope of recognition; in the mood of departure something is born that can only be called the germ of resurrection. The germ of resurrection lives in that which is dying. But what is the essence of this *Last Address*?

Rudolf Steiner looks back once more to the beginning of his activity in the realm of spiritual science; to the year 1902 in which he held the lectures that appeared later as the book *Christianity as Mystical Fact*.[2] What matters in this book is that at its centre the one who was the writer of the Gospel of St. John, Lazarus-John, is mentioned by name more or less for the first time. This was said in simple but unmistakable words in this the first (or almost the first) of Rudolf Steiner's books in the realm of spiritual science.

Now at the end of 1924—the year in which he gave us, among hundreds of lectures on other themes, the eighty karma lectures in which he traced the destinies of the leading personalities, especially those of the nineteenth century—Rudolf Steiner turns once more in his *Last Address* to the being whom he had indicated at the beginning of his karmic investigations, namely the being of Elias-John. In this way an arch is built uniting with the arch of Lazarus-John, because Rudolf Steiner reveals for the first time that John the Baptist and John the Evengelist are the same personality. Then he traces the path through the Christian era of this same being, who later became the painter Raphael, and who not so long ago was the poet Novalis.

The extraordinary thing about this *Last Address* is that Rudolf Steiner opens the gates, as it were, and allows us to look at the period of 252 years which passed between the death of Raphael in 1520 and the birth of Novalis in 1772, and we are permitted to follow the path of this soul through the spheres of the heavenly planets. At the end of the address Rudolf Steiner calls upon mankind by suddenly revealing how important it will be for men to come forward; for men to unite and become leaders of true Michaelmas festivals. Perhaps I should read you the paragraph in which he says this:

> If, in the near future, in four times twelve human beings, the Michael Thought becomes fully alive—four times twelve human beings, that is, who are recognized not by themselves, but by the Leadership of the Goetheanum in Dornach—if in four times twelve such human beings, leaders arise having the mood of soul that belongs to the Michael festival, then we can look up to the light that through the Michael stream and the Michael activity will be shed abroad in the future among mankind.[3]

We should inscribe this into our hearts because it belongs to the last words which Rudolf Steiner spoke to the community of members of the Anthroposophical Society. It is a call to form a community around four times twelve people, and that this community should stand in the sign of a Michaelmas festival renewed out of the Spirit. Then Rudolf Steiner places a seal onto what is to come by speaking the closing words of the address; the words of the great Michael meditation. This, in a nutshell, is the content of the *Last Address*.

If we consider this address as the crowning of all that happened in the previous months, then we can see how from April or May of the previous year (1923) onward, Rudolf Steiner directs our attention in an ever stronger, ever more decided way to Michael. He points out that it is the aim of Michael to awaken us so that we may become his pupils.

There is a special lecture held in Berlin on 23rd May 1923 in which Rudolf Steiner points out with great urgency—for the first time, as far as I am aware—the need to institute a new Michaelmas festival. This lecture deserves our study, for it is the last he held in Berlin, and therefore again a farewell with a note of sorrow.

Rudolf Steiner begins the lecture by turning back to the burning of the first Goetheanum. He speaks about this event in very impressive words and makes some essential remarks, of which I would like to read just one sentence:

> For even if some kind of building for our purposes should arise at the same place—which should definitely come about—it cannot become a full replacement of the old Goetheanum, because of the difficult circumstances of our time.[4]

He then breaks off and begins to speak about the study of man. He describes the acquisition of walking, speaking and thinking in the first three years of the child, and how on coming to earth from the spiritual world the human soul brings these faculties with it through previous spiritual meetings and experiences, and how they then awaken as true humanity in the small child. He speaks at length about sleeping and waking, about death and rebirth, and finally at the end of an extremely long lecture which is filled with all the new discoveries of a spiritual scientist of that time, he suddenly points to Michael and to the future festival of Michaelmas which did not yet exist. Of course, old Michaelmas festivals were still celebrated at that time—the word 'Michael' was even printed in the calendar on the 29th September and farming festivals were celebrated then—but for the most part mankind had completely forgotten that a Michael festival once stood behind the Harvest festival. We would have to go back to pre-Christian times in order to discover that festivals of resurrection were celebrated within the Mysteries at this time of year, in autumn.

However, in our time something new should begin. I will read you some passages from this lecture because these are the first words which should lead to the renewal of the festival of Michael:

> He who fathoms the secrets of the earth's circuit during the course of the year will know that the Michael force is now descending again through the Nature-forces—the Michael force which did not descend in former centuries. Thus we can face the leafless autumn, inasmuch as we look towards the approach of the Michael force out of the clouds.[5]

Later he continues:

> When, however, the festivals which we celebrate without understanding them, will again be understood, then we shall have the strength to establish out of a spiritual understanding of the year's course, a festival which only now for present-day humanity, has any real significance: this will be the Michael Festival. It will be a festival in the last days of September, when autumn approaches, the leaves wither, the trees grow bare and Nature faces death—just as it faces a new budding life at Easter time—and when we experience in Nature's fading life, how the soul of the earth is then united with the earth and brings with it Michael out of the clouds.[6]

During autumn the soul of the earth is inhaled into the body of the earth, into the circumstances of man, and thereby into the souls of men. Since 1879 the Michael-power has united with this inhaling and streams in more and more in our time. This process, which happens every year but which men mostly overlook because they sleep through it, should bring about something which Rudolf Steiner describes in the following way:

> Far more important than other reflections on social conditions—which can lead to no results in our present chaotic conditions, unless they contain the spirit—would be this: that a number of open-minded people should come together for the purpose of instituting again on earth something proceeding out of the universe, as, for instance, a Michael Festival. This would be the worthy counterpart of the Easter Festival, but a festival taking place in autumn, an autumn festival. If people could determine upon something, the motive to which can be found only in the spiritual world, something which can kindle feelings of fellowship amongst those who assemble at such a festival—arising out of the fullness and freshness of the human heart through immediate contact—then something would exist which could bind men together again socially.
>
> For in the past, festivals used to bind human beings strongly together. Just think, for instance, of all that has been done and said and thought in connection with festivals for the whole of civilization.[7]

These are weighty words which should not only be confimed intellectually but should be taken to heart, because only then will they gain the power of will. Then, at the end of these deliberations, Rudolf Steiner says:

> But the courage would have to be found amongst them not merely to discuss external social reforms, etc., but to do something that connects the earth with the heavens, that re-connects physical with spiritual conditions.
>
> Thus something would again take place amongst men, constituting a mighty impulse for the continuation of our civilization and our whole human life; because the Spirit would once more be introduced into earthly conditions.[8]

In such words we hear very clearly how the future Michael festival must be a festival of community; not a festival of the withdrawing individual, but a festival of the individual who wants to become a member of the whole community. This is what matters.

If we look at the lecture as a whole, the last lecture held in Berlin from which I have quoted, one thing becomes clear, which is the following. The Goetheanum ceased to exist and the moment it disappeared there arose the impulse to establish and institute a Michael festival which should work towards the formation of communities. You see, what we should learn from this lecture is a Michaelic recognition, namely that temples, buildings or any architectural works of art which are true, are always connected with social impulses whether secret or public; hence the names 'mason' and 'freemason'. The craftsmen and builders who built the cathedrals and churches could only do so by virtue of the fact that they themselves were a guild, for cathedrals and churches are erected in order to make a community possible. The impulse to become a community or a congregation asks for a building, or first erects a building in order to be able to work in it.

It is one of the secrets of architecture that it immediately causes social structure or social formation. Just as the Goetheanum arose and vanished, so also forms of community will have to arise out of Goetheanistic impulses. The church as a building unites the community of the believers; those who build the church are the circle of the ones who know. That this is so becomes clear from another part of Rudolf Steiner's work, namely from two lectures held in Stuttgart[9] ten years before 1923, also in the month of May, in which for the first time he points to the Michael impulse in our time. He does this at the precise moment when the decision had been taken to erect the Goetheanum on the hill of Dornach.

We can say that the Goetheanum arose and vanished surrounded by a Michael impulse. In the Michael festivals, the Goethanum should reappear, forming and building communities. If this is done in the right way, it cannot any longer be destroyed by flames. This is one of the things to which I wanted to draw your attention.

The other is a strange fact which might belong to those signs of the time to which Rudolf Steiner refers in this lecture; namely that on September 28th 1864, sixty years before the *Last Address*, Karl Marx founded the first Socialist International in St. Martin's Hall in London. Before that many workers' unions had been founded, but from the middle of the last century onwards the proletariat which had awoken at that time tried to become a power which makes history, and it is now a hundred years since the international movement of workers was established. This is also an important sign of the times.

This event took place fifteen years before the beginning of the age of Michael. Workers gathered from all over the world and for the first time began to realise that they were a united power. It was indeed a Michaelic impulse, for it transcended nations and was taken up by the powers of will of those men who wanted to become leaders, and justifiably did so. However, it was not the fault of the workmen themselves that things developed differently, but rather the fault of the intellectuals who led them in an anti-Michaelic way. It is important to consider this.

Now let us look back to what I tried to indicate last Sunday concerning the Karlstejn. In the same way as the Goetheanum, this was also a building which was intended to be community-forming. Arising out of Rosicrucian impulses, it was meant to point to social-political impulses which should have become reality; impulses such as, for instance, the Golden Edict about which I spoke at length. But it was too early; nobody could understand it, and therefore the impulse had to withdraw again.

This complex building is a threefold one. I described it to you before and perhaps you will permit me to repeat it again briefly. The first part is the Imperial Palace in which Karl IV acted socially. There are the reception rooms, the dining rooms and bedrooms; everything that is necessary for the unfolding of the outer might of a personality. If you walk through these rooms, even today you have the impression that they must have been filled with all that the economic power and craftsmanship of those days could produce in stone, precious stones, clay and other materials.

From this building a little bridge leads to the second, the middle building, which is dominated by the Lady Chapel on the walls of which were depicted scenes from the Book of Revelation. From this second building, which is entirely independent of the first and rises above it, another bridge leads to the third building which is a kind of square tower, somewhat higher than the second building and very much higher than the first. On entering it one ascends a flight of stairs, guided and accompanied on both sides by a series of pictures which describe the making of bread and wine by the work of man. Then one opens the door and enters the chapel. I have described how its walls are covered with semi-precious stones and that on the upper part of the walls are numerous pictures of saints and martyrs, each set in gold. The documents of the Holy Roman Empire were kept in this chapel, but it was also a chapel for meditation and the Christian cult.

The description of these three buildings indicates the three spheres of the social organism. The Imperial Palace, filled with all the treasures of the earth, suggests the sphere of the economic life. Independent of this is the sphere of the legal life and again independent of these is the tower with the Chapel of the Holy Cross, the sphere of the spiritual life. The coming form of the social order of mankind is anticipated architecturally in this group of buildings which, full of mysteries, was built in central Europe out of Rosicrucian impulses.

But how can we understand this more clearly? If we describe the economic, legal and spiritual life in this way, we can ask ourselves where, in truth, are these three spheres to be found? They do not develop merely because people work together, or that one judges the other and draws up laws, or the fact that some people are artists, poets or scientists. For these three spheres of social life simply are; they exist. If we ask the fundamental question of where they can be found, then the following answer, among others, may be given.

The sphere of the economic life is our Mother Earth, for out of the earth, through human labour, comes all that we need for life. We also receive water, stones, the minerals, clay and fibre. The earth has given everything to us in immeasurable abundance so far, and the new world which has arisen in the last hundred years is no contradiction to this archetypal image. Mother Earth is the homeland of all that can be called the economic life.

And what of the legal life? Why is the Lady Chapel decorated with scenes from the Book of Revelation? It is because the Book of Revelation describes the entry of the Logos into the realm of the earth and of mankind. The legal sphere is the sphere surrounding the earth; the sphere of language. Therefore we say that 'judgment is pronounced'—law and order express themselves in words alone. The human word filled by the word of God is the law according to which we live and work here on earth.

What do we meet in the Chapel of the Holy Cross? There saints and martyrs and all those who have died gaze down at us, and if we really want to understand the spiritual life we must learn that it is the sphere in which the dead and the unborn have their homeland. Spiritual life becomes active where the living communicate with those who have crossed the threshold or who are beyond the threshold. The ancient teachers of wisdom who no longer come down to dwell on earth, the angelic beings, the unborn—all these form the background of spiritual life. It is into this sphere that Michael shines and radiates, calling us, gazing at us, waiting for us to recognise him. This is the call which goes out to us today. It is the call that sounds forth from Michael's messengers when they urge men to come to the wedding meal. However, the one goes to his fields, the other has to give his daughter in marriage, the third to fill his purse, and as a result the call fades away for many, the call which Rudolf Steiner once spoke in a new form in these verses:[10]

> Springing from Powers of the Sun,
> Radiant Spirit-powers, blessing all Worlds!
> For Michael's garment of rays
> Ye are predestined by Thought Divine.

Then there appears the face which shines through the sphere of the unborn and of the dead, saying:

> He, the Christ-messenger, revealeth in you—
> Bearing mankind aloft—the sacred Will of Worlds.

It is radiant power that appears, and out of the radiance the

the Logos now streams forth:

> Ye, the radiant Beings of Ether-Worlds,
> Bear the Christ-Word to Man.

It streams down to men.

> Thus shall the Herald of Christ appear
> To the thirstily waiting souls,
> To whom your Word of Light shines forth
> In cosmic age of Spirit-Man.

This is the second part, and describes the second sphere. It calls men to the Kingly Wedding and turning to men it says:

> Ye, disciples of Spirit-Knowledge,
> Take Michael's Wisdom-beckoning,
> Take the Word of Love of the Will of Worlds
> Into your souls' aspiring, actively!

Listen to the call, it says, and join the Kingly Wedding.

With these words Rudolf Steiner placed in our hands a tool for the forming of Michael communities to celebrate Michael festivals; not to miss one's fellowman by sleeping, but to meet him awake in one's willing. This is what matters in our time, which is a Michael-time; a time in which man should never lose sight, or knowledge of, the Michael festival striving to become the core of community-building.

Third Lecture

Föhrenbühl, 29th September 1964.

Yesterday evening we tried to raise some aspects of Rudolf Steiner's *Last Address* into consciousness, because forty years have now passed since it was held on the 28th September 1924. It seems to me that in our deliberations we came to recognise an important aspect which is not always seen or understood in the right way, namely that architectural style and building forms are intimately connected with what is built up in the social realm; in short, with community-building.

I believe this is a very important realisation. We were able to recollect how through the event of the burning of the Goetheanum—when the outer building went up in flames, and the beauty and grandeur of that mighty work of architecture perished—how at that moment Rudolf Steiner had to call upon a new impulse; namely to rebuild what had been destroyed outwardly as wood, concrete and glass in a new way. This impulse was to build a new society, an Anthroposophical Society with new aims. These two events, the burning of the Goetheanum and the formation of the General Anthroposophical Society through the Christmas Foundation Meeting 1923, are closely connected. They are as intimately connected as building in stone and building in the social realm are always connected in history. This is what I meant yesterday in saying that the knowledgeable (the Freemasons) erect the buildings in order that the less knowledgeable can congregate in them—be it a temple or circus, church or mosque—for common work or common activity: in short, for community. This is something we should not lose sight of, especially in view of the fact that we planned to study the various forms of communities and community building this winter.

A further aspect should be added to this which is peculiar to our time. We referred to it yesterday and I would like to do so once more today in order that Rudolf Steiner's words can resound here. We said that after the burning of the Goetheanum Rudolf Steiner wove the building of communities into a light-filled Michael-activity. After the Goetheanum was destroyed he made us understand that a consciousness must begin to awaken for the celebrating of Michael festivals, because only through the celebrating of such Michael festivals can community building develop. On the 23rd May 1923 in Berlin he said the following:

> When, however, the festivals which we celebrate without understanding them, will again be understood, then we shall have the strength to establish out of a spiritual understanding of the year's course, a festival which only now for present-day humanity, has real significance: this will be the Michael Festival. It will be a festival in the last days of September, when autumn approaches, the leaves wither, the trees grow bare and Nature faces death—just as it faces a new budding life at Easter time—and when we experience in Nature's fading life, how the soul of the earth is then united with the earth and brings with it Michael out of the clouds. When we acquire the strength to establish such a festival out of the spirit—a festival that brings with it once more a feeling of fellowship into our social life—then we shall have established it spiritually: for we shall then have founded something in our midst which has the spirit at its source. Far more important than other reflections on social conditions—which can lead to no results in our present chaotic conditions, unless they contain the spirit—would be this: that a number of open-minded people should come together for the purpose of instituting again on earth something proceeding out of the universe, as, for instance, a *Michael Festival*. This would be the worthy counterpart of the Easter Festival, but a festival taking place in autumn, an autumn festival.

> If people could determine upon something, the motive to which can be found only in the spiritual world, something which can kindle feelings of fellowship amongst those who assemble at such a festival—arising out of the fullness and freshness of the human heart through immediate contact—then something would exist which could bind men together again socially.[1]

This is the important point because it was the essence of the architecture and form of the Goetheanum. It will only find its social resurrection if the celebrating of true Michael festivals by communities of men becomes more and more established. However, something else arises from these considerations, namely the fact that it is not only the building activity itself which is connected with the social realm, but also that during the building process, and then within these buildings, festivals are celebrated. Festive moments of the circle of the year are held fast (the word 'festival' is derived from 'to hold *fast*') in order that they can be inscribed into the human soul in such a way that those who celebrate together form a union, an order, a community.

One of the many reasons why contemporary social life is in a state of such complete decline is that our time has gradually forgotten to acknowledge the importance of celebrating festivals, and this is because people today are actually ashamed when they prepare to celebrate a festival in common. This is the reason. Well, these are words of introduction in order to round off what was said yesterday.

If we are to continue what we began yesterday evening, we must turn to something else. Let us ask how the Goetheanum was built. As a background we saw how building is connected with social structure, and that social structures are linked with the celebrating of festivals both within and around architectonic structures, so that out of them social forms may arise. If we look back, we realise that it is just fifty years since the First World War cast its dreadful shadow over mankind, and we may acknowledge how the Goetheanum arose as an island of peace during the storms of that war. Moreover, it is an important image for the history of our century that in this island enclave on the Dornach hill near Basle a group of people erected a building, and that this small group of people consisted of representatives of all those nations that were at war with each other in the countries surrounding this enclave. They erected a building from which a certain impulse could go forth.

Between the years 1914 and 1918/1919 something of special importance came to fruition. Superficially, it could be thought to have ripened parallel to the emergence of the Goetheanum, but in reality it did so in close connection, in intimate relationship with the development of that building. I shall try to describe very briefly what this was.

In the years 1916 and 1917 two fundamental works by Rudolf Steiner appeared. They are very little known today, and are not even translated into English because they have not been taken as seriously as they should have been. *Riddles of the Human Being*[2] was published in 1916, and was followed in 1917 by the book *Riddles of the Soul*.[3] The titles already indicate that Rudolf Steiner wanted to show the connection between them. If you read the book *Riddles of the Human Being*, you will find that he looks back to the time of the 19th century and tries to discover the threads which lead to those personalities who still represented a genuine spirituality in the cultural life of that period. He describes the three great philosophers Fichte, Hegel and Schelling, portraying them as the last twilight of the entire European spiritual life within which, however, already appeared the germ of a new spirit-light. He outlines the mighty points of departure taken in the works of a philosopher such as Immanuel Hermann Fichte, the son of Johann Gottlieb, who perceives the content of future anthroposophy through the power of his intellectual, yet all-embracing, consciousness. Fichte even uses the word 'anthroposophy', by which he means the new spiritualised knowledge of man, which he foresees but is as yet unable to present in full clarity himself. Rudolf Steiner then turns to personalities like Karl Christian Planck, Wilhelm Heinrich Preuss, on many of whom dawns the first inkling of reincarnation and karma, and he discusses, for instance, poets of Austria's cultural life who were full of spirituality. This is the content of the book *Riddles of the Human Being*, and if you read it over again you will realise how threads were taken up in it which should have formed a bridge to what was later revealed as spiritual science at the beginning of the Light Age.

The other book that was published a year later is called *Riddles of the Soul*. Here a different note resounds, for it turns not to the past, but to the future. The book starts on a discord with a sharp analysis of the work of the contemporary psychologist and philosopher Max Dessoir, who is heavily criticised by Rudolf Steiner. Then follows an appreciation of the psychologist and philosopher Franz Brentano who had died a short time before, and about whom much could be said as he was indeed a precursor of an anthroposophical psychology. Following this, Rudolf Steiner sketches a new knowledge of man–which he himself calls an outline presentation–in which the twelve senses of man are described, and where he points out for the first time the threefold structure of the soul and the threefold structure of the human physical organisation. He also describes the unity of the nervous system not as a motor-sensory apparatus, but solely as a sensory apparatus. Furthermore, the knowledge of man is widened from many other aspects.

What does this really signify? In the book *Riddles of the Soul* the foundation is laid for a Michaelic spiritual science, and this Michaelic knowledge of man is the prerequisite for something which should also have developed during that time, namely the idea of the threefold structure of the social organism. We surely see in this a mutual connection with the building of the Goetheanum, and realise that within the Goetheanum a Michaelic knowledge of man, a Michaelic natural science, was meant to grow in order that around the completed Goetheanum something else could develop, namely a social organism which would radiate into the surrounding peoples of Europe.

If we are able to understand this then we will gain some insight into the divine thoughts that are connected with the building of the Goetheanum. A building was to be constructed within which natural science and all the materialistic knowledge of that time should be permeated by spirit-recognition and thereby become Michaelic. From this place messengers should carry order, social order, out into the decaying society of that period which was shaken by the murder, the millionfold murder of the First World War—shaken by the collapse of the morality of the past; shaken by the collapse of spiritual knowledge. These were the intentions.

This would have been possible to a degree, because for the renewal of a Michaelic natural science no clairvoyance is needed, but purely and simply the courage of spirit-recognition. Soon after the Christmas Foundation Meeting, in a lecture given on 13th January 1924,[4] Rudolf Steiner described how spirit-recognition could develop in the course of history. In the beginning of this lecture he points out the fact that the time in which we live has acquired a special nature with regard to recognition. In earlier times, he says, it was the case that the initiates could see into the world, into Creation, and that within this world they met the spirit of the creative, formative powers. He describes how initates of the Old Persian epoch, for instance, beheld the forms of the earth and how within these—whether animal or plant forms, stones or minerals, or the surface of the earth itself—they met spiritual activity as spiritual images. Later, in the Egyptian period, the initates looked into the watery element; in the Greek period the Spirit-vision showed itself in the element of air like a *Fata Morgana*. At the beginning of the European period, the beginning of the Middle Ages, the last initiates, for instance individual Rosicrucians, tried to experience this mirroring of the spirit within the element of warmth. Therefore it was necessary for them to make use of auxiliary means. They studied and absorbed the knowledge of the earthly world, (we may recall such individuals as Faust, Paracelsus and others), and took it into sleep; carried it as knowledge into the spirit and waited for the spiritual answer which revealed to them in pictorial symbols what they should know and were allowed to know.

Rudolf Steiner points out that in our time it is no longer necessary to carry this knowledge into sleep, but that it is possible, by a particular effort of thinking, to gain the answer during waking consciousness. This is done by studying contemporary natural science, absorbing it and then carrying it towards Michael from whom the earthly knowledge is then received back, transformed into spiritual knowledge.

> The possibility has remained until this present. It is so indeed, my dear friends. If you are touched by the Rosicrucian principle as here intended, study the system of Haeckel, with all its materialism; study it, and at the same time permeate yourselves with the methods of cognition indicated in *Knowledge of the Higher Worlds and its Attainment*.[5] Take what you learn in Haeckel's *Anthropogenesis: the Ancestors of Man*.[6] In that form it may very likely repel you. Learn it nevertheless; learn all that can be learned about it by outer, Natural Science, and carry it towards the Gods; then you will understand what is related about evolution in my *Occult Science*.[7]
>
> Such is the connection between the feeble, shadowy knowledge which man can acquire here with his physical body, and that which the Gods can give him, if with the proper spirit he duly prepares himself by the learning of this knowledge. But man must first bring towards them what he can learn here on Earth, for in truth the times have changed.[8]

This should have happened in the Goetheanum, and indeed in all places where the impulse of the Goetheanum worked, or should have worked. Had it done so, a comprehensive, Michaelic knowledge of man would have been attained, and the Michaelic messengers would have gone out from the Goetheanum in order to establish the reality of a threefold social organism. Historically, it was a terrible disaster that fire destroyed the Goetheanum and that consequently the centre of this activity was wiped out, because what had begun to take shape around it as a social organism has only been partly realised.

You no doubt remember the passage which we read yesterday, in which Rudolf Steiner says that no other building will really be able to replace the first Goetheanum. We have experienced the truth of this. However, there is something else which should be mentioned.

While still holding fast to the recognition that to build architecturally and to build in the social realm are parallel activities, let us recall the Karlstejn, in which we could see indications of the image of the threefold social organism. Then let us turn from the Karlstejn, which was built in the fourteenth century, to the Goetheanum which was built in the twentieth and ask: What was its intention? What did it try to express? Such questions are permissable; they are fully justified. Was it also an image of the threefold social organism? No doubt the Goetheanum should have become a building of the spiritual life; the spiritual life which is a part of the threefold social organism. This spiritual life should have found its realisation in the Goetheanum building as the esoteric background of social life. In a lecture held on 23rd April 1919, which he called *Esoteric Prelude to the Exoteric Work on the Social Question*, Rudolf Steiner describes this in the following way.

> All that is formed out in the human head, all that gives to the human head its configuration and form, points to prenatal life, points to that which man brings with him through birth from the spiritual worlds—be it from the spiritual world itself, be it from former earthly lives—into physical life. If one is able to see a connection of all the individual faculties of man—be they spiritual or manual faculties—to the forming of the head, then one will be led further in one's vision till one is able to trace back to prenatal life all that results from individual faculties.
>
> You see, it is this that leads the spiritual scientist to an elucidation which is most significant for him, an elucidation of the question: what is physical spirit-life? Physical spirit-life, my dear friends, exists here on earth, because we as men bring something with us at birth. Physical spirit-life, as far as I have spoken about it to you today, does not only evolve out of this physical world, it arises out of those impulses which we bring through birth

> out of the spiritual world into physical existence. By being men who bring into physical existence reverberations of a supersensible existence, we shape in this physical world, in the society of man, all that is contained in physical spirit-life. No art would exist, no science would exist, no educational impulse would exist, no children could be educated, no schooling could be given if we would not bring something through our birth impulses, from the prenatal life into the physical life.[9]

This describes the human head which we all carry, and by so doing are guaranteed the knowledge that we have come from a prenatal existence which is much more real than the world in which we live now, our sensory world. It is the guarantor of our spiritual life.

Yesterday I described what is now supported by these words of Rudolf Steiner. The actual realm of spiritual life is the one in which the dead and those who are to be reborn weave and work, and from which come all our impulses. And an image, an artistic metamorphosis of the human head is the shape of the Goetheanum. Imagine once more the ground plan consisting of the large and the small hall, covered by the cupola. Here *(see diagram on page 118)* are the windows, here the Christ-statue, here the pulpit, here the pillars—twelve on this side and seven on this.

What does this represent? It is nothing else but the shape of our head: this is the forehead, this is the back of the head and the windows are the senses. Everything else is simply the architecture, the world architecture which every one of us carries as the image of prenatal spiritual activity. The fact that the Christ-statue stands here can only be understood if we remember that in the past centuries an entirely new organ[10] was formed by the activity of high spiritual beings within the frontal bone; that organ in which a spiritual scientific recognition, the Christ-recognition of our time, can be born.

You see, this is the ground plan of the building of which mankind is now deprived. Without it a centre of active spiritual life was taken away, and thereby the morality of the legal life could

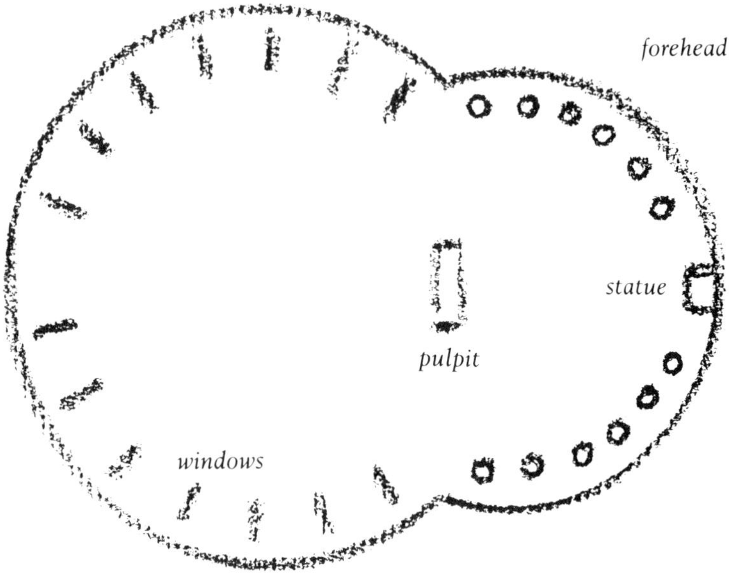

no longer develop in the way it was meant to and so could not influence the economic life. This has given rise to the continuously increasing catastrophy in which we are forced to live today, and from which there is almost no way out. But what actually happened?

World economy went crazy. The result of the chaotic rise in production all over the world is that the consumers—which is to say mankind—multiply in an explosive way. Production does not rise because of the growing population, but as an effect of rising production more and more men must be born. As a result, what could be called a severe asthmatic condition in the economic life sets in. Excessive production causes breathing in, breathing in and yet more breathing in, but the breathing out process is missing—

people today are prevented from dying. Old people are not able to return to the spiritual world; they are artificially preserved here on earth as living corpses. This is the result of what I have tried to describe. Well, it is not necessary to talk further about this today. However, in considering what I have tried to show you, another question can be raised. Have you ever asked yourselves in which architectural style the first Goetheanum was built? Is it completely isolated from its time, almost as though it were in a vacuum? Or, if it *is* a phenomenon of our time—and this seems to be the case, after all I have tried to say—where does it belong? Indeed, it is extremely fascinating to review the various metamorphoses of style against the background realisation that architecture is connected with social form.

If we look back we can see that in the nineteenth century no coherent style existed. Instead, a kind of eclecticism ruled. If you walk along the ring road of Vienna, for example, you can experience this to the full, seeing Greek, neo-Gothic and Gothic styles all copied with more or less accuracy. If this were not permeated by my childhood memories I would say it is a kind of confectionery style! In Berlin, Munich, Paris—indeed, in all the towns that were rebuilt during the nineteenth century—you will find the same thing. Going further back we come to Rococo, then Baroque. Baroque changes into the Classic style, and Classic into High Gothic which then becomes the Gothic style proper. Gothic then changes into Romanesque, and before Romanesque the Basilicas, then further back into all that comprises the primitive Christian art of the catacombs, roofed over by Roman architecture with its baths and theatres, circuses and palaces, and thence to the Greek temple. We could go still further back but it is not necessary at the moment.

However, we should not merely look at this, we should also try to experience it inwardly. What great differences there are between a Greek temple, a Roman bath or palace, the early Christian buildings, the Basilicas, the Romanesque style! They all develop and metamorphose, as do all man's expressions—his gestures, clothes, shoes; his thoughts, his speech, his actions. Everything is in a process of continual change; a continuous culture that is metamorphosed again and again. Beginning with the Greek *polis*, it forms social structures which develop further to the Roman ceasars, then to the decay of all social structure and its reconstitution by the empires of the later kings and popes. If we look at this in an active way we will see that at the end of the nineteenth and the beginning of the twentieth century a new style, both of building and of life, tried to evolve; a style which can be seen in its entirety only now that we have gained some distance from it. It is a style which expresses itself in the same manner in music, art, drama, poetry and painting; a style which today we call, somewhat disparagingly, *Jugendstil* (Youth style).

However, if we trace the group of people in which this style came to expression, we will discover that all of them were contemporaries of Rudolf Steiner. They were all born either at the beginning or the middle of the eighteen sixties. Gustav Mahler, Henry van der Velde, Gerhart Hauptman, Eugenie delle Grazie, Emil Nolde, Edward Munch or Aristide Maillol—all belonged to this developing style which in the end did not fully unfold. Everybody took something from it, splintered it, sexualized and intellectualized it, until finally artists such as Gustav Klimt and Egon Schiele appeared who led it into Mannerism.

It is very interesting to ask where the origin of *Jugendstil* lies. To answer this question we have to refer to a period during the eighteen sixties in England when the so-called Pre-Raphaelite movement developed. At that time something new began to unfold out of which arose a man like William Morris, for instance, who attempted something quite specific. He did not merely want to paint a picture or design a house, but he strove for a refinement of style in every aspect of life, be it in clothing, interior design or furniture. In this way something new and active was intended to be brought about whereby man can become truly human.

But this intention was also wiped out. It was swept aside by the emergence of the various 'isms'—Expressionism, Cubism and the like. However wonderful such impulses as 'The Blue Rider' and the '*Bauhaus*' were they all vanished, except in one instance and that was the Goetheanum and what began to develop around it as the new Goetheanistic style. This is the elevation, the first real spiritualisation, of the *Jugendstil* impulse, and it is from this that we will have to progress after the horrors of today's art and the collapse of every contemporary form. However, this rebuilding will only be possible after the destruction which is to come. Rudolf Steiner stated exactly when the new Goetheanum buildings would arise all over Europe—in the seventies of the coming century.

If we look back once again to these changes in style and ask what causes them, with the help of spiritual science we can learn to know that they are brought about by those leading spiritual beings who take over the guidance of mankind every three hundred years. The work of Michael, preceded by his many servants preparing for his activity, and beginning to develop his style, brought about a first blossom in the Goetheanum. Michael was preceded by Gabriel, in whose age developed all that was called Baroque and Rococo, and before which came the High Gothic and Gothic styles. We could no doubt continue to follow this back through the centuries. You see, everything that developed at the end of the last century and at the beginning of this was crowned by the Goetheanum. The Goetheanum was the first perfection of what can be called the Youth style, and we should recognise the activity of Michael in it.

Behind all this chaos, all this disintegration and decay, Michael stands radiantly within and above mankind, as is described in the Michael Meditation.[11] We can unite ourselves with his being by turning to the description which Rudolf Steiner gave of him, and by living with it, because through this description appears the image of the one who is the master-builder of our time.

> Michael is a being who reveals nothing if we do not bring him something from our diligent spiritual work on Earth. Michael is a silent Spirit—silent and taciturn. The other ruling Archangels are talkative Spirits—in a spiritual sense, of course; but Michael is taciturn. He is a Spirit who speaks very little. At most he will give sparing indications, for what we learn from Michael is not really the word, but—if I may so express it—the look, the power, the

> direction of his gaze.
>
> This is because Michael concerns himself most of all with that which men create out of the Spirit. He lives with the consequences of all that men have created. The other Spirits live more with the causes; Michael lives with the consequences. The other Spirits kindle in man the impulses for that which he shall do. Michael will be the true spiritual hero of freedom; he lets men do, and he then takes what becomes of human deeds, receives it and carries it on and out into the cosmos, to continue in the cosmos what men themselves cannot yet do with it.[12]

This is an image of the being of Michael. However, through the fact that this being works, and that sometimes he interrupts his waiting by beckoning to man and calling him gently to recollect that he himself is a spirit-being; by the fact that Michael waits for what we do and not for what is demanded of us, the opportunity is placed in our hands to develop what is most fundamental for our time—initiative.

The adversary powers are those which want to lift every burden from man so that he would totter half-conscious and lost in dreams throughout day and night. To awaken initiative, and out of this initiative to form communities in contrast to all the social structures presently around us; to celebrate Michael festivals within these communities and thereby receive new impulses; to carry the image of the Goetheanum as an image of the new structure of community within ourselves—these are seeds for the preparation of a hopeful future. Everything else is irrelevant, secondary or merely additional, for what matters today is to celebrate the Kingly Wedding wherever possible, both with those who are worthy and those who are unworthy, in order that the tables be filled where the common meal can be celebrated. This alone means to serve Michael.

Man as a Social Being and the Mission of Conscience

Five Lectures

Föhrenbühl, Christmas 1964 to Epiphany 1965

The Archetypal Phenomenon of Social Science

Föhrenbühl, Third Sunday in Advent, 13th December 1964.

Many weeks have passed since I last spoke here.[1] Let us now try to look back over all that has happened between 30th September and today, 13th December. Indeed, many public events have occurred in the course of the last two months which have increased world tension, both politically and in the realm of human relations, raising it to a much higher level than was the case at Michaelmas. You no doubt remember all the events that have taken place, for instance in the middle of October.* In both East and West new phenomena have appeared which now reveal more strongly, more pointedly what is actually happening in the world today.

As events take place with such rapidity, the individual all too easily forgets what has happened during previous weeks and months, let alone over the past year. The strong, and in my opinion extremely portentous, move towards the destruction of mankind caused by the political changes in Great Britain, the elections in America, the fall of Khrushchev, and now by the increasing urgency of events in Africa, shows that things are beginning to happen with such swiftness that we are no longer able to follow them with our consciousness, let alone with our feeling.

---

* *Footnote*. Reference is to a number of world events: the first bombing raids on Vietnam ordered by President Johnson; the American election campaign between the right wing Senator Goldwater and President Johnson; the entrenchment of the Cold War as Breshnev emerges as First Secretary after Khrushchev is deposed; the detonation of its first atomic bomb by China; the unilateral declaration of independence by Southern Rhodesia; Belgian troops invade the Congo to release hostages and the massacre of missionaries; the election of Harold Wilson to lead Britain into the European Economic Community.

We can say that in the East a radicalising process has set in, and that in the West a lameness is developing which is constantly aggravated by a dreadful poverty in ideas. From the South the tide of nationalism has begun to flood Middle Europe* and now threatens to drown it completely. What this reveals cannot be adequately described in simple words, but only by using images, for instance by saying that the three beasts now show their faces more and more openly, and that the more clearly they appear the less they are seen. In the West appear illness and death; in the East selfishness; in the Middle ever-increasing doubt. I have to mention these matters, not in order to be negative—that is not my intention—but in order to point out the phenomena which can be perceived by those who want to see. However, it will not be possible to take this further today: perhaps we may do so next Sunday.

We are now in the time of Advent. If we look into our souls we may acknowledge the reality of the words spoken at the beginning of the Act of Consecration of Man during Advent. They describe the soul 'deeply musing' in front of the altar and how a veil conceals the soul from the gaze of the spirit eye. During the past few days an image of this state of soul could be clearly experienced in the mist which shrouded the light of day, the light of the sun. What happens within the soul was reflected outside in nature. In the growing stillness of the human soul we could feel how the mood of Advent gradually awakens into clarity. But what is this Advent mood?

Because a veil covers the soul gradually concealing it from the gaze of the spirit eye, and because of the growing stillness—almost a becoming blind—the power of listening becomes stronger. Hearing becomes clearer (as is always the case when someone goes blind), and something appears which could be called the awakening of the voice of conscience. Everything I tried to say at the beginning by way of introduction arose out of this awakening

* This refers more widely than to the geographical area of central Europe, implying also a spiritual mission for 'Middle Europe' whose culture is intended to nurture the balance between extremes in mankind.

of the voice of conscience.

If we try to follow the verses of the *Calendar of the Soul*[2] in Advent, which accompany us during this time, we may notice that the voice of conscience begins to resound from a particular organ; from the heart. (I do not know if any of you have seen my small contribution to this question which has recently been printed.[3] I would like to add a few words to it.) In the first Advent verse the soul speaks, firstly to itself:

> Can I conceive true Being *[35]*
> That it might find itself anew
> In the soul's productive urge?

And then answers itself:

> I feel power being lent to me
> To live myself in the world's own self
> With all humility as part thereof.

This attitude of living oneself 'in the world's own self with all humility as part thereof' is the beginning of Advent. Man begins to experience himself as one among many thousands of candles, perhaps we may even say 'ego candles'. Just as these candles form part of the wreath of mankind, so each single self should try to become a member of the mighty World-Self. Not only I as an individual, but thousands and thousands of other individuals, all form the candles on the Advent wreath* of the World-Self.

Then in the following week something happens which will cause a mighty event within the soul. The *Calendar of the Soul* verse says:

> Now speaks within my being's depth *[36]*
> To revelation pressing,
> Mysteriously, the Cosmic Word:

And the Cosmic Word says:

> Imbue thou with my spirit light
> The aims of all thy labour
> To sacrifice thyself through Me.

---

* A reference to the old custom of lighting candles in a wreath of evergreen branches during the four weeks of Advent.

This is in the second week of Advent. But what does it mean to 'imbue with my spirit light the aims of all thy labour, to sacrifice thyself through Me'? The Word, the World-Word speaks, saying that from its own light all these 'Ego candles', these 'self-candles' should now be lit and begin to shine, to radiate into the darkness of this time of the year. Thousands and thousands of them shine and every human Ego is one of them.

Now today, on this Sunday, the third Advent week begins, the mood of which is nothing less than is expressed in the *Calendar of the Soul* verse:

> To carry Spirit-light into World's Winter-night *[37]*
> Is now the blissful impulse of my heart.

Now the heart begins to speak and says: I take this candle, this light, and carry it into the World's Winter-night, blissfully, joyously.

> To carry spirit-light into World's Winter-night
> Is now the blissful impulse of my heart
> That shining seeds of soul
> In grounds of World take root
> And Word Divine through senses' gloom resounds
> Transfiguring all existence.

When this has happened something else arises:

> And Word Divine through senses' gloom resounds
> Transfiguring all existence.

The 'World's Winter-night' has been lit up and the Divine Word begins to resound in the darkness. The realm of tone has been reached. The veiled soul receives the Word and prophetically proclaims what will come to pass at Christmas. This is one aspect of Advent.

There is also another aspect, a diametrically opposite element however, which belongs just as much to Advent as the miracle which we have tried to illustrate by way of an image. The content of Advent time, which we meet every day in our Gospel readings, has an entirely different character. This content is revealed in

Christ's prophecies of the destruction of the world, and His reappearance, which were given to the disciples on the Mount of Olives in the days between Palm Sunday and Good Friday. This is the second aspect of Advent. It is not stillness, but mighty catastrophies; not Divine Word, but destruction; not redemption, but sternest warning. Here the call is: 'Let him which is on the housetop not come down. Neither let him which is in the field return back. Let them which be in Judaea flee into the mountains', and: 'pray ye that your flight be not in winter.' (Matthew 24: 16–20.)

We have to place these two aspects side by side in order to gain a true picture of Advent. We are urged to awaken those winter sounds from within ourselves to light up the darkness at the approach of the wonder of Christmas, while at the same time images of the most dreadful catastrophies arise; catastrophies, moreover, which have continuously taken place before our eyes and ears over the last twenty or thirty years. These are some of the apocalyptic series of events which will lead, step by step, to the end of earth existence. It is in one of these apocalyptic times that we live today: an Advent time for all mankind. Yet in this apocalyptic Advent of mankind an inner Advent is also contained. It would be wrong to use the word concealed here, but rather to say that even within the almighty hubbub and destruction of the mechanised world there is contained a stillness within the individual's own soul. Shining within the darkness of agnostic materialism is the light of the human Ego on the Advent wreath of the World-Self.

There is man, and there is the world; neither one nor the other alone but both together have to be taken into account. Advent means that we must unite the decline with the ascent. How these can be united, how man today can find his way through these conflicting events we shall perhaps discuss later, but for the moment it will be left as a question. Today I wish to present mainly questions in order that some answers can be given next Sunday.

On 12th December 1918, during Advent, shortly after the end of the First World War, Rudolf Steiner held a lecture in Bern which was published under the title *Social and Antisocial Forces in the Human Being.*[4] In the course of this lecture he describes social and antisocial drives and then says that one can recognise these drives as the archetypal phenomenon of all social science. For this reason I thought that in the course of our efforts to learn to understand man as a social being we should become acquainted with this archetypal phenomenon.

In this lecture Rudolf Steiner first characterises what has entered mankind since 1848 with the publication of the Communist Manifesto. He then goes on to say that although people repeatedly discuss the social element within man, they overlook some of the fundamental facets of human nature; namely that if we are to speak of social drives, then at the same time we must also include antisocial drives. He illustrates this by saying:

> Just as little as a pendulum can swing to one side only, as little can social impulses of men be expressed by only one side. This is because the social impulses of man are quite naturally opposed by antisocial impulses in the human being. Precisely because one finds social impulses or drives in human nature, one also finds the opposite.[5]

Here again we confront a phenomenon of diametric opposites, not in the image of Advent which I used before, but within man. Man is a social being only by virtue of the fact that within him are social as well as antisocial drives. This must be taken into consideration first of all. I would like to try to approach this complex question with exactitude, because it concerns a mighty archetypal phenomenon. Rudolf Steiner says:

> What really happens, not merely in that which presents itself to the senses, but in the total situation, when one person stands opposite another, when one person meets another? Nothing less than that a certain force works from one person to the other. The meeting of one with another leads to the working of a certain force between them. We cannot confront another person in life in indifference, not even in mere thoughts and feelings, even though we may be separated from them by distance. If we

> have any kind of relation to other people, or any communication with them, then a force flows between us creating a bond. It is this fact which lies at the basis of social life and which, when broadened, is really the foundation for the social structure of humanity.
>
> One sees this phenomenon most clearly when one thinks of the direct interchange between two people. The impression which one person makes on the other has the effect of lulling the other to sleep. Thus we frequently find in social life that one person gets lulled to sleepiness by the other with whom he has interchange. As a physicist might say: a 'latent tendency' is always there for one man to lull another to sleep in social relationships.[6]

Well, of course, we do not realise this so easily, for if someone falls asleep in a lecture it is definitely not a social phenomenon! It has nothing, or only very little, to do with social behaviour. Rudolf Steiner is pointing out the fact that the tendency in all concomitance of man is ever and again a falling asleep. But I say 'tendency' because in this lecture Rudolf Steiner asserts that the task for man in the age of the Consciousness-soul is to become as *awake* as possible; that the task is to lift up into consciousness, and to experience consciously, all that has so far been unconscious or only half conscious. This means that the present age calls for just the opposite of what tries to emerge in man as a social drive; it calls for awakeness, for consciousness, for individualisation, and this is an antisocial drive.

> In the relationship between people the social impulse ought to develop. Yet it can only develop during sleep. Therefore in the relationship between people a tendency is shown for one person to dull the consciousness of the other so that a social relation may be established between them. This striking fact is evident to one who studies the *realities* of life. Above all things, our interchange with one another leads to dulling the consciousness of one another, in the interests of a social impulse between people. [And

> he continues] In this situation a tendency to keep awake has an antisocial character—the assertion of one's individuality, of one's personality, in opposition to the social structure of society.[7]

You see, this is the archetypal social phenomenon. In every human meeting, hundreds of times a day—whether between the same people meeting from morning to night, or between different people meeting only occasionally—one puts the other to sleep. But the other must hold his own ground: he wakes up and thereby becomes antisocial. We are trying to learn to see through this phenomenon, and I believe that we can begin to understand it by considering another lecture which Rudolf Steiner held some months later. It is from the cycle entitled *Study of Man* which was given in Stuttgart in August 1919 at the inauguration of the first Waldorf School. In the eighth lecture Rudolf Steiner speaks about the twelve senses of man. He introduces the teachers to the whole realm of the senses, and then begins to describe the sense of Ego in the following way.

> When you confront another man something like the following happens. You perceive a man for a short time; he makes an impression on you. This impression disturbs you inwardly; you feel that the man, who is really a similar being to yourself makes an impression on you like an attack. The result is that you 'defend' yourself in your inner being, that you oppose yourself to this attack, that you become inwardly aggressive towards him. This feeling abates and your aggression ceases; hence he can now make another impression upon you. Then your aggressive force has time to rise again, and again you have an aggressive feeling. Once more it abates and the other makes a fresh impression upon you and so on. That is the relationship which exists when one man meets another and perceives his Ego: giving yourself up to the other human being—inwardly warding him off; giving yourself up again—warding him off: sympathy—antipathy; sympathy—antipathy.[8]

Here the background of this archetyptal phenomenon is described again, for in sympathy there lies the tendency to fall asleep; in antipathy the tendency to wake up. We may now realise that this describes the sense of Ego in man, and that the social and the antisocial drives are, so to speak, identical with all that we carry within ourselves as the highest sense, namely the sense of Ego.

May I remind you that at Easter this year I tried to point out the connection between the three highest senses and the threefold structure of the social organism.[9] We spoke about the sense of word, of thought and of Ego, relating them to the economic, the legal and the spiritual life. Now the sense of Ego begins to reveal itself as the archetypai social phenomenon. The next question is: What is this process of falling asleep and reawakening?

Rudolf Steiner continues his description in the same lecture:

> This however is not all. In that sympathy is active you sleep into the other human being; in that antipathy is active you wake up again, and so on. [Here Rudolf Steiner uses the same expressions as for the description of the social and antisocial drives.] There is this quick alternation in vibrations between waking and sleeping when we meet another man. We owe this alternation [and please pay particular attention to these words] to the organ of the sense of Ego. Thus this organ for the perception of the Ego is organised in such a way that it apprehends the Ego of another in a sleeping, not in a waking will and then quickly carries over this apprehension accomplished in sleep, to the region of knowledge, i.e., to the nervous system. Thus when we view the matter truly, the principal thing in the perception of another man is after all the will, but essentially a will which acts in a state of sleep, not wakefulness. Thus we are constantly weaving moments of sleep into the act of perception of another Ego. What lies between them is indeed knowledge, that is immediately carried over into the domain of the nervous system. So that I can really call the perception of another a process of knowledge, but I must know that this process of

> knowledge is only a metamorphosis of a sleeping process of the will. Thus this sense process is really a process of the will, only we do not recognise it as such. We do not bring into conscious life all the knowledge which we experience in sleep.[10]

I hope that what these social and antisocial drives are is becoming clearer from the point of view of the knowledge of man. They comprise the sense of Ego in a process of continuous alternation between sleeping and waking: sleeping in the unconscious will of the lower man and waking in the clash between the sleeping will and the nervous system, which results in waking becoming recognition. This means that when we meet a fellow human being, or if groups of people meet other groups, then the will weaves, at first unconsciously, from man to man. However, within this sea of unconscious will, waves of the sleeping will surge up and beat against the rock of the nervous system. I recognise the other—antipathy: I fall asleep in the other—sympathy: the will again surges up—antipathy. In the recognition of the other person the antisocial drive is expressed, while in the falling asleep in the other person the social drive is made manifest. Awakening to one's fellow men has its begining in the continual coming and going of the sea of will, in the ebb and flow of our volition. Neither one nor the other suffices, but both together in rhythmical interchange between coming and going, give rise to the archetypal social phenomenon.

Earlier we drew attention to the words: 'There is this quick alternation in vibrations between waking and sleeping when we meet another person. We owe this alternation to the organ of the sense of Ego.' If we wish to take a step further into the phenomenon of social and antisocial drives, we must ask ourselves what this organ of the Ego is. As far as I know, Rudolf Steiner gave two tentative answers to this question. The first, given in 1919 is, and I quote:

> The organ for the perception of Egos is spread out over the whole human being and consists of a very fine substantiality,

> and on this account people do not talk about this 'organ for perceiving the Ego'.[11]

Three years before, on 2nd September 1916, Rudolf Steiner spoke in the following way about the sense for the perception of the Ego of another human being:

> The perception of Ego has its organ just as seeing and hearing. But the organ for the perception of Egos is formed in such a way that although it has its starting-point in the head, the realm of the entire body, in so far as it is dependent on the head, forms the organ for the perception of our fellow man's Ego. To some extent one could also say: the head is an organ of perception for the Ego of the other in so far as the whole human being is attached to it and its faculty for the perception of the Ego radiates through the whole human being. Man as far as he is at rest, as far as he is the motionless human figure which has so to speak the head as its centre, is the organ of perception for the Ego of the other. In this way the organ of perception for the Ego of the other human being is the biggest organ of perception which we have and we ourselves are as physical man the biggest organ of perception which we have.[12]

For the sake of emphasis, may I repeat:

> In this way the organ of perception for the Ego of the other human being is the biggest organ of perception which we have and we ourselves are as physical man the biggest organ of perception which we have.

The head as centre—in so far as all other parts are attached to it—means only that the head is the end result. It is transformed from the previous life in which it existed in the shape of the body, and is now able to form for itself a new body, and thereby becomes an Ego organ; however, an organ not for perceiving itself but for perceiving the Ego of our fellow man. If we begin to grasp this not merely intellectually but in all its reality, we may realise that we can never see ourselves unless we are able to perceive ourselves clairvoyantly.

Then the remarkable fact emerges that while our own self always remains hidden from us, we can nevertheless perceive all other Egos, and that through our whole body we are a mirror for all the others, and we do this in the rhythm of falling asleep and waking up. This brings to light not only the archetypal phenomenon of social science, but also the fundamental law of all social activity, which can be outlined as follows: 'I can never claim for myself a reward for my own work, but am supported by my fellow man. I acknowledge that the work of my fellow man provides my livelihood, while he trusts that my work will contribute economically and socially to his.'* This is so because each individual perceives the other as an Ego.

Do you now see how senseless it is for people, whether young or old, to continually proclaim that they refuse to be influenced? Such stupidity is a misunderstanding of spiritual science! An individual can only be uninfluenced if he withdraws to a cave, stops eating and tries to avoid being met by anyone. But the moment he becomes man, he is a man among other men. He mirrors his fellow men and is himself mirrored in them. However, he knows about them only when he asserts his antisocial nature, just as they only know him when they are antisocial. He lives through them because they sleep and thereby meet him in their sympathy, just as they live through him because he falls asleep in them and thereby meets them in his sympathy. This is the archetypal social phenomenon.

Here again we find diametric opposites, similar to the ones which we met earlier when we described the time of Advent. We can begin to think about this; however, we should rather try to direct it more and more into the consciousness of daily life. It is human existence; it is the secret, or one of the secrets, of communion, for just as the carrier of the unconscious will which enters our fellow man socially in the state of sleep is the blood, the wine, so the awakening in the recognition of our fellow man is the nerve, the bread. These are preliminaries to the sacrament which, without noticing it, we have to carry out ever and again until what is

---

* This is König's free rendering of what Rudolf Steiner called a fundamental social law in his essays *Anthroposophy and the Social Question.*[13]

indicated in the apocalyptic verses of the Advent gospel is revealed, namely Christ appearing in the clouds. Today He appears in the veils of the soul which are placed before the spirit eye.

In the same lecture on the social and antisocial forces in the human being which we quoted earlier, and which is indeed an Advent lecture, Rudolf Steiner says the following:

> We have often said that just in our age a reappearance of the Christ in the ether realm will take place. This reappearance of the Christ is indeed not far off. That He is coming again is no cause for pessimism, nor should it give rise to a nebulous longing and a desire for soul-warming, self-seeking, theosophical theories. The Christ Impulse has various forms but in His present form He wishes to help humanity realise that spiritual wisdom is now being revealed by the spiritual world. This wisdom wants to be realised and the Christ Impulse will be a help in this realisation.[14]

This is what matters in our time. This is a kind of opening to our deliberations, which I hope will be possible to continue in the coming Sundays.

Man as a Social Being during Advent and Christmas

Föhrenbühl, Fourth Sunday in Advent, 20th December 1964

Last Sunday we tried to study what Rudolf Steiner calls the archetypal phenomenon of all social science, the social and antisocial drives in man. We tried to learn in more detail about these social and antisocial drives with the aid of a special lecture given in 1918, a truly Advent lecture, in which Rudolf Steiner describes the activity and function of the sense of Ego. In the course of our deliberations we came to understand that it is through the activity of this highest of the twelve senses that we not only sense the reality of the existence of another's Ego, but can also have a direct experience of it.

In lectures given to the teachers of the first Waldorf School, in which Rudolf Steiner explains that the activity of the sense of Ego is such that we 'fall asleep' socially in our fellow man, and then immediately 'awaken' again antisocially in order to preserve ourselves, we learned that this is a kind of higher breathing process which happens within seconds, allowing us to gain an immediate experience of the 'I' of another human being.

If we take this earnestly and do not just let it file past our intellect but, being awake human beings here on earth, rather try to experience it fully and give it its due place in the image of the world which we are gradually building up, then we may call this activity an 'evening-morning' relationship. It is an 'evening' relationship because we 'fall asleep' in our fellow man, and a 'morning' relationship because we 'awaken' through our fellow man. Considering this we may begin to realise how the process through which we go each day—namely going to sleep in the evening, and entering the spiritual world; then waking up in the morning and walking through the day more or less awake with our higher being–is one which takes place continually on a minute scale, in a fraction of a second, in the realm of the sense of Ego when we experience our fellow men and they experience us. So we can say that we enter into the being of the other, and that, for a short while, the other person (because he is a spiritual being) is the spiritual world into which we enter between evening and morning. We 'awaken' by meeting him and then he represents, by virtue of his outer being, of his sheaths, what we otherwise experience as the World Will of the world within ourself.

In conclusion, we can say that we lose ourselves lovingly in the being of the other, an 'evening' experience, and that we 'awaken' by rejecting the sheaths of the other, a 'morning' experience. This mighty tension between evening and morning makes us conscious of the Ego of our fellow man. All this comprises the archetypal function of all social life. This is the first aspect.

Then, at the end of our deliberations, we searched for the organ which carries the sense of Ego. Just as the eye is the organ of the sense of sight, the ear is the organ of the sense of hearing and the organ of the sense of touch is the skin, so the sense of Ego also has an organ. Rudolf Steiner describes it in a passage which we quoted last time saying:

> The entire man, the physical man in as far as he is head and the remainder of his bodily structure is attached to this head, this whole is the organ of the sense of Ego.

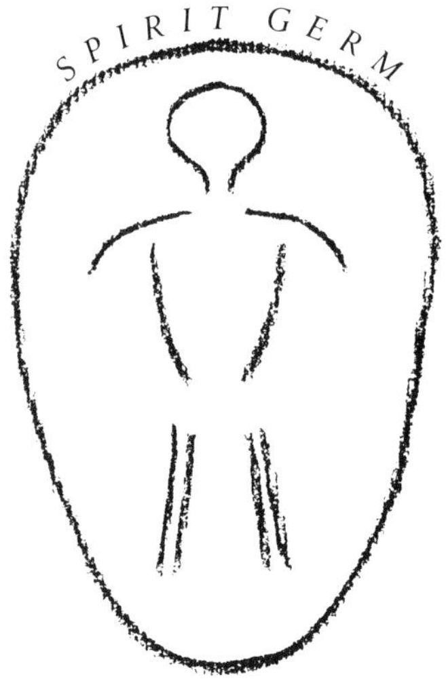

It would have to be drawn something like this:

Then Rudolf Steiner concludes his description with the following sentences which I shall read once more, because we shall begin our deliberations with them today.

> Man as far as he is at rest, as far as he is the motionless human figure which has so to speak the head as its centre, is the organ of perception for the Ego of the other. In this way the organ of perception for the Ego of the other human being is the biggest organ of perception which we have and we ourselves are as physical man the biggest organ of perception which we have.

Let me repeat; 'the organ of perception for the Ego of the other human being is the biggest organ of perception which we have' and therefore we ourselves, as physical man, are this organ. What Rudolf Steiner is pointing to here is a veiled though open secret, namely that man has a sense organ for the perception of Ego, but at the same time he himself *is* the sense organ. We can say that, as body, *I am* the organ of perception of the sense of Ego, while at the same time, as Ego, *I have* an organ for the perception of other Egos. Such deliberations reveal these two sides of the human Ego, namely of the 'I am' and the 'I have'; of being and having; of head and limbs; of past and future; in short, the 'I' that is, and the 'I' that has.

Man *has* this sense organ, and at the same time he *is* the sense organ. But the 'being' and the 'having' can only be understood when taken together—the 'having' in the evening, the 'being' in the morning: 'having' in the loving, losing of oneself in the other; 'being' in the rejecting of, the recognition of, the other. Only when both these facets of human existence on earth are taken together do they comprise the sense of Ego in man. They comprise the phenomenon of man as a social being. This is the most important thing that we should place once again before our souls in remembering our previous work.

However, the question immediately arises: What is this motionless human figure, this head and its attached body, which each one of us carries in common with all the other millions of humanity? What is this head which was once the trunk and limbs in a previous incarnation, and what is this body which will become the head in the coming incarnation? What is this archetypal image of man which makes us all equal although we carry it in such extremely varied ways—not only by being short or tall, thin or fat, but by everyone having his own individual figure, and in this figure there being imprinted the twofoldness of the head which comes from the previous life and the remainder of the body which is, so to speak, the hope for the coming existence? What really is this figure?

There is, in fact, only one answer to this question. We know that this figure is what Rudolf Steiner described in his later years as the 'spirit germ' of man. It is not the physical-material body which is visible, but the invisible physical structure which consists of a head and the attached trunk and limbs.* For every man and in every incarnation, during the time between death and rebirth, the structure of the spirit germ is created ever anew by the power of spiritual hierarchies together with the power of those human souls who, in the spiritual world, accompany the Ego of man.

Rudolf Steiner described the forming of this spirit germ in a remarkable way in a lecture held in Christiania (Oslo) at Whitsun, on 17th May 1923. It is important that we learn to know what the sense of Ego is; to know what strives in the physical realms towards the archetypal phenomenon of the social life. Rudolf Steiner first describes how after death man rises into the spiritual world, goes through the spheres of Kamaloka and then enters the devachanic world. He continues:

> Man is a spirit among spirits. But what he now beholds as his world is the wonder of the human organisation as cosmos, as the whole world. Just as we are surrounded here by mountains, rivers, stars, clouds, so man in his wonderful organisation is our surrounding, our world, when we live as spirits among spirits. We look out, we look—if I may express myself in an imaginative way—right and left into the spiritual world: just as here rocks, rivers,

* It might be helpful for the reader to bear in mind the distinction between all the many visible triangles that can be constructed, and the invisible, purely imaginary concept 'triangle'.

> mountains are everywhere, so there man is everywhere. Man is the world. And we are occupied with this world which is actually man. Just as we build machines, keep books, sew jackets, make shoes, just as we write something here on earth, just as we weave in this way all that is called the content of civilization, of culture—so we weave there the web of mankind, together with the spirits of the higher hierarchies and disembodied men. We weave mankind out of the cosmos. Here on earth we are a perfected man. There we prepare the spirit germ of the earthly man. This is the great secret, that the heavenly occupation of man consists in weaving together with spirits of the higher hierarchies the great spirit germ for the later earthly man. We weave in vast spiritual dimensions in the spirit-cosmos the web of our own earthly man which we become when we descend again to earthly life. Our work is a work on the earthly man carried out together with the gods.[1]

This is work, spiritual work, which is accomplished in the spiritual world. It is accomplished together with those who are karmically connected with us, and with the spirits of all the hierarchies. There we weave out of Man, out of the Adam Kadmon of the cosmos, our own human garment, mighty and great. However, the closer we approach the earth, (which means the nearer we come to our own birth), the more this human garment shrinks; the smaller, the shorter, the narrower it becomes, and at a certain moment, namely when our future parents prepare the physical germ, we lose the spirit germ and it unites with the physical germ. This spirit germ is the figure of man about which we spoke before.

We also have to take something else into account with great exactitude. All men, every single one, have the same spirit germ. For every man, be he large or small, rich or poor, fat or thin, black or white, yellow or brown, the spirit germ is identical. In the same lecture Rudolf Steiner says:

> The human physical body acquires individuality only through the circumstance of its being permeated by the ether body. Otherwise, all physical bodies would be exactly alike; for all human beings, while dwelling in the spiritual world, weave identical spiritual germs for their physical body.[2]

So the spirit germ which we lose, which unites with the physical germ, and after seventeen days from conception becomes the cup to receive the ether body, the astral body and the Ego: this spirit germ is the same for all mankind.

You see, all this is of fundamental importance to our understanding of the archetypal phenomenon of social activity. We all carry in us the same spirit germ as an organ for the sense of Ego, yet we have physical bodies of every conceivable variation. This diversity only arises through the influence of our ether body which we weave from the powers of the moon sphere in the seventeen days after we have lost touch with our spirit germ, and into which is woven our karma. This happens when the material substance of the earthly world unites with the being of the spirit germ and the ether body. Thus we can imagine that the spirit germ unites with the physical germ, and in the first seventeen days fashions the archetypal image of man. Then heredity begins to work from below, and the karma of man begins to work from above. It is this which makes our bodies in their form and substance as individual and diverse as they are. But hidden under this diversity we all bear the same spirit germ, the same achetypal figure, whether we are large or small, young or old, black or white. This is the reason we recognise other people as beings like ourselves, for it is the same figure which we all carry within us. This is the fundamental basis for the equality of all men: it is the archetypal phenomenon of the sphere of rights in which we are all equal. What this means is that in this figure we carry within us an immaculate–and I use this word deliberately–an immaculate image of the human form. This immaculate image is the organ of the sense of Ego, and both together–the organ and the sense–form the archetypal phenomenon of all social activity.

Now let us summarise this once more. We are trying to vividly imagine the immense variety and power of the work done on the spirit germ between death and a new birth. We cannot apply the concepts of the earthly world to this work, but if we were to refine such concepts thoroughly, we might say that through the work of the spirits, 'modelling', 'singing', 'writing', 'music-making', 'hammering' and 'filing' are all practised in boundless variety so that for every single human being the archetypal image of man is woven anew in every incarnation.

Once we have fully grasped this and been able to make this step in understanding, we may remember how last Sunday we considered the polarity which confronts us every year during Advent. One side of this polarity was described as an inner stillness which tries to grow as the soul's veil spreads before the gaze of the spirit eye, bringing about the experience spoken of in the beginning of the Act of Consecration of Man: that the working of the Father-ground of the world can be heard in the depths of the soul. This means that with the falling of dusk the Word, the creative Word, begins to resound in the depths of our souls. The other side of the polarity of Advent is that we stand in the midst of apocalyptic events; that we have to behold death and destruction; sun and moon are darkened and the stars fall from the skies; that need and misery spread and that the call is heard: 'Let him which is on the housetop not come down, neither let him which is in the field return back' and: 'pray ye that your flight be not in winter.' The polarity is this: outer tumult, outer need, and inner stillness.

Perhaps we can begin to feel that this is in fact the same image which we described before, but in a different form. On the one hand it is the mighty work of hierarchical powers in co-operation with the human individuality and all those spirits of men which surround it; that is, the weaving of the immaculate human figure which is nothing other than the image of God. This figure is clothed by descending with the ether body and the physical body; it is permeated by the feelings and desires of the astral body, and it is continuously moulded by the Ego. On entering into the earthly world it begins to submit itself to its destiny, and also begins to order itself into the destiny of mankind. On the other hand, however, this archetypal image will enter earth existence again and again: it must make mistakes and carry the pain of sin; it must suffer entanglements; it must experience happiness and disaster and persevere through them. In expressing it like this we can at the same time add that every single man is consequently a part of the apocalypse: every one of us, in this sense, is of an apocalyptic nature. Nevertheless, within this apocalyptic nature we carry the pure, immaculate image of God by which we can recognise our fellow human beings.

To be a man among other men is indeed the destiny of our existence, and to be so in such a way that we continually try to fit our own karma into that of mankind, into the immediate surroundings in which we live. In these words, which point to the co-ordination of one's own karma with the karma of mankind, is contained the drama of being man on earth. There is nothing more dramatic than the attempt of the individual either to become happy, which means to bring his own karma into harmony with the karma of mankind, or to be unhappy, which means to be in opposition to the karma of mankind.

We shall now consider this statement further. You see, from the moment that the social question arose in the course of civilisation, people have tried ever again to achieve their goal by reform: their goal being to make as many people as happy as possible. This is the background of all reform, whether justified or not, whether tyrannical or well-meaning; whether the reformers are socialists or monarchists, republicans or democrats, bolshevists or anarchists, because in the background their wish—whether just or unjust, religious or utilitarian—is always to make people happy, or to give them a life which suits them.

Let us ask ourselves what this really means. It requires a rather extensive answer, for the problem of happiness and luck is indeed connected with the time of Advent and Christmas. Towards the end of Advent, sometimes even at the beginning of Advent, the wish arises in everyone, or certainly in many people—and I sincerely hope in every one of us—to make as large a number of people (be it even only a few), as happy as possible in the very near future. The wish arises to remember this or that person who we may have forgotten over the past months, to think of them and give an appropriate gift. We feel the wish to help someone who is poor, or make peace before Christmas with someone with whom we have recently quarrelled. This is perfectly justified because it has its origin in the same urge, the same wish that is the source of all reform. One could say, to be very flippant about it, that all social reformers have something of Santa Claus about them! They would like to be as kind as possible, and would like to make other people happy. Well, of course, today this has gone a little astray because a very profitable business can be built out of making others happy, but let us not pursue this for the moment.

After having made a sufficient number of one's fellow men happy, a feeling enters the soul which can quite rightly be called peace. We give happiness in order to gain peace, which means to be happy ourselves. In Advent and at Christmas this is one of the fundamental experiences we can have. We should remember this so as to begin to deal with these instincts in a conscious way, in order not to act simply out of wishes and desires but out of the knowledge that in the time before Christmas it is man's natural wish to make others happy, so that peace can come to earth and enter the hearts of men when Christmas arrives. Perhaps it is strange to realise this.

Today, in the twentieth century, happiness and luck have taken on different forms from the ones they had in the time of our parents and grandparents. In the nineteenth century luck still played a powerful role as a concept in the life of men. At that time people still imagined the goddess of fortune spinning her wheel. Fortune was not merely a supplement to life, for people were still said to be lucky or unlucky. Search the literature of the nineteenth century and you will discover how numerous the novels are which have as their theme the change from luck to disaster; how some people are haunted by bad luck from birth, while others are lucky fellows who succeed in everything.

Well, today we would no doubt say these are Victorian concepts, which is true to a certain extent. For although these concepts disappeared at the end of the Kali Yuga—and must now be replaced by new ones, for there is no doubt that good and bad luck do exist—we must go much farther back to discover their origins. Only when we come to the Graeco-Latin period do we find that gods of fortune existed: Tyche in Greece, Fortuna in Rome. Both were goddesses, mother goddesses to whom certain powers and symbols were attributed. They carried the fruit-basket, the horn of plenty, filled with immense gifts, and they also carried the wheel. We can sense that behind Tyche as well as Fortuna there was indeed a presence like that of the all-embracing mother goddess, Demeter. She gave of her gifts, and when the wheel turned from good to bad luck, and from bad luck back to good, the image of Persephone was repeated: Persephone, the lucky-unlucky daughter of Demeter, who has to spend half her life on earth and the other half in the underworld.

Here we meet something which, as I said, is an old concept that must be transformed today. In a lecture held in Berlin during Advent, on 7th December 1911, entitled *Good Fortune, its Reality and Semblance*, Rudolf Steiner said:

> Man's strange need for luck is rooted in the fact that he continuously has the urge not to be alone in his thinking, in his feeling, in his entire inner being, but to be in one accord with all that works and weaves in his surrounding. Man actually speaks about luck if he does not want success, an effect to depend on him only, but to depend on something else.[3]

What is this other factor? It is our surroundings! When someone attempts something, and from all sides help is given him, his intentions are fulfilled yet he knows that he has not brought about this success himself, rather—as was said in earlier times—he was lucky. If we try to translate this into modern terms, what does it mean? We can indeed be lucky on the most varied levels. At the most basic there is the animal satisfaction of being able to fulfil one's drives and desires. There is also another quite different joy, which is described in such a wonderful way in Rudolf Steiner's autobiography *The Course of My Life*.[4] He relates how in his childhood he experienced the greatest happiness at the recognition of geometrical structures; for instance, that two parallel lines meet only in the infinite. This is the joy of recognition. There is also the joy of the deed, and the joy of giving. Luck and joy are always the meeting of one's own intentions with those of one's surroundings. Bad luck, however, arises when man and world do not meet: '...bad luck releases in man an experience of being shut out from the world, as if the contact with the world were interrupted', Rudolf Steiner says.

If we look below the superficial experience of joy it is in fact what I have drawn attention to before in saying that when one's own karma begins to fit into the karma of humanity there is good luck, but when one's own karma is excluded from the karma of humanity there is bad luck. We experience this continually. For example, we know how on some days we can be in full harmony with everything around us; how everything we do succeeds, and how joy then fills our soul. And we all know how on other days everything is against us; we drop everything, or we continually get dirty, and nothing succeeds. There is always the same contrast, whether in greater or lesser circumstances. Commanders of armies can be borne along on the waves of luck, which means on the waves of world karma, only to fall into the depths of disaster later because world karma is no longer in harmony with their personal karma. This is at the root of all luck.

Now let us read once more the Advent verses of the *Calendar of the Soul* recalling the first one which says:

> I feel power being lent to me *[35]*
> To live myself in the world's own self
> With all humility as part thereof".

This is luck. It is the Advent joy described earlier, and the root of this joy is that I:

> . . conceive true Being *[35]*
> That it may find itself anew
> In the soul's productive urge.

This is, in fact, the joy of recognition. In the second verse of the second Advent week the World-Word says:

Imbue thou with my spirit light *[36]*

[which means with the spirit light of the World-Word]

The aims of all thy labour

[the aims of thy labour, meaning the working of your karma]

To sacrifice thyself through Me.

The first Advent verse is the joy of recognition; the second is the joy of deed, and this is continued in the third verse with the words:

To carry Spirit-light into World's Winter-night *[37]*
Is now the blissful impulse of my heart.

[which is the joy of mutual giving, for then:]

World Divine through senses' gloom resounds
Transfiguring all existence.

Perhaps I may now say that these are the three degrees of joy of the first three Advent Sundays. This is the true joy that builds man up as a social being in Advent and Christmas time. Everyone is renewed, not in connection with others but alone, individually, and in the renewal he becomes a social being in the joy of recognition, the joy of doing and the joy of mutual giving. This is in order to be able to enter on this day, the fourth Sunday of Advent, into the realm of the fourth Advent verse, from which so much flows on into the approaching Holy Nights.

From today, from the fourth Advent Sunday onwards, the light of Christmas begins to shine. We should not wait until the 24th of December, for the forecourt has been crossed during the first three weeks of Advent, and today we already stand within the sanctuary. Only on the first Holy Night do we enter the tabernacle of the twelve Holy Nights. This clearly shows in the *Calendar of the Soul*, in the verse which Rudolf Steiner entitles 'Mood of Christmas'. This mood spreads over the whole week. It is the peace of the Spirit which begins to radiate.

I feel as disenchanted *[38]*
In my soul's womb the spirit-child;
In brightness of the heart
It has begotten the Holy World-Word,
The heavenly fruit of Hope,
That grows rejoicing into farthest worlds
From out of my being's ground divine.

This verse has three parts. The first part describes the birth of the spirit-child in the soul's womb:

I feel as disenchanted
In my soul's womb the spirit-child;

while in the second part the second birth is announced:

In brightness of the heart
It [the spirit-child] has begotten the Holy World-Word,
The heavenly fruit of Hope,

In the spirit-child is born the heavenly fruit of hope, the Holy World-Word. Then comes the third part which proclaims the third birth:

That grows rejoicing into farthest worlds
From out of my being's ground divine.

This heavenly fruit of hope is the continuation of the activity of the Word Divine. But what is being indicated here?

We cannot really use the word 'indicated', and we can hardly say 'described', but perhaps what we may say is that the birth of the higher man within us is *shown* here so that we can follow it with our experience. Let us look in detail at what is said:

I feel as disenchanted
In my soul's womb the spirit-child,

Wonder awakens in us; we wonder at the spirit-child that is born in the soul's womb. If we experience the brightness of heart wherein the heavenly fruit of hope is formed as World-Word, then love permeates our soul. If we go out into the farthest world into which this World-Word grows, rejoicing 'from out of my being's ground divine', then we hear the bells of our conscience ringing. Wonder, love, conscience. This is Manas, Buddhi and Atman beginning to appear, revealed in the peace of the spirit.

However, translated into words which we know, this means: 'The Spirit of God reveals himself in the heights and He brings peace to men on earth in whose hearts there dwells good will'. 'The Spirit of God reveals himself in the heights'—in *wonder* we stand before him. 'He brings peace to men on earth'—in our souls awakens *love*. 'In whose hearts there dwells good will'—in order that the pure bells of our *conscience* can ring out. This is the message of Christmas. In this Christmas message the true man reveals himself as a social being, for only with Manas, Buddhi and Atman as seeds can he become a man among men; can he become the archetype of all community; can he become the likeness of God.

The Heavenly Fruit of Hope and Human Conscience

Föhrenbühl, Holy Nights, 27th December 1964.

We have now entered the time of the Holy Nights, the time of Advent and Christmas being concluded. Last Sunday we described how we are led through the forecourt of Advent into the sanctuary of Christmas and now, since the night between the 24th and 25th, we have entered a kind of tabernacle in the cycle of the year the existence of which usually passes unheeded by most people, although it is certainly there.

In order to recall actively and in common all the preparatory work in which we were engaged before Christmas, let me try to summarise briefly what can be called the archetypal image of all social behaviour. This is the sense of Ego which is given to man as the highest of his twelve senses, and within which is expressed the reality of those social and antisocial drives which fill us all. We realised that the organ for the sense of Ego is the figure of man, and that it can be identified with what Rudolf Steiner described as the 'spirit germ'. In the last lecture we called it 'the immaculate archetypal image of the human figure' which, with the help of all the spirit beings, is woven for every man each time he incarnates. The spirit germ is at first as expansive and mighty as the universe, but it gradually contracts and becomes smaller until finally it is that which every one of us carries in himself as the immaculate figure of man, as the likeness of God.

Today we can call this spirit germ the permanent promise of Christmas which we carry with us as earthly men; a promise of Christmas which makes it possible for us to endure the battle for existence. Indeed, I would not hesitate to say that the spirit germ is the covenant which God made with mankind, for by it we are connected to the divine world at all times. Through this spirit germ we have the permanent promise that we may return to the Father ground of all existence, for the spirit germ is the 'prodigal son' which we take with us down to earth, and carry with us throughout life. Thus the spirit germ touches one of the most intimate secrets of the festival of Christmas. This is the first point.

The second is that last time we also pondered about something which in everyday language is called luck. We tried to gain a first inkling, a first understanding of luck, and remembered that the Romans called it 'Fortuna', and that luck was a goddess. With the help of Rudolf Steiner's indications we began to understand that luck is the state in which the karma of humanity and the karma of the human individuality are held in mutual balance. To be lucky means to be able to order one's own destiny into the destiny of mankind; to be in harmony with what is not our own destiny, but is the destiny of our surroundings and of humanity.

That this is possible is due to the spirit germ, for the spirit germ not only leads us back into the spiritual worlds from which we came but, by carrying within us the archetypal figure of head, trunk and limbs—not the substance thereof but solely the form—we continually bear within us the secret of Christmas. We bear the archetypal image of the Godhead; we carry the child; we carry the beggar; we carry what is hinted at in the gospel when Christ says: 'Except ye be converted and become as little children, ye shall not enter the kingdom of heaven'. This is all Christmas: it is an indication of the innermost grace of the spiritual world towards man; an indication of the endowment which we receive for every new life and which we are allowed to carry with us. We should always remember this.

Now let us turn once more to the Christmas verse of the *Calendar of the Soul*:

> I feel as disenchanted *[38]*
> In my soul's womb the spirit-child;
> In brightness of the heart
> It has begotten the Holy World-Word,
> The heavenly fruit of Hope,
> That grows rejoicing into farthest worlds
> From out of my being's ground divine.

You will remember we said that this verse has three parts. However, I do not want to repeat it all now but to point out that in the middle part the serious meditant is confronted by something mysterious in the words:

> In brightness of the heart
> It [the spirit-child] has begotten the Holy World-Word,
> The heavenly fruit of Hope.

It says that this World-Word is the 'heavenly fruit of Hope'. Here the word 'hope' suddenly appears and we may wonder what this means. Indeed, we must approach such works as the *Calendar of the Soul* as earnestly and as exactly as we would approach the gospels, which means we must investigate each word and be wakeful where an expression such as 'the heavenly fruit of Hope' appears. But why hope; what is hope?

We know that hope is one of the Christian virtues. St. Paul, for example, is intensely preoccupied with it in his Letter to the Romans but, in Chapter 13 of his first Letter to the Corinthians, which is well known to us all, he also gives hope a most intimate place, next to charity and faith. Is this an activity of the soul, a spiritual fruit of man, or is it a drive, a desire, a feeling, a thought, an idea, a will-impulse? What is hope? We cannot be satisfied by simply saying: Well, it is a virtue. Which Christian virtue is it? There is an old Rabbinic saying which runs: 'All creation is created perfect; only man is founded on hope'. All creation is perfect—which means complete—but only man remains open, depending on hope. Now there is a strange verse by Rudolf Steiner which says:

> In the Head the power of Faith
> In the Heart the might of Love
> In the full human being strong Hope
> Holds and sustains life.

Here we find the power of faith in the head; the might of love in the heart, and then in the full human being strong hope, which holds and sustains life. This means that the entire human being is the bearer of hope. With this we have made an important step forward; not one of complete understanding perhaps, but at least a divining.

There is a lecture given by Rudolf Steiner on 14th June 1911 in Vienna which takes faith, love and hope as its theme. There Rudolf Steiner speaks in a particularly enlightening way about these three virtues. I would like to dwell on all three of them, because only then can the meaning of hope be taken fully into our consciousness, and I will use Rudolf Steiner's own words, because I believe that in this way we shall perceive the archetypal power living in faith, love and hope more clearly. In this lecture he says:

> If we look at this with a view to the evolution of the world and of mankind, then we will remember that during the moon-stage of the earth the astral body was given in addition to man. What is this astral body? It consists out of powers which have to take hold of something, which must always cling to something. We experience these powers in their effect as faith, as power of faith. The astral body is the source of faith itself. Therefore it has to receive food, it has to develop, it has to live. The longing for food is the longing of faith. If this power of faith cannot be satisfied, if faith is deprived of one thing after the other which it could hold, then the astral body becomes ill and through it the physical man himself becomes ill.[1]

You see, Rudolf Steiner calls the entire astral body the bearer of the power of faith. Indeed, in one passage he even identifies the astral body with the power of faith. Imagine what this means! We have a body of faith and through it we live and involve ourselves in the world. Out of this body of faith the virtue of faith is born. Then he continues:

> Let us remember that on the Old Sun man received the ether body in its predisposition and that the fiery, light-filled, shining element of the sun is the predisposition of the ether body: in it is only the other side of love—what love is in the spirit: light is love. In the ether body is given

> to us in this way the love and the longing for love and we can call the ether body with full right the body of love, light and love.[2]

In this way love lives within us. Love as a formative power is inborn in us, just as faith, as an active power, is also in us. We are filled with love by virtue of our carrying living ether sheaths. These are not fantastic illusions, dead ideas or ethical concepts; they are living realities. Then about hope Rudolf Steiner says the following:

> The third fundamental power is hope. The human soul must hope, everybody knows this. Men walk about in the world dissatisfied and searching and far too often one finds people to whom everything seems to be stale, to whom nothing gives satisfaction, through whose fingers everything runs like water; it is dark around them, without prospect, seemingly without hope.[3]

Then Rudolf Steiner continues—and we should really take this to our hearts:

> The fundamental theosophical teachings about karma and reincarnation give satisfaction to the power of hope in the human soul; they offer the lasting element which leads into the future. What is a deed, a thought, or a word if separated from man? Man and his deeds, man and his thoughts belong together, and it is impossible to consider an evil deed or an offence as being atoned for unless the wrongdoer himself has made amends for it. The law of causality says here: The life of man is bound up with man and he must go from incarnation to incarnation... It will take only a short while until the teaching of reincarnation and karma will be recognised by ordinary science, and thereby something will be restored to mankind of which it has been deprived by materialistic science; namely hope.[4]

It is my belief that we cannot impress into our minds deeply enough that hope is founded upon the absolute conviction of repeated earthly lives. If this conviction is not born in man, or if it does not become reality in and through us, then all hope for mankind will be lost. We could even say that then mankind will lose Christmas. This has very nearly happened already. However, to continue:

> The germ of physical man was formed on Old Saturn. In which way? It was formed there spiritually out of that which shall last—namely out of hope.[5]

Can we begin to understand this? Can we start to divine that the germ of our entire existence was spiritually formed, as the archetypal figure of our body, in hope? It *is* hope! Rudolf Steiner goes on:

> Therefore the physical body can rightly be called the body of hope! The specific property of the physical body is its density. If the waves of soul life beat more and more onto the physical body and penetrate more and more into it, then it becomes permeated by the hope, by the certainty that something will develop out of it which lasts for ever, which is immortal. This longing for the satisfaction of hope, for a continuation of life, is a consequence of the power of hope which lives in the human soul.[6]

In these words an essential truth is unveiled, for in them the true meaning of the words 'the heavenly fruit of Hope' is recognised, because hope is the primeval germ out of which we have grown and developed. We carry this primeval germ in us, as was said before, as the Christmas promise of the Godhead to man. Out of hope springs the heavenly hope of Christmas, when the spirit awakens in us; when the spirit-child reveals itself in the womb of the soul. When, two thousand years ago, the great Christmastide of mankind drew near and Christ was born on earth, then the heavenly fruit of hope was born into waiting mankind. What is this heavenly fruit?

The heavenly fruit of hope is what we would call human conscience. Rudolf Steiner described in great detail (and after him a number of scientists have done the same, thereby confirming his findings), that human conscience first awoke in the individual in the pre-Christmastide of mankind's history—in approximately the fourth or fifth century B.C. It was then that the heavenly fruit arose in us out of the power of hope. This happened only once in history; now however, it happens millions of times but individually, in each single human being—as a Christmas event—if we only want it. Therefore we can say that one of the innermost events of Christmas time is the birth of conscience. It is the heavenly fruit which arises out of hope; hope which is the spirit germ of man, the archetypal image in us of all social existence—the hope out of which we have all been born and out of which awakens the voice of conscience. Conscience awakens in order to greet the light of the world which descends upon us as a Christmas event; the same light of the world that shone two thousand years ago into the darkness of the earthly night.

We can now recall that in the lecture last Sunday we concluded by describing how wonder is contained in the first part of the Christmas verse of the *Calendar of the Soul*:

> I feel as disenchanted *[38]*
> In my soul's womb the spirit-child.

while in the second part compassion is expressed:

> In brightness of the heart
> It has begotten the Holy World-Word
> The heavenly fruit of Hope.

and in the third part conscience:

> That grows rejoicing into farthest worlds
> From out of my being's ground divine.

At this point I will only indicate something that we shall continue next time, namely that out of faith arises wonder; out of love comes compassion, and out of hope is born conscience. If you refer back to the Easter lectures which were held here,[7] you will remember that out of these three powers of wonder, compassion and conscience the future social structure, namely the sheaths of the Christ, can be woven by man. Hope and conscience—these are further secrets of Christmas which lead us into the sphere where we are all brothers. We are brothers to all men because we all have the same spirit germ, and because we are all imperfect; yet we are built out of hope. We are brothers because out of hope we can ever and again give birth to conscience. This is the jubilation of Christmas, if we can somehow grasp that conscience is born in every single human brother out of those archetypal determinants which have their origin in the physical existence of our human form, and in all that we carry in us as the immaculate image of the Godhead. This is Christmas.

If, with these revelations, we approach the gate of the Holy Nights as child, as beggar, as human brother, and if we have formed from them a staff with which we may knock at the portal and the gate opens, then we meet the *Calendar of the Soul* verse which introduces this week. It says:

> To Spirit-revelation yielded *[39]*
> I win the Universal Being's light.
> The strength of thought grows on
> In clarity to give myself to me.
> From thinking's power springs awakening
> Feeling of Self.

This verse, too, has a threefold structure as do most of the verses of the *Calendar of the Soul*. In the first part the sphere of the Holy Nights appears:

> To Spirit-revelation yielded
> I win the Universal Being's light.

The result of it, the consequence, is a reflection within the human soul which then recognises itself and realises:

> The strength of thought grows on
> In clarity to give myself to me.

Such an expression as 'myself to me' does not appear frequently in the *Calendar of the Soul*. Only in certain very important passages do the words 'myself to me' occur. It is like a concentration, like a kernel which forms itself within a fruit, and then it continues:

> From thinking's power springs awakening
> Feeling of Self.

The question is: What does 'feeling of Self' actually mean? This is also an expression which cannot be taken as lightly as any ordinary expression might. Rudolf Steiner does not use these words arbitrarily; he means them very exactly. If you read through the entire *Calendar of the Soul* you will only find this expression 'feeling of Self' in one other passage, namely in the Michaelmas verse:

> Nature, I bear within my Will *[26]*
> The motherhood of thy existence
> And by the might of my Will's fire
> My Spirit's impulses are steeled
> That they might bring to birth
> Feeling of Self
> To bear myself in me.

Here even the expression 'bring to birth' is used. At Michaelmas the 'feeling of Self' is born out of the Spirit's impulses and this 'feeling of Self' is the power which makes it possible 'to bear myself in me'. Here, in tracing the exactitude of spiritual science, are discoveries filled indeed with bliss!

We can proceed further and ask where else Rudolf Steiner uses the expression 'feeling of Self'? What does he want to denote by it? We can say quite definitely that by this expression he points out something which we all experience at times and which cannot be called other than a feeling, and yet it is a feeling of one's self. It is the experience we have when at times, and only when thinking of it, we not only *know that we are*, but we know that we know that we are. To only know that we are means to be conscious of our self, but *to know that we know that we are*, goes much further. It means that generations of our own Egohood appear above us and look at our deeds and our thoughts. It means that we are not only self-conscious, but conscious of our self-consciousness. This is the 'feeling of Self'. The knowledge that *we know that we are* is the other form of conscience. The one is *conscientia*, conscience; the other is the German word *Gewissen* (collective knowledge). It is instructive to read how philosophers from Thomas Aquinas to Jaspers have tried to fathom *Gewissen*. They all speak about this knowledge of the knowledge of the self. This is what is denoted by the expression 'feeling of Self'.

It might by now amaze us to discover that Rudolf Steiner speaks about this 'feeling of Self' once more in the lecture we referred to last time where we found the description of the spirit germ; a lecture from the cycle *Man's Being, his Destiny and World Evolution* which was held in Christiania (Oslo) at Whitsun 1923. In that lecture he describes how man does not weave the spirit germ here on earth, but during the course of his development between death and rebirth. He weaves it together with all the hierarchical beings. When it is completed, however, the human soul gradually loses sight of those individual spirit beings with whom he has woven and formed the spirit germ; his conscious awareness of them as single spirit beings start to blend and become blurred until gradually the sight of them is lost. Rudolf Steiner says:

> When living then in a general spiritual world [because the individualities of the spiritual world have become blurred] a stronger feeling of self arises in you than you had before. Before this time you were in your self in such a way that you were as though united with the spiritual world experiencing its individualities. Now you feel the spiritual world so to speak only like a general spirituality; but you yourself feel stronger. The intensity of the feeling of one's own self awakes. Thereby the need for a new earthly life gradually arises again in man. With the awakening of the feeling of self, the need arises for a new earthly life.[8]

It is in the spiritual world that the knowledge of the knowledge of one's own self begins. The revelations of individual spiritual beings disperse, and man begins to collect himself anew from the spiritual meetings which he has had. He has to turn to himself and, at this world-moment of his existence, a higher feeling of self awakens. This is the other side of conscience which he then takes with him into earthly life. During the time that the feeling of self awakens in the spiritual world, he still lives as a soul in the sun realm; yet this divining of the feeling of self means, in other words, the divining of the angel which will now lead him to his earthly life. A longing now arises; the gaze of man enters time and he looks down at the generations into which he will gradually have to order himself.

This feeling of self then leads him out of the sphere of the sun into the sphere of the moon where he takes up what he left there at the end of his last life, namely his own destiny. The feeling of self leads him back so that he can take up his own destiny and unite with it again, and thus he shoulders it like a rucksack and, burdened by it, returns to the earthly world. He is led by his *daimon*,* by his feeling of self, which can then be woken up in a Michaelic way in the Christmas night, and in the Holy Nights which follow, out of the sphere of the sun existence in which we live during this time.

> To Spirit-revelation yielded *[39]*
> I win the Universal Being's light.

Thus in a preparatory way we can awaken in ourselves the feeling of self at Michaelmas, and then more fully at Christmas, by grace of the Godhead, we can awaken the higher part of our conscience.

Now let us look back over what we have tried to describe. Firstly there is the heavenly fruit of hope which we learned to know as conscience born out of the brightness of the heart; and then there is the feeling of self springing from the power of thinking, which we also recognised as conscience. Both were born at Christmas two thousand years ago and since then are born again and again. The 'light that gave warmth to simple shepherds' hearts' is the heavenly fruit of hope; the 'light that enlightened the wise heads

---

* *Daimonion*, a classical term from Heraclitus for guardian spirit, loosely interpreted today as one's fate.

of kings' is the feeling of self. It is World Conscience itself, the Light Divine, the Sun of Christ, which warms our hearts and enlightens our heads, in order to awaken in mankind the heavenly fruit of hope—conscience and the feeling of self—to a divining of our higher existence:

> That Good may become
> What from our hearts we would found
> And from our heads direct
> With single purpose.[9]

In this way individual conscience and World Conscience unite; in this way man and Christ unite. This can be called a Christmas recognition, and I hope that it will help in making this festival a little more inward; this festival which is nowadays in great danger of becoming an entirely outer one.

Human Conscience and the Two Jesus Children*

Föhrenbühl, Holy Nights, 3rd January 1965.

Last Sunday we continued our deliberations by studying the expression 'the heavenly fruit of Hope' from the Christmas verse of the *Calendar of the Soul*. We considered not only man as a social being, but also the inner being of man. Indeed it was because we tried to do justice to the festival of Christmas out of spiritual science that we were so moved last time by the expression 'the heavenly fruit of Hope'. We felt compelled to ask: What is hope? Following indications given by Rudolf Steiner on this subject, we found that hope can be called the most ancient heritage of mankind. Rudolf Steiner says that hope was there at the very beginning of all evolution as the primal organisation of our bodily existence, and he does not hesitate to call the physical body, as it was then formed, the body of hope.

This is quite fundamental and it gave us the possibility to discover, step by step, that what is described in the *Calendar of the Soul* as 'the heavenly fruit of Hope' can also be called human conscience. Our body of hope, which is identical with what we previously called the spirit germ of man, namely the untouched, heavenly form-existence of our body, is the crib in which the spirit child—human conscience—is born. It is this which is common to all men and makes us all equal; it is this which we can experience again and again in such an intimate way as the equality we share

---

* Karl König refers to one of the 'open secrets' of the New Testament, always known in esoteric circles but an unresolved puzzle to theological scholars for centuries, concerning the different descriptions of the birth of Jesus given in the gospels of St. Matthew and St. Luke. Rudolf Steiner revealed that historically there were two Jesus children and that the gospels present, not a contradiction, but very precise accounts of two *separate* births, one at Christmas and the other at Epiphany.

with all who have a human countenance, whether rich or poor, young or old, saint or sinner. Every one of us has this body of hope, and in each of us is woven the spirit germ from which conscience is born anew each Christmas. This is the jubilation which can penetrate human hearts if they are still receptive to it.

Then we continued a little further and we found that conscience unfolded and developed in the course of the evolution of mankind. It did not merely remain how it was at the beginning of its development. At first when in Greece (and later by Paul) it was called *syneidesis*, and then in Rome *conscientia*, conscience was the admonisher, the cautioner in us. This it still is today, for it is the voice of conscience which calls us, which warns us, which indicates that we should do this or not do that, or reminds us that we have forgotten something. It calls us again and again and we use the word 'calls' because it is just that: a voice.

However, the further evolution of conscience was of such a nature that it did not remain simply an admonisher, that is, a *syneidesis* and *conscientia*. The German word *Gewissen* (collective knowledge) indicates a new step in its evolution, namely that conscience is something which allows us to know that we know, and also lets us know that we do not know. It gives us knowledge beyond our knowledge; consciousness beyond our self-consciousness, so that we now have a second form of conscience guiding us.

We were able to trace this further in the following verse of the *Calendar of the Soul*, the verse for last week, where the very distinctive expression 'feeling of Self' appears. Trying to understand the meaning of this phrase, we found it mentioned in the lecture where Rudolf Steiner speaks about life between death and rebirth. There he describes the world moment when the supersensible man, working together with all the divine beings and with those human souls who he will meet in a future life, suddenly ceases to recognize their individuality in all its manifoldness. He can no longer stand opposite them seeing them eye to eye; he knows that there is only spirit existence. It all melts into something generalised, into something which could be called revelation but which is no longer immediate individual spirit meeting. The moment this change takes place there arises within him the longing to return to earth. He 'recollects' himself and remembers that he is a man on the way to earth. This gives him the special feeling which Rudolf Steiner calls the 'feeling of Self'. Yet at the very moment when this 'feeling of Self' awakens within him beyond the threshold, the spirit germ which was expanded over the far cosmos contracts, enwrapping his soul-spirit being and carrying him like a boat through the waters of the spirit to the shores of the sphere of human existence where he starts the descent to earth. It is essential that we come to realise more and more that the spirit germ, the body of hope and the 'feeling of Self' have their origin in that realm from which every one, humanity's many millions, form their earthly shell each time they descend to earth. In this is hidden what actually leads to the development of conscience within mankind.

Considering this 'feeling of Self' once more we may ask when it arose in the history of mankind. We then discover—and we mentioned this in the lecture before last—that it points to the strange phenomenon called luck. Luck was once an outer occurrence, but it became 'feeling of Self' the moment it turned inward, and the medieval saying 'everyone forges his own luck' is not an aphorism to be smiled at but is—as indeed many proverbs are—a gift of the spirit which, if traced back, lead to the sources of Rosicrucian knowledge. The Rosicrucians sent this into the world for the moral guidance of mankind. Fairy-tales, legends and proverbs educated humanity during the Middle Ages; alongside religion these were the sources of inspiration. The more that religion was disregarded in human souls, the more it was necessary for images in the form of fairy-tales, contents of the feeling-life in legends, and thought-contents in proverbs to be instilled into mankind. The saying 'everyone forges his own luck' is just such a pearl of moral wisdom.

Today things are no longer as they were in Greece and Rome when luck was still experienced as a living goddess. Tyche, Fortuna at that time were met as outer goddesses, just as before the fifth century B.C. the Erinnyes (Furies) confronted men as goddesses of destiny and vengence instead of conscience. Both turned inward: outer conscience became our inner voice; outer luck became the second part of conscience, the 'feeling of Self'. This will have to enter our consciousness more and more and become a necessity similar to drinking and eating. For indeed, if we are lucky today—which means if we succeed in such a way that joy fills our hearts—then we should realise immediately that it is not through our own merit, but by grace which has been bestowed on us. Luck hints at something which still rests in the lap of the future, and we can only accept luck if we try to become worthy of it. This means that we cannot simply accept it, put it into our pocket like a sum of money, and be pleased about it. Rather, we should know and be admonished by the knowledge that luck is an advance payment, on account as it were, for our future existence either in the present life or in a following one. If this is not consciously understood, and we fail to lift up a lucky occurrence or unforeseen success so that it may lead to future achievements, then we are not yet able to forge our own luck.

If bad luck befalls us, or if sorrow and pain move us or even overwhelm us, then we should feel with the same certainty that it comes from the past, from our very own past. If somebody hits you, or if the world beats you down, then it is you yourself who hits, who beats you down for reasons which are hidden from you, but which have their origin in the past of your own being. Only if we realise this will we know, or begin to know, that we forge our own luck—or our own bad luck, which is the same thing.

You see, I pointed out to you that the expression 'feeling of Self' appears only twice in the *Calendar of the Soul*. For the first time in the Michaelmas verse:

> Nature, I bear within my Will *[26]*
> The motherhood of thy existence
> And by the might of my Will's fire
> My Spirit's impulses are steeled
> That they might bring to birth
> Feeling of Self
> To bear myself in me.

Here we can almost see into the forge of our existence:

And by the might of my Will's fire
My Spirit's impulses are steeled
That they may bring to birth
Feeling of Self.

The forge of my will steels the iron of my spirit's impulses in order that the sword of my 'feeling of Self' is forged out of it. Then, in the verse for last week:

To Spirit-revelation yielded *[39]*
I win the Universal Being's light.
The strength of thought grows on
In clarity to give myself to me.
From thinking's power springs awakening
Feeling of Self.

This is the 'feeling of Self' which makes us able to forge our own destiny. It is the other form of conscience. This was one of the fundamental images which we gained in our common work last Sunday when we were able to discover that on one side there is the admonishing, warning conscience, which can be called the 'heavenly fruit of Hope', and on the other a conscience which we have learned to see as the 'feeling of Self', an inwardly turned form of what once, and even today, appeared to men as luck. This led us finally to the last part of the *Foundation Stone Meditation* in which Rudolf Steiner says that 'at the turning-point of time the Spirit-Light of the World' appeared, and he pointed out the fact that this Spirit-Light of the World worked in a twofold way into earthly existence; by giving warmth to simple shepherd's hearts, and by enlightening the wise heads of kings. There we can directly perceive how *syneidesis-conscientia*, the 'heavenly fruit of Hope', is what is kindled by the Spirit-Light in the simple shepherds' hearts, while it is the 'feeling of Self' that is enlightened in the wise heads of kings. (I am trying to put this as clearly as possible so that we may understand each other properly and not confuse the issue.)

Rudolf Steiner urged us to realise that the advent of conscience within man is heralded in the fifth century B.C. in Athens, in the work of the great Greek dramatists between Aeschylus and Euripides. The rise of conscience is the preparation of humanity to receive the Mystery of Golgotha, for without the one the other would not have been possible. We should try to visualise the birth of conscience again and again in a living way, for in reality it is also the birth of Europe. The birth of conscience is the birth of a growing recognition for what we now call the Mystery of Golgotha. What came to life during the four centuries before Christ, and grew in single individuals, whether they were heathen or Jew—most notably in figures such as St. Paul—had been prepared by the deed of Buddha in 550 B.C. when he rose from Bodhisattva to Buddha. It is, however, only one part of the evolution of conscience in mankind. The other is that in the fourth post-Atlantean epoch mankind received its actual mission on earth. Man began to develop a 'feeling of Self', to experience the voice of God in his own soul, in order that the guidance he had previously been given from above could be transformed into the power to make him the 'man who takes himself in hand'. This does not lie in the thinking man, the feeling or the willing man, but in the whole man in whom conscience awakens in all its diversity.

Only through the fact that conscience can awaken is the recognition of Christ and the recognition of the Mystery of Golgotha at all possible, for we do not grasp the gospel if we only think it, feel it, or will it—or even if we feel it willingly or feel it thinkingly. The awakening of conscience is something utterly new; it is a sphere previously unknown to man—a new realm within his soul. The Spirit-Light, the Light of Christ, the might of the inner Sun of the World shines into simple shepherds' hearts and there awakens *syneidesis*; it shines on to the wise heads of kings and there the 'feeling of Self' arises for the first time.

The choir of angels resounds from the clouds and admonishes the shepherds, because it is a voice of conscience. It says to them: 'Fear not, for behold I bring you good tidings of great joy which shall be to all people. Go to Bethlehem'. This is the heavenly voice of conscience which begins to stir in the shepherds' hearts. *Syneidesis, conscientia* awakens in them for the first time and they go full of fear, yet with an inner joy, to the stable at Bethlehem and there they find what has been foretold. They find the child 'wrapped in swaddling-clothes lying in a manger'. Why is this expressly described in the gospel? The child, naked, bare, and wrapped only in swaddling-clothes is the symbol for what now awakens in the shepherds; a dim consciousness of the body of hope, of this untouched, eternal spirit germ which is the archetypal image of all human form. And the shepherds sense that they may be like this child, for they also carry within them—or so they feel—this archetypal form. This is the essence of the journey to the crib of the Nathanic child; for in this Luke child the body of hope, the untouched archetypal human form which has not yet gone through any earthly incarnation, has become physically visible for the first time. Hence the words: 'And this shall be a sign unto you'.

It is entirely different with the kings. No voice sounds for them, no angel proclaims to them, and it seems as if they might be deaf. But in them the inner eye has opened and the star appears. The star leads them only if they themselves try to follow it; if they endeavour to observe its coming and going, and pursue it in thought and deed and if, out of the innermost desire of their highest nature, they try to keep it continuously visible. For they know that this star is the being who was their teacher six hundred years ago, whose name at that time was Zarathas, and it is he who now leads them. For the moment they can only divine why, but they hope to know when he descends upon them. This, however, does not happen, for the star leads them not to a hut, but into a grotto where the child awaits them on its mother's lap, bathed in sparkling crystal light, in the radiance of starlight which has come down to earth. This is not the child in the crib, but the child who, merely by His existence, challenges Herod's right to the throne. This is the child to whom gifts of milk, a lamb and a fleece cannot be given, but to whom is offered the gifts of the whole evolution of mankind: gold, frankincense and myrrh. These are the symbols of rulership: gold as a crown, silver-frankincense as a sceptre, iron-myrrh as a sword. This is the awakened 'feeling of Self' which has taken its dwelling on earth.

Both the Nathanic and the Solomonic children are heralds representating what is beginning to develop within the whole of humanity as conscience. This is the meaning of the imagery. Both children later move to Nazareth—the Nathanic child soon, the Solomonic child about three and a half years later—and there *syneidesis-conscientia* and 'feeling of Self' grow up side by side. Why in Nazareth? What is its importance?

You will be unable to find the historical Nazareth on any map or in any document, and yet it was a village, a settlement of the order of the Essenes which was still in existence at that time. Nazareth had been founded by one of the five pupils of Jeshu ben Pandira (Jesus son of Pandira), that great inspirer of the order of the Essenes, who lived approximately a hundred and twenty years before Christ. This 'third Jesus' had five pupils whose names were Mathai, Natkai, Nezer, Boni and Thoma. The third pupil, Nezer, had immersed himself especially profoundly in the teachings of the Nazarites—meaning into the secret doctrines of the Jewish religion—and it was he who established the settlement of Nezereth, or Nazareth. In this settlement the families of both the Solomonic child and the Nathanic child took up their dwelling. As a result something united in Nazareth in life, in soul and spirit, which brought about the end of the spiritual stream of the Essenes. What did the Essenes strive for?

Rudolf Steiner describes the two paths of initiation which were fundamental to the Essenes. One led into the depths of the soul, which today we would call the mystic path. It led the pupil towards the goal he desired to reach if he tried to become united with the spiritual being who worked through Abraham. To do this he had to go back through the generations, which means through the blood, passing into the depths of his own bodily existence in order to reach that past from which he himself hailed according to heredity, according to the lineage of blood. He had to pass six times seven, forty-two generations in order to reach where Father Abraham, permeated by a mighty spirit being, had become the primeval father of the Jewish people who were to be the preparers of the body of Christ. This path of initiation now found its living fulfilment on earth in the Solomonic child.

The other path led out into the expanses of the firmament, where the Essenes could reach the all-embracing Godhead. Twelve times seven steps, the twelve-fold revolving of the planets through the zodiac, had to be attained in order to reach the place of origin, the very source of all human existence. Now, however, this source was to be found on earth in the Nathanic child.

The endeavour of the Essenes was in fact aimed at developing human conscience. In creating the two paths of initiation, they attempted to acheive what later the simple heart and the enlightened head would develop. It is a remarkable deed of world conscience that during the last two decades the historic documents of the Essenes have been found, so that mankind is now suddenly confronted with the truth of what until then it had treated superficially or completely denied, namely that we have before us the mighty teachings of the Essenes as a preparation for Christianity! It is really incomprehensible that the truths described by Rudolf Steiner from his spiritual investigations, for instance in 1910 and 1911, have not been recognised in a clearer, more pronounced way until now, when historians and scientists confirm them word for word. People now accept this as if it were self-evident instead of realising that it is a miracle.

These two children grew up in Nazareth, the one turned entirely inward, the other full of wisdom, until they reached the age of twelve. Then both families set out in the company of many others in order to take them to the temple in Jerusalem to have them undergo the rite of initiation into manhood. This rite is called *Bar Mitzva* in the Hebrew language: we would call it confirmation. Now the festival of Easter, the feast of the Passover in Jewish tradition, has as its basis those special events which are connected with the forming of the Jewish people: the exodus from Egypt, the deeds of Moses and the passage through the Red Sea. We can see this forming of the Israelites' destiny as a preparation for the Mystery of Golgotha. We should however, become aware that one of these two Jesus children—the Solomonic child, who is the being of Zarathustra—met Easter in its Jewish form directly as his own destiny. For it was the powers of Zarathustra, working through the being of Moses, that accomplished the deeds which were later commemorated in the most festive and high-spirited way. It was he himself who had led the exodus from Egypt, who raised up the serpent into a staff, who held back the waters of the Red Sea, and who formed the Israelite people. Now, at his meeting 'Easter' when he is ready to enter manhood, the memory of all this reawakens in him. He can behold his own past and while beholding it he leaves his body and enters into the purest medium which then existed on earth: the immaculate body of the archetypal image of man carried by the being of the Nathan child. He enters the body of the Luke Jesus and out of this arises the discourse with the scribes in the temple which is related in the Gospel of St. Luke. The abandoned body of the Solomonic child still walked about on earth for a few weeks and then it died. We can say of the newly-integrated body, in which the golden star of Zarathustra shone within the archetypal image of warmth of the spirit germ, that conscience walked on earth. For eighteen years*—a full moon-node—it went out to men and through its very existence shattered them, awakening the best in every man just as conscience does.

If you read some of the descriptions which Rudolf Steiner gave in the lecture cycle called the *Fifth Gospel*[2], you will begin to understand a little of what is alluded to here. A special development took place over the next few years. At first those surrounding the young Jesus of Nazareth had a very high opinion of him, just because of the mighty answers he had given in the temple. They saw in him the up and coming scribe, so to speak, the one who would reach an extraordinarily high degree of knowledge of the scriptures, and consequently were full of immense hope. They began to drink in his every word. He, however, became more and more taciturn. The 'conscience of man' stopped speaking because something was preparing itself in order that world conscience, not human conscience, would speak once again. We know from the first chapter of the Gospel of St. John how John twice points out the wandering figure of Jesus, each time in a different way. We are able to experience what he means when he

* i.e. until the Baptism in the River Jordan.

says: 'Behold the Lamb of God which taketh away the sin of the world'. This is Jesus of Nazareth; this is human conscience to which world conscience, although silent for centuries, had once spoken in the form of the Bath-Kol, saying:

AUM, Amen!
The Evils hold sway,
Witness of Egoity becoming free,
Selfhood-Guilt through others incurred,
Experienced in the Daily Bread,
Wherein the Will of the Heavens does not rule,
In that Man severed himself from Your Kingdom
And forgot Your Names
Ye Fathers in the Heavens.[2]

This is the voice of world conscience resounding in the soul of human conscience, in Jesus of Nazareth, expressing the primal debt of mankind, into which the Christ has to pour Himself in order to transform it so that it becomes:

Our Father which art in heaven . . .

Out of this we may see or even experience what it means to immerse oneself in an intimate way in the nature of human conscience. It was said earlier that conscience is identical with the rise of Europe; with the Christianising of mankind. Apart from Rudolf Steiner there has, as far as I know, only ever lived one other human being who pointed out how far reaching, how mighty and yet how utterly unmastered conscience is. This was the being of St. John. It was he into whose hands Christ gave the destiny of the Holy Spirit when He spoke from the cross saying: "Behold thy mother". John, in one of his later lives as the individuality Novalis, spoke about the all-embracing nature of conscience. We find it written at the end of the unfinished novel *Henry von Ofterdingen*. The passage is like a promise, like something pointing into the future which Novalis had left behind in order to take up again in a future life. It is contained in a talk which Henry of Ofterdingen (who should not be confused with the minnesinger) has with a pilgrim called Sylvester. Sylvester tells him about different cloud-formations and describes how they can even change into evil forms, and then:

> "When will the time come," asks Henry, "when all fear, all pain, all need and all evil is removed from the universe?"
>
> "When there is only *one* power—the power of conscience. When nature has become chaste and moral. There is only *one* cause for evil—common *weakness*; and this weakness is nothing else than limited moral receptiveness; and lack of interest in freedom."
>
> "Please help me to understand the nature of conscience."
>
> "If I could do that, I would be God, for conscience arises in the very act of understanding it."

Let us mark these words 'conscience arises in the very act of understanding it'. Henry then asks:

> "Even conscience, this power which generates the universe and meaning, this germ of all personality, appears to me to be like the spirit of the world poem, like the accident of the eternal, romantic confluence of the endlessly changeable totality of life."
>
> "Worthy pilgrim" Sylvester replied, "conscience appears in every serious completion, in every embodied truth. Every inclination and skill which reflection turns into a world-image becomes a phenomenon, a transmutation of conscience. Indeed all development leads to what can only be called freedom, regardless of the fact that thereby not simply a mere concept but the creative basis of all existence is to be designated. This freedom is mastery. The master exercises unfettered power in a purposeful, definite, and deliberate manner. The objects of his art are his and subject to his pleasure, and they do not shackle or cramp him. And precisely this all-embracing freedom, mastery, or sovereignty is the essence, the drive of conscience. In him is revealed the holy peculiarity, the immediate creativity of personality, and every act of the

> master is at the same time a proclamation of the lofty, simple, uncomplicated world—God's word."
>
> "...Conscience, to be sure" Sylvester responded, "is the inborn mediator of every human being. It is the representative of God on earth and hence for so many the highest and the ultimate. But how far removed was that former science, which was called ethics or moral doctrine, from the pure form of this sublime, comprehensive personal thought. Conscience is man's most peculiar essence in full transfiguration, the divine primal man."[3]

Such words, spoken by one who is so deeply, so immediately connected with the Mystery of Golgotha, should time and again be recalled in our souls, for something is revealed in these words that we meet in the *Calendar of the Soul* verse for this week which says:

> When in Spirit-depths I am, *[40]*
> Then in the grounds of Soul
> Out of the heart's worlds of love
> Empty illusions of my self-bound nature
> Imbue themselves with fire of Cosmic Word.

The 'heart's worlds of love' is the sphere to which Novalis bears witness. It is the all-embracing world-heart from which springs the conscience of man; from which conscience ever again rekindles its warmth, dispelling the 'empty illusions of our self-bound nature' by virtue of the fact that the fiery power of the Cosmic Word begins to work from this sphere.

We shall return to this once more on January 6th.

The Further Development of Conscience and the New Clairvoyance as Power of the Good

Föhrenbühl, Epiphany, 6th January 1965.

This will be the last in this cycle of five lectures which, starting from man as a social being, has developed step by step—with the guidance, so to speak, of the twelve Holy Nights—into a beholding of the inner man in as far as he has to become a social being here on earth. We shall try to conclude our recent deliberations, and then look forwards to those issues which I have in mind for our common work at Easter. By looking back as well as forward—as befits the day of Epiphany—we shall conclude this cycle and turn to what we will soon place before our souls.

If by way of an inner exercise we begin to perceive the natural landscape in which we are privileged to live, we will gradually come to recognise what weaves between things in that landscape and learn to understand the intervals between its tones and chords, so to speak. We could make it an inner task during the numerous journeys between Brachenreuthe and Föhrenbühl* not merely to look at everything we see in physical form and shape such as plants, trees, hills, mountains, animals, houses and so on, but rather to observe the interweaving of nature. We should try to observe the weaving of the garment which forms and re-forms itself around all these things: the interplay of clouds; the rising of the mists and how the light breaks through; how cold hardens the landscape and how warmth gives it width; how contours form and disappear. In this way we would learn not simply to look at but also to inwardly experience and accompany this immensely varied and wonderful interplay of nature. For it is far more exalted than what has already become hardened into physical, earthly form.

---

* Two centres of the Camphill Movement near the Lake of Constance in Germany.

We will then be able to experience that behind the apparent irregularity in all these phenomena—a sudden thunderstorm, hail, approaching rain, a blizzard, bright sunshine, drought—there is not haphazard arbitrariness but regular law, and this regularity reveals itself when, for instance, we look up at the star constellations which shine down on us from the firmament at night. We cannot define exactly what the light and colour is, for it is revelation; it is 'Being' out of which emanates all that I have just tried to describe. The revelation of the interweaving of nature is nothing but the power of the ethereal world continuously revealing itself to our senses. It is the ethereal world from which every living thing is born and then dies. Behind it works that spirit realm from which pours the order of all existence, even if we are as yet far from recognising it. And what happens when we practise the *Calender of the Soul* is that we begin to recognise the intervals between the chords and tones of our soul. The law that appears behind it is full of being: it is what we may call the Cosmic Word.

The *Foundation Stone Meditation* says:

> For the Christ-Will in this horizon's Round
> Reigns in the rhythms of the World, blessing the soul.

The *Calendar of the Soul* teaches us to experience this. In this way we have been accompanied by the *Calendar of the Soul* through Advent and Christmas, and have now arrived at the verse which I quoted only briefly last time:

> When in Spirit-depths I am, *[40]*
> Then in the grounds of Soul
> Out of the heart's worlds of love
> Empty illusions of my self-bound nature
> Imbue themselves with fire of Cosmic Word.

What is the meaning of this verse? A single sentence consisting of the words 'When in Spirit-depths I am' characterises the situation in which the soul can be this week. Then something happens; a process is taking place in the depths of the soul ('then in the grounds of Soul') and again a particular situation is described, for we can find the words 'out of the heart's worlds of love' if we have the ability to dwell in spirit depths. In these depths the sphere of the 'heart's worlds of love' opens up, and out of these worlds of love of the heart streams the fiery power of the Cosmic Word. You see, already in the introductory verse of Christmastide we discover the spirit child that is born in the soul's womb:

> In brightness of the heart *[38]*
> It has begotten the Holy World-Word.

Now we meet the same thing again. Out of the heart's world of love the fire of the Cosmic Word is born; out of the brightness of the heart the holy World-Word is begotten.

These are the realms we enter into during the Holy Nights at the turning point of the year. This is the time when Olaf Åsteson[1] has his spiritual encounters, so similar to those richly described by Dante in the *Divine Comedy*. These are all truths. If however, we penetrate behind the images of Olaf Åsteson and the *Divine Comedy* into the very depths of this time, then we will experience the fire of the divine Word arising in the spirit depths of the heart's worlds of love, and the Cosmic Word, which brings law and order into all that we encounter in the weaving of nature, wiping away the 'empty illusions of one's self-bound nature'. The divine Word works throughout the whole year, but this is not such an immediate experience because it is the still, small voice of conscience within that constantly renews itself. If this voice were not actively at work, if it did not resound and guide us, helping us to keep the right measure, we would be suffocated by the empty illusions of our pecularities and vanities. We can see in imagination how the first historic steps towards inner order in the realm of the soul—order in our selfish peculiarities and empty illusions—were taken at the time when the Cosmic Word took its dwelling in the body of Jesus of Nazareth; when conscience evolved in man through Christ having entered the earth.

All this becomes clear on studying closely those gospel passages in which John the Baptist begins to speak. This is the mighty call of St. John, for he is the very first to awaken the conscience of his contemporaries. It did not exist before; it is unique. Now Elias-

John calls up in a fiery way what has never before been called up in men: *meta noete*–change your thinking–means start to awaken your conscience at last! 'Repent ye', he calls, 'for the kingdom of heaven is at hand'. 'Prepare ye the way of the Lord, make His paths straight', (Matthew, chapter 3). 'I baptise you with water: but one mightier than I commeth...He shall baptise you with the Holy Ghost and with fire', (Luke, chapter 3). We find the same words used over again: 'the fire of the Cosmic Word' in the *Calendar of the Soul* verse, and 'to baptise with the Holy Spirit' in the gospel. And in the third chapter of the Gospel of St. Luke we find, 'He will throughly purge his floor and will gather the wheat into his garner; but the chaff he will burn with fire unquenchable', while in the *Calendar of the Soul* it says 'empty illusions of self-bound nature are dissolved in the fire of the Cosmic Word'. The mighty power of the word of St. John resounds through this verse for the week of Epiphany.

You see, what in fact happened at the turning-point of time was that the conscience of men was called up. John's baptising means in reality that he began to awaken conscience in order to prepare that realm in men into which Christ could enter. In this world moment, while John called up the voice of conscience in men, the archetypal image of conscience itself, Jesus of Nazareth, wandered through the Holy Land, inwardly sorrowing for the spiritual failure of the Jewish people and for the voice of the Bath-Kol having grown silent. Conscience was awakened in men by St. John, while the archetypal image of conscience walked through the Holy Land. Both events together were the preparation for the mighty event which we know as Epiphany; the baptism in Jordan which could be carried out by no one but St. John, because out of the power of his own conscience he could baptise the archetypal image of conscience.

We may ask from where did St. John have the power to call up the conscience of men? This power came from nowhere else but his association with the order of the Essenes, of which he was a member. We already spoke about this order last Sunday when it was pointed out that about a hundred and twenty years before the Mystery of Golgotha the order of the Essenes had been penetrated by the teachings of that mighty personality known to us today as Jeshu ben Pandira. We know of this from documents that have only recently come to light, but it had already been disclosed earlier by Rudolf Steiner, and through certain ancient Talmudic documents. Who really was Jeshu ben Pandira, Jesus son of Pandira?

Rudolf Steiner often referred to Jeshu ben Pandira, but always in a special way. In the lectures which he gave on the Gospel of St. Matthew, he says in one passage:

> In Jeshu ben Pandira we have to see a personality standing under the guardianship of the Bodhisattva who is the successor of that Bodhisattva who was born as the son of King Suddhodana and become Buddha in his later life. The facts are therefore clear—a stream, a preparatory stream which was accesory to the main Christian stream, originated from the Buddha's successor, from the present Bodhisattva, who later on will become the Maitreya Buddha and who sent his emissaries into the Essene communities.[2]

This could not be expressed more clearly for those who have preoccupied themselves with this subject: Jeshu ben Pandira is a messenger of the Bodhisattva who came after Buddha.

I would like to make a few digressions here which will lead us away from the course of this lecture for a moment. I think it is necessary to do so because my impression is that we need to gradually broaden our understanding of these complex matters. Rudolf Steiner describes how the history of mankind is under the guidance of various spiritual beings. We know that in our time, for instance, we are under the guidance of the Archangel Michael. Since 1879 he has taken on the guidance of mankind and will continue to do so for the next three hundred to five hundred years. In the period preceding it, which we will also speak about later, the mighty being of the Archangel Gabriel held the guidance of mankind. In this way the seven Archangels alternate in their task as time-spirits. However, many more spirit beings also exist, among which are the twelve who in Eastern esotericism are called the Bodhisattvas. The Bodhisattvas form a spirit lodge in the centre of which is the Cosmic Word itself inspiring them. These twelve are servants of Christ, of the Cosmic Word, and one after the other each has to accomplish certain tasks within the evolution of mankind. A Bodhisattva needs about five thousand years to undertake his mission for mankind, and when this mission is completed he rises from being a Bodhisattva to a Buddha, for Buddha is not a name but an office. The last one to rise to the office of Buddha did so in 550 B.C., and for the preceding five thousand years had been a Bodhisattva. If we ponder about this we can see how from 5500 B.C. to 550 B.C. the Bodhisattva who then became the Gautama Buddha was active. When this Buddha who is so well known rose to the rank of Buddha he handed over the crown, so to speak, of the guidance of mankind to the Bodhisattva who is now active, and who will become the Maitreya Buddha in about the year 4500 A.D.

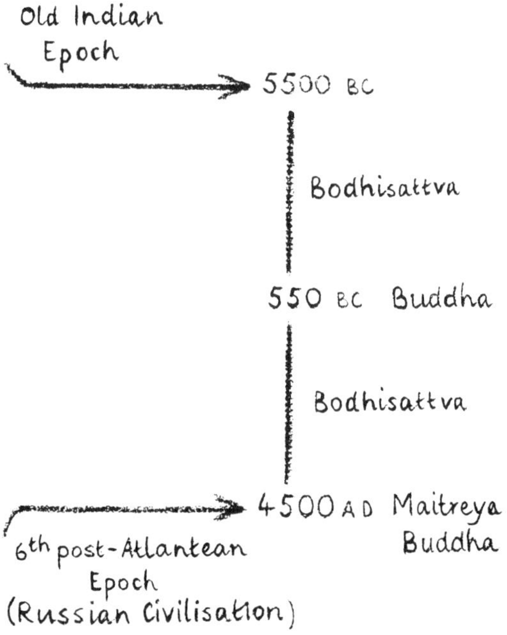

If we wish to establish this a little more firmly in our historic conscience, then we must realise that in 5500 B.C., which means during the time that the Holy Rishis were still the teachers of mankind, the mission of that Bodhisattva began who later became Gautama Buddha and who handed on the guiding mission to the Bodhisattva of our own time who will become the Maitreya Buddha in the year 4500. This falls in the period which we may call the Russian cultural epoch, the sixth epoch of the post-Atlantean age. Each of the twelve Bodhisattvas has a task. Gautama Buddha is described in occultism as the bringer of compassion and love. It was he who gradually awoke in man the loving and compassionate feeling for his fellow man.

The mission of the presently active Bodhisattva is different. He is the bringer of what can be called the good. He is the bringer of an absolute morality which is active in men whether they want it to be or not. Rudolf Steiner has described in many ways how this will happen. The power of the word of this Bodhisattva will be such that through him the good in man will become magically active. On one occasion Rudolf Steiner said that we cannot yet describe in existing words how mighty the power of the word of that Bodhisattva will be: he will proclaim the good and simply by the fact of his proclaiming it, it will be there.

This is a necessary digression in order to outline the difference between a Buddha and a Bodhisattva; what the previous Bodhisattva was and what the present one is. A Bodhisattva either incarnates himself or else works through his messenger, for instance Jeshu ben Pandira, who he permeates but with whom he is not identical here on earth. A Buddha, however, does not incarnate; he influences the evolution of mankind from the heights of spirit realms.

Now, having made this digression, let us return to what we have called the archetypal image of conscience. After the event in the temple at Jerusalem the Solomonic child sacrificed itself and its Ego, the Ego of Zarathustra, takes dwelling in the body of the Nathanic child. For the coming eighteen years, until the baptism in the Jordan, the two Jesus children were united, and accordingly their being was twofold: *conscientia*, the archetypal image of conscience, and 'feeling of Self' (*Gewissen*). Conscience, the quiet within oneself, and 'feeling of Self', the knowledge of self-knowledge, are together as one. But the question arises: Who is it that now carries Zarathustra within himself?

Rudolf Steiner gives an answer to this question. Especially in the lectures on the Gospel of St. Luke,[3] but also in other passages, he describes how the Nathanic child to whom the shepherds came had never previously incarnated on earth. He calls this child the sister-soul of Adam. Adam entered earthly incarnation, but his sister-soul was as if preserved so that later it could enter a human body immaculate and unsullied by the Fall and its necessary consequences. Since the Fall this pure Nathanic being had gradually approached ever nearer to the earth from the heights of the spirit world and was recognised and venerated in the various religions. The Indians, for instance, called it Krishna. In the wonderful song of the Bhagavad Gita we read how Krishna teaches Arjuna, the son of the king, through the mouth of the charioteer, and suddenly in the midst of battle Arjuna awakens to the discovery of his own self-consciousness, of which he had not been aware until then. This is world destiny revealed. Rudolf Steiner tells us in the fifth lecture of *The Occult Significance of the Bhagavad Gita* that:

> Krishna is this individuality in the evolution of mankind who did preparatory spiritual work on the human organisation for centuries and centuries, so that man was gradually enabled to enter into the age of self-consciousness from the eighth, seventh century B.C. onwards. How does Krishna appear, the builder of the human egoity, the builder of human self-consciousness? He had to speak in front of Arjuna in words which are entirely permeated and penetrated by self-consciousness! Thus we understand Krishna from a different aspect as the divine builder of that which prepared and brought about self-consciousness in man.[4]

Spirit beings become active within human souls and thereby in them new stages of consciousness can arise. Self-consciousness dawns through the activity of Krishna; compassion and love through the activity of Buddha, and conscience emerges through the activity of Jesus about whom we spoke at such length. Now imagine that this Krishna being who brings self-consciousness to man, this sister-soul of Adam, incarnates on earth a few centuries after the Bodhisattva had become Gautama Buddha. He arrives amidst great poverty, wrapped in swaddling clothes. Yet he brings with him the Buddha himself; for the supersensible sheaths of the Buddha, (called in the old Indian terminology the Nirmanakaya of Buddha), unite with this Krishna-Adam-child, and this becomes the power out of which human conscience begins to develop. The Essenes perceived this power, and John the Baptist carried it in his heart. This power radiated outwards to the surrounding people. It is the Nirmanakaya of Buddha that sings as those angelic voices which appear to the shepherds directing them to go and seek the child; 'Ye shall find the babe...' All this can be found in the hidden background of the history of mankind. Compassion and love unite with self-consciousness. They are beings who come down to earth as immaculate body and bring about conscience in man. This is one aspect.

The other aspect of what we tried to describe is Zarathustra. He is that golden star who appears to the three Magi and leads them to Bethlehem, and out of whom is then fashioned the other form of conscience, which we called 'feeling of Self'. Now please note carefully: it is the other Bodhisattva, the one who had earlier sent Jeshu ben Pandira into the order of the Essenes, who will now accompany the other Jesus child; Zarathustra is accompanied by that Bodhisattva who will become the Maitreya Buddha in 4500 A.D. I would like to explain this by means of a passage from Rudolf Steiner. We know that such exalted beings as Zarathustra for instance, continue working throughout history, although they continue working in ways that cannot be measured by any human standards. For instance, they do not incarnate as we ordinary human beings must. We have to return to the spiritual world in order to purify ourselves before we are able to start anew, but such beings accomplish this differently. Rudolf Steiner says:

> The Zarathustra ego was so mature that it did not need to pass again through Devachan. After a comparatively short interval and with the help of the etheric body we have just described, it was able to build up a new physical body. This led to the birth for the first time of a being who thenceforth appeared again and again, returning in a new incarnation after a comparatively short interval between death and a new birth. [So every hundred years this being appears on earth.] This being having found his discarded etheric body in the way described, wended his way through the history of humanity. He became, as you can imagine, the chief helper of those who wished to understand the great event of Palestine, wending his way through the evolving periods under the name of the 'Master Jesus', incarnating on our earth again and again as a guide and leader of the spiritual stream we call the Christian. He is the inspirer of those who wish to understand Christianity in its living evolution; he inspired, within the esoteric schools, those called to foster unremittingly the teaching of Christianity. We find him behind the great spiritual figures of Christianity, always teaching what the great event of Palestine really signifies.[5]

So behind Zarathustra stands that Bodhisattva who will become the Maitreya Buddha. This is the other secret. The sister-soul of Adam unites itself with the Bodhisattva who became the Gautama Buddha in 550 B.C. But Zarathustra is active century after century and behind him works the being who will become Maitreya Buddha, the bringer of the good. This has to be made clear first of all because, you see, it is actually the case that such beings must be active behind all Christian communities today which develop out of the honesty of the heart, for men are unable to do this alone.

We have spoken about the activity of Krishna through whom people attained the 'feeling of Self' approximately in the ninth, eighth and seventh centuries B.C. and how then, through his co-operation with Buddha, conscience came about. Now, in more recent centuries, under the guardianship of this Master Jesus, under the guardianship of this Bodhisattva, something else has taken place as if behind a veil, and yet it can be known. Under this guardianship spiritual beings have begun to work in the frontal part of the human brain. Where the region of the 'feeling of Self' lies, about which we have spoken at such length, work has been done in the human brain since the time of Copernicus, approximately since the fifteenth and sixteenth centuries. An organ has been developed which although it cannot be perceived physically nevertheless exists. It is an organ out of which the power of a new clairvoyance will gradually evolve. Rudolf Steiner says that:

> Powers which today have entered the striving human souls, which are used today in order to gather spiritual knowledge, these very powers worked in the last four centuries in the human organism as creative powers. Let us take the entire period from Copernicus to the last third of the 19th century, [which means up to the year 1879], during this period mysterious powers worked on our bodily organisation...[in order to form a new organ, a delicate organ in the human forehead].[6]

Rudolf Steiner indicates that these mysterious powers were the powers of the Archangel Gabriel. If we undertake to study an indication of this kind earnestly we begin to realise its depth, for Gabriel is the one who announced to Mary the coming of the Nathan Jesus child, and also proclaimed to Joseph the coming of the other, the Zarathustra Jesus. In addition, if we allow not the hundreds but the thousands of pictorial representations of the Annunciation by European painters in the fifteenth, sixteenth, seventeenth and eighteenth centuries to pass before our inner eye, we may see in every variation of form and colour how an angel comes carrying a lily, with Mary kneeling before him. This image, which we see depicted on the stage each year at Christmas and which our children drink in so eagerly, can prompt us to ask what it really represents.

This is something far greater than it appears, for it illustrates how the powers of Gabriel have caused a lily-shaped organ to grow in the frontal part of the human brain out of which the new clairvoyance may now be born. This is the background of the earlier images of the Annunciation. It is entirely unconscious, and yet profoundly effective. On the numerous Christmas cards which we all receive we can often see the form of that organ from which future powers will issue. These powers will bring about the following: out of the 'feeling of Self' will develop the power of clairvoyance. This clairvoyant power is present in order that now, under the guidance of the Bodhisattva, a transformation can take place in us whereby we progress from a recognition of space to a recognition of time. This means that we will no longer be enclosed between birth and death, but that we will learn to experience in an immediate and ever more powerful way that we come from the spiritual world, and will return there; that we have been on earth before and we shall be here again. The time for this is now upon us. Until now, man could only lift up his eyes as far as the firmament, but this will be broken through for the organ now exists with which we shall learn to look at past and future events, just as now we can look at space. Then space will become time.

This is connected with a further fact which Rudolf Steiner disclosed when he spoke about the future evolution of conscience. In a lecture given on 8th May 1910 he explained that conscience will further develop in such a way that it will function as described in the following passage:

> As a parallel to the appearance of the Event of Damascus a great number of people in the course of the twentieth century will experience something like the following: As soon as they have acted in some way they will learn to contemplate their deed; they will become more thoughtful, they will have an inner image of the deed. At first only a few people will experience this, but the numbers will continually increase during the next two or three thousand years. As soon as they have done something the image will be there; at first they will not know what it is; but those who have studied Spiritual Science will say: This

> is an image! It is no dream; it is an image, showing the karmic fulfilment of the act I have just committed! [This will begin in the 20th century.] The more incarnations a man has during which he cultivates and perfects his conscience, the more is he doing towards the acquisition of that higher faculty through which in the form of spiritual vision the voice of God will once more speak to him, the voice of God which was formerly experienced in a different way. Aeschylus still represented his Orestes as having a vision before him of what had been brought about by his evil actions; he was compelled to see the results of these actions in the external world. The new capacity in the course of development for the soul is such that men will see the effects of their deeds in pictures of the future. That is the new stage.[7]

In this new stage, space-consciousness will be transformed into time-consciousness. Out of the 'feeling of Self' will emerge clairvoyant vision, and out of conscience will be gained the immediate knowledge of reincarnation and karma through inborn images.

This is the essence of our deliberations during the Holy Nights. It all points towards the greatest event of this century which is growing ever more mighty and far-reaching, namely the reappearance of Christ in the clouds; His reappearance in the ether realm. It is this realm which we should more and more begin to master with the help of the understanding that we have started to gain tonight. There, in the ether realm, He can be seen with the aid of a transformed conscience, and the transformed 'feeling of Self'. The passage by Novalis from which I read last Sunday asked: 'Help me to understand the nature of conscience'. The answer was: 'If I could do that, I would be God, for conscience arises in the very act of understanding it'. However, we must endeavour to develop conscience in us, in mankind, by trying to understand it. Then we shall become servants of the Good, servants of that Bodhisattva who tries to guide those who today strive for a new Christianity.

This effort will be continued at Easter when we will try to allow the other part of the body of hope, which with the help of Rudolf Steiner's insight we call the phantom, to arise as an image before us. However, until then we should try to work strongly on what we have achieved in our common work so far and for this the verse of the coming week can be a guiding star to which we may aspire:

The Soul's creative power *[41]*
Now strives from out the heart's deep ground
To kindle into rightful action
Forces of Gods in human life,
Itself to fashion
In human love and human work.

Re-awakening and Resurrection

Four Easter Lectures.

Föhrenbühl, Easter 1965.

World Breath and World Pulse

Föhrenbühl, Palm Sunday, 11th April 1965.

The lectures I have decided to give this Easter will have a quite definite subject. An overall title for them could be: 'World Pulse and World Breath', a vast theme of which I hope I am able to convey a few aspects.

Let us begin our deliberations today, Palm Sunday, the day which opens Holy Week. Today the Passion begins, and in each one of us those world images arise which were inscribed into the earth and the human soul when, two thousand years ago, the Mystery of Golgotha took place. It was as if during the seven days from Palm Sunday to Easter Sunday something happened which was like the point of balance, the Ego point, of all earth existence. In reality we can only imagine this correctly if we realise that the eyes of the hierarchies and of all creation—the eyes of the universe, so to speak—gazed on Jerusalem and Bethany which were at the centre of these events. It was as if the world stood still: the world breath stopped; the world heartbeat ceased. It was as if seven 'world-minutes' passed in complete silence and that in the silence minute seeds began to sprout—but minute only from the point of view of the world—which continued growing, radiating a power of life throughout the centuries.

During Passion Week world images arose which have accompanied mankind ever since: the Lord entering Jerusalem on the ass; Christ casting the money-changers out of the Temple; the Lord in the circle of the disciples cursing the fig tree; Christ on the Mount of Olives relating the apocalypse to the disciples, revealing to them vision after vision of the future; Christ being anointed by Mary Magdalene before his death. Image follows image: the last supper, the garden of Gethsemane, the capture, the judgment, the walk to Golgotha, the crucifixion, the burial, the women going to the tomb during Easter night, the event of the resurrection. Then follow three appearances of the resurrected One: first to Mary Magdalene on Easter Sunday, then to the two disciples on the road to Emmaus and in the evening to the whole circle of the disciples. These are images which continually accompany the human soul if it tries to enter the coming days of Holy Week with a believing and awakened consciousness. Indeed, these are events in every human soul, provided that it is willing to make them conscious by bringing them to mind each day, even if only for a short while whether in the evening or the morning, trying to imagine Jerusalem and Bethany and, gropingly perhaps, striving to behold what happened at that time.

By doing this we may also remember that a new year is now beginning. In fact, Passion Week is the last week of the previous year, which began on Easter Sunday and took its course through the circle of the past twelve months. In Passion Week the year draws to a close and on Easter morning it starts anew.

Nowadays, we celebrate the beginning of a new year in January, but in previous ages it was celebrated at a variety of times. For instance, in the third post-Atlantean epoch the year began at midsummer, not only in Egypt and Babylon, but in all those regions where the high culture of the Druids spread in all its dignified magnificence. In those days the sun was revered and at the moment when the light of the great Sun Being began to decrease they experienced that on earth something new developed within the soul of man.

Later, from the earliest beginnings of the influence of Judaism, the peoples of the Middle East celebrated new year at Michaelmas; and even to the present day the Jewish year begins with the harvest. When the corn was harvested they sensed that a new year was beginning, and they tried to experience their own rising power of thought and Ego together with the waning sun. At that time Michael was still the countenance of Christ.

Later still, when Christ was born at Christmas, the beginning of the year was celebrated on 25th December, and this practice continued into the Middle Ages until, with the introduction of the

Gregorian calendar, it was moved to 1st January. Just as in primeval times, so nowadays there is a repetition of change. Gradually we may begin to feel that in our time the year should really begin on Easter Sunday, and that this particular day should be celebrated as the true beginning of the year. This is the real reason behind the struggle for the introduction of a fixed Easter, because a date fixed by man according to earthly considerations is in reality the opposite of what is needed, namely the emergence of Easter as a new time to begin the year. The truth is that the breath of the year begins with the day of resurrection; a new 'year-breath' sets in. The shadow of this event is what really compels us to battle for the preservation of Easter as a festival directed by the cosmos.

Perhaps some of you may remember the passage in Goethe's *Faust* in which Faust tries to explain this to Wagner during the so-called 'Easter walk' when he says:

> Released from ice are brook and river
> By the quickening glance of the gracious spring
> The colours of hope to the valley cling
> And weak old winter himself must shiver
> Withdrawn to the mountains, crownless king:
> Whence, ever retreating, he sends again
> Impotent showers of sleet that darkle
> In belts across the green o' the plain
> But the sun will permit no white to sparkle;
> Every form in development moveth;
> He will brighten the world with the tints he loveth.

In these words Goethe describes what we all experience at this time of year. The ice crust of the earth has melted and an exhaling begins which leads all the developing, sprouting growth from the depths of the earth into the fullness of nature. However, as Rudolf Steiner has pointed out, this breath exhales only from the earth and alone it could never bring forth the Easter which strives to emerge, for this breath has to be met by another breath.

Let us turn to the *Calendar of the Soul*[1] and with its help try to understand some of the secrets of existence. The first verse, the verse of Easter week, (which starts on Easter Sunday irrespective of the actual date on which Easter falls), begins with the following words:

> When from out the worlds of space [1]
> The sun speaks to human sense.

This means that two streams of breath begin to meet. Rising from man and the earth there is the stream of earth breath, towards which a cosmic breath streams from the cosmos. This is meant quite concretely, and later I will explain what it means. It is the breathing of the year; the meeting and release of these two breathing processes which begin at Easter. One breathing process ascends from the earth, the other descends from the cosmos, and both meet and begin to interpenetrate. They unite and intermingle completely at St. John's tide, when the world breath kisses the earth breath. Thereafter they begin to separate further and further from each other through the following weeks and months, until in autumn the world breath again returns to the heights and the earth breath enters the depths. At Christmas they are furthest apart, being completely separated from each other. In the course of winter, during January, February and March, they begin to strive towards each other again in order to join hands as it were, at Easter. During Passion Week we are at the end of the world-year of breath. Earth breath and world breath join hands in order to gradually come near to each other.

Now listen to the last verse of the *Calendar of the Soul* which is used from Palm Sunday onwards:

> When from depths of soul [52]
> The spirit wends to world existence.

This is the verse for the present week. We should turn to it every day and ask ourselves: What does 'spirit' mean here? These lines point to the breathing process. However, this is only part of the answer, because a response immediately resounds from outside:

> And beauty gushes from the widths of space

We should try to experience the reality of 'beauty gushing from the widths of space'. Then we are told what is behind this beautiful sheen:

> Then out from farthest heavens
> The force of life draws into human forms
> And, working powerfully, unites
> The spirit's with the human being.

This is the mutual breathing process which takes place and which opens up the world year out of the depths of the soul. Out of the depths of the earth the spirit turns to world existence. From the world existence an answer is given, for from the 'gushing beauty' which we meet comes the force of life out of the cosmos which, working powerfully, unites the spirit's being with the human being. The question now arises which, if we take the *Calendar of the Soul* literally and try to understand it, really is a profound question: What is this force of life, which 'out from farthest heavens draws into human forms'? Is it just a phrase, or is it much more than words: is it a living activity? Let us study the verses for Passiontide and those of the weeks leading up to Passiontide once more. In them a very special word is used in two places, a word which was in fact created by Rudolf Steiner and which therefore demands our particular attention as to its meaning. The word is *Werdelust*, meaning 'rapture of becoming'.* When Carnival week is over and Lent begins, the 47th verse of the *Calender of the Soul* says:

> Now rapture of becoming would arise *[47]*
> From out the lap of worlds
> Quickening the senses' glory.

Then something is told about man himself:

> May it find my thinking's might
> Well armed by powers divine
> Which strongly live within my inner being.

---

* Several renderings of this unusual word exist in different translations. The reader may wish to compare these with the form used here.

For the present let us ponder the first three lines:

Now rapture of becoming would arise
From out the lap of worlds
Quickening the senses glory

The soul divines that 'Carnival' (meaning 'goodbye to the flesh') has passed, and something new is beginning. In the 'lap of worlds' the process of development begins to move and in it can be heard the budding 'rapture of becoming'. *Werdelust* appears again three weeks later in the verse for the second week of Lent, but then in an entirely different context:

Now speaks unto the human 'I', *[50]*
Mightily revealing
And setting free its being's force
The world-being's rapture of becoming.

Here the 'rapture of becoming' is no longer in the 'lap of worlds' but is beginning to resound of itself. In this instance, three weeks later than the first, the heavens have opened and the 'rapture of becoming' appears and begins to exchange words with the human 'I':

Now speaks unto the human 'I',
Mightily revealing
And setting free its being's force
The world-being's rapture of becoming.

and the 'rapture of becoming' says:

Bearing my life into thee
Out of the spell of its enchantment
I shall attain my own true goal.

This is a meeting of active powers, a meeting of the world-being's 'rapture of becoming' and the human 'I'. But what does this really mean?

A conversation develops in which the embracing world breath, which begins to join hands with the earth breath, turns to the human 'I'. But is this world breath, this 'rapture of becoming' which arises out of the 'lap of worlds', the same as the world 'I'? We know that there are verses in the *Calendar of the Soul* which are related to each other as polar opposites, for instance verses 52 and 1; verses 51 and 2 etc., and that these polarities, as far as I understand them, express universal laws. We may now wonder whether the post-Easter verses, which are the polar opposites of those pre-Easter verses which speak about the 'rapture of becoming', can provide us with help concerning these questions. Let us take the verse for the second Sunday of Lent first:

> Now speaks unto the human 'I',
> Mightily revealing
> And setting free its being's force
> The world-being's rapture of becoming:

and compare it with its polar opposite verse, that of the third week after Easter. We find:

> Now speaks unto the cosmic All, *[3]*
> Forgetting self
> And mindful of its origin,
> The growing human 'I':

Here the strange and mighty polarity is indicated again. That which is outside, namely 'rapture of becoming', turns to the human 'I', and when the human 'I' begins to unfold after Easter it corresponds to the 'rapture of becoming'. One could almost say that the 'rapture of becoming' is the world 'I'. It speaks to the human 'I' which, after having been addressed and having gone through the time of Easter, then begins to grow and turns to the cosmic All.

If we go back to the verse which provided us with the word *Werdelust*, 'rapture of becoming':

> Now rapture of becoming would arise *[47]*
> From out the lap of worlds
> Quickening the senses' glory.

we find in the polar opposite verse after Easter:

From out of narrow selfhood is arisen [6]
Myself, and finds itself
As cosmic revelation
In powers of space and time;

From this it can be seen that the 'rapture of becoming' is the world 'I', and that in man, as though from inside, it corresponds to the human 'I'. Keeping this polarity in mind, let us listen to the following:

From out the lap of worlds *would arise*
From out of narrow selfhood *is arisen*

In these words resurrection begins to resound—the world 'I' strives to arise; the human 'I' is risen. The resurrection has taken place in the course of this period. This is the first point I would like to make.

There is also something else in the verses of Palm Sunday and Easter Sunday, which appears to me to be very important because it is a polarity that concerns all men. In one verse it says:

And beauty gushes from the widths of space [52]

In spite of the fact that images of pain and sorrow rise in our souls during Passion Week, nevertheless 'beauty gushes from the widths of space', and when Easter Sunday comes then what is beauty outside changes into joy from the profound depths of the human soul. Beauty and joy accompany us at Easter time in spite of the Passion. The eternal beauty of existence and the lasting joy of the human heart are both part of the process of resurrection. Both are part of that great breathing process, of that cosmic laughter and weeping which permeates the whole world-earth-year. In man the heart laughs; it begins to jubilate during Easter time and joy breaks forth from human hearts. This is not merely a phrase; it becomes a truth that men begin to experience joy at Easter, just as they do when they look at beauty. This is surely connected with the fact that only a joyful face can be really beautiful and that only beauty can create real joy in the human heart. Well, this much can be said to begin with about this whole world of breath.

Although we live as men on earth from conception to death, in actual fact we do not fully permeate our body. We believe we do, and so perhaps it should not be denied at the outset, but in reality we do not live in the substances, or in the anabolic and catabolic processes of composition and decomposition of the body. We live in the earthly and cosmic forces that work through the body, and everything that affects us as mechanical agencies such as the power of gravity or centrifugal forces. At the same time we live *within* our earthly existence as breath and pulse. By earthly existence I do not mean the physical substances, but existence which is expressed by the body as organisation in the breath and pulse. We neither live in the heart or lung, nor in the liver or kidneys. We carry all these organs in us, and the older we become the more we realise that they are merely ballast which we are quite unable to permeate as yet. As men we live in our breathing and our pulse, existing in them both. Therefore, having spoken about breath it is now justifiable to ask where the pulse of the cosmos is to be found. Turning again to the *Calendar of the Soul*, the first verse, the Easter verse, says:

> When from out of the worlds of space *[1]*
> The sun doth speak to human sense
> And joy from out of the soul's profundity
> Unites itself with light in the beholding.

Now compare these first four lines with the first three lines of the last verse, that of Palm Sunday:

> When from depths of soul *[52]*
> The spirit wends to world existence
> And beauty gushes from the widths of space

There is nothing further; but the first verse continues:

> And joy from out of the soul's profundity *[1]*
> Unites itself with light in the beholding

The statements of spiritual investigation are so exact, for the words 'unites itself with light in the beholding' mean that just as breath and pulse unite with each other, so also the joy that rises out of the soul's depths unites with 'light in the beholding'. However, the rising, growing light is not identical with the breath of the 'rapture of becoming', the breath of the world 'I' about which we have just spoken, but it is something new. It is the light which illuminates the whole world. It is that light which is spoken of in Genesis when the Word proclaims 'Let there be light'. At that moment life begins to grow within creation. Life begins to flow, begins to form and shape itself. This is the beginning of all circulation; the beginning of all blood circulation which leads finally to the heart and the pulse.

Consider the cosmic breath outside, the 'rapture of becoming', which unites with the rising earth breath. These two unite in summer, then draw apart again until they are fully separate in the depths of winter. The rising and falling light radiates as pulse through this yearly breathing process of inhaling and exhaling. The light works in such a way that it creates from within those tides which since time immemorial have become the four great festivals of the year: Easter, St John's, Michaelmas and Christmas, or whatever they have been called in pre-Christian and Christian times. In this way we can experience one half of the year exhaling, the other half of the year inhaling.

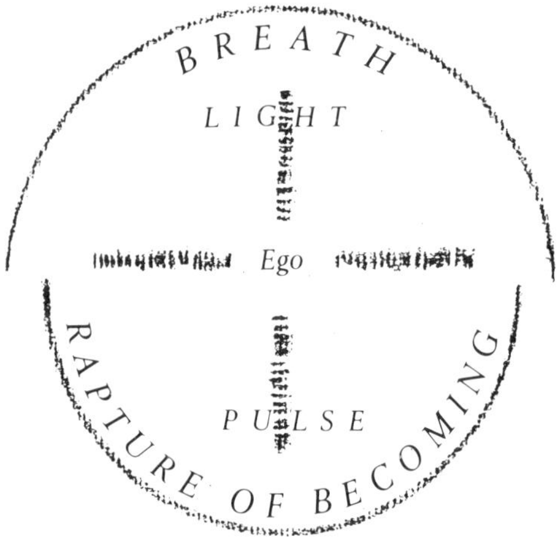

Here *(see diagram)* is the earthly breath into which work Easter, St John's, Michaelmas and Christmas, and thus the fourfold pulse is born. Here is light, and here is pulse; here is breath, and here 'rapture of becoming', and both meet in the Ego.

When contemplating this image and observing the interplay of pulse and breath, of world pulse and world breath in which each breath is permeated four times by the pulse, I began to realise that this is the archetypal image of the Holy Mass which even in the most ancient Mysteries has always been celebrated in a fourfold way as Gospel Reading, Offering, Transubstantiation and Communion. In winter, when the world breath appears after Christmas and the human soul has prepared itself for the Act of Consecration of the year by having gone through the first weeks of January, when the inner strength gained at Christmas begins to radiate outwards, then the eternal Gospel is being proclaimed. Then comes Easter, and what both man and the earth receive at Eastertide is carried into the spring, into the Offering. At St. John's tide the world breath resounds into this Offering and unites with it in order that in summer the Transubstantiation can take place over the whole earth and within the human soul. Then follows Michaelmas. The light has now given itself up and begins to fade; the world breath having united itself with the earthly breath begins to recede, so that now man and earth receive the Communion. This comes to an end at Christmas, when another new year of the Holy Mass of the earth begins. The Gospel Reading takes place and everything starts anew. Thus we can say that at Easter the breathing year of the earth and of man begins; and if we want to understand the pulse, then we have to picture the image of the cosmic Mass of the course of the year which starts during the Holy Nights.

These deliberations were a very first beginning in which our approach has been from the realm of nature and the realm of man. Next time we shall try to understand it a little more from within. Let us remember the words 'rise, risen, resurrection' for on these everything depends.

Human Breath and Human Pulse

Föhrenbühl, 14th April 1965

Performances such as those just given* can lead deeply into all that should be experienced by human hearts in these days. They call up the images I hinted at on Palm Sunday and make us ready for a conscious experience of Passion Week. In earlier times this experience was different; it was much more immediate then, more heartfelt and more human. Today it is hardly possible, even among those who understand it, to muster sufficient inner strength, sufficient inner will to lay aside the daily business and turn to what is most fundamental in our existence. We are therefore extremely grateful to our friends for helping to arouse these sentiments and feelings in us.

Before we continue with our reflections about Easter, let me briefly recapitulate what was said on Palm Sunday. You will remember how, with the help of the *Calendar of the Soul*, we tried to approach the world events taking place at this time in the cycle of the year by paying particular attention to the verses for the weeks before and after Easter. We spoke about the double breathing process which takes place within the totality of earth existence, one rising from the earth, the other descending from cosmic expanses, and we followed the way these two streams begin to meet each other. It is a decisive fact that these two great breaths set the new year in motion.

Through these verses we then turned our gaze towards everything that confronts us as beauty in the external world, and considered the joy of the human heart which streams towards it: beauty from without; joy from within. Beauty and joy accompany

* It is thought that verses from the *Calendar of the Soul* were performed in eurythmy.

these two great breathing processes. Then, discovering something quite remarkable and, I believe, very profound, we realised that behind beauty is that force which in the *Calendar of the Soul* Rudolf Steiner calls *Werdelust*, 'rapture of becoming'; while within or behind joy, the 'I' and the Self arise, corresponding to the 'rapture of becoming'.

To this I briefly added that man does not only live in the realm of breath—and nor does the world—but that breath is accompanied by the rhythm of the pulse which, at least in most instances, is identical with the rhythm of the heart. If we search consciously for the origin of what we know as the human pulse that is experienced within as the pulsebeat, it is to be found nowhere else save where light weaves in space. The rising and falling of light during the course of the year is mirrored within man as the beat of his pulse. Thus it can be said that just as the breath of the world is revealed by the inhaling and exhaling of the year, so the pulse of the world is experienced as the fourfold beat of the great festivals: St. John's, Michaelmas, Christmas and Easter. And this pulse accompanies the breath.

Today we can add that the festivals of the world breath were, and still are, heathen and mighty, while the festivals of the world light are Christian and inward. Just as we must learn to distinguish between world breath and light outside, and between human breath and pulse within, so we should learn to differentiate between the heathen elements which still exist in our festivals, and the Christian, inward festivals of light that must gradually replace them. We know that the Christmas festival necessarily contains many heathen traits, as does the festival of Easter. St. John's is hardly Christianised as yet, while Michaelmas is only gradually starting to become a Christian, inward festival through the work of Rudolf Steiner. However, concerning the relationship of pulse and breath outside in the world, and inside in man, something else should still be added, and it is from this point that I would like to begin today.

In the last lecture it was said that it is not at all true that man really lives in his physical body. Man is a spirit-soul being, an individuality, before he descends to earth at birth, so it would be succumbing to error to believe that he lives in material substances such as bone or muscle, or in the organs, or even in such processes as metabolism or the circulation. All the materials, substances and processes are not really our own. We wear them just as we wear a garment which we put on in the morning and take off at night. They are rather like ballast, packing, cover, or decoration, and no doubt every man has his own individual substances. In fact, this is a great problem for surgery today and is especially frustrating for the modern surgeon undertaking organ transplants because he is unable to replace a liver, or exchange one kidney for another, with the same ease as fitting spare parts to a car. Such people hold the callous view that it is senseless to conceive of man as being built individually because they believe that there cannot really be any differences in matter. Yet the material substances of our bodies, our organs, tissues and fluids, are only so individual because our ether body is always permeated by our soul-spirit individuality. Nevertheless, the substances themselves do not belong to us. If we ask where we really live, we have to say that we live in the rhythm of our breathing, although *not* in the substances of our breathing, and in the rhythm of our pulse. One should make it a point to engage in the meditative task of imagining how one lives as soul in the rhythm of one's breath; how one lives as Ego in the rhythm of one's pulse; not in the circulating blood, nor in the substances of the breathing process, but solely in their rhythms.

An important further aspect is that from the very first day, from the moment of our birth, we begin to breathe. We could also say, and it would be quite correct to express it like this, that the moment a child begins to breathe it is born. However, this holds good only for the breath, because the pulse begins long before birth at the moment when the fertilised ovum divides into two and begins to grow. We breathe only from the moment of birth, but our pulse begins to beat in the first days of our existence shortly after conception. This is an important difference to notice. Of course, the scientists will say that the embryo and the foetus also breathes because the mother's blood provides it with oxygen and removes carbon dioxide, and that therefore this is a breathing process too, but it is, in fact, a process of nutrition. What is called cellular respiration has hardly anything to do with breathing in the sense of inhaling and exhaling air into and out of the depths of the body. Therefore we can say that the pulse sets in soon after conception, whereas breathing begins only at birth, and that we live in both, for they carry us through our existence on earth. Pulse and breath are the great rhythms within which we truly live.

We can now ask the following: How does the pulse work in us, and we in it? and, What does the breath and our soul bring about through the pulse? It is really not very difficult to learn, or rather to experience, how the Ego lives and works in the pulse, and how the soul lives and works in the breath. In our pulse and through our blood we find a relationship to the power of uprightness within us which encounters gravity; a relationship that gives rise to the power of will in us. Our pulse binds us to the earth; it keeps us in the realm of warmth, allowing us to experience will and encounter gravity. It leads downwards into the depths of our existence to where we continually strive to establish our morality. Breath, however, is different. It helps us to find our way into the realm of language which is aroused in us as children, and through which the power of thinking develops. One path leads from breath upwards through language to thought and wisdom; the other leads downwards from pulse through the power of uprightness and gravity, to the will and into morality. Thus from the breath the path leads up to the larynx where language awakens and speech carries thinking, while from the pulse the path leads in an entirely different direction, in and out, to and from the heart, awakening warmth and entering into that realm which we recognise in life as morality. Let us keep this before us as an image.

Now we must consider a further question: How are breath and pulse related to each other? This can be answered in no other way than by saying that death sets in the moment breathing begins, and that although the pulse continually struggles to counteract the death process, breath is the stronger. Breath destroys; pulse strives to enliven. Breath becomes ever stronger day by day; pulse becomes weaker year by year until finally death occurs when the breath of life has overcome the pulse of existence. So a battle rages continually throughout life; a battle in which the Ego endeavours to maintain life by means of the pulse, while the soul tries to destroy life through the breath which increases in power until death overtakes us.

When we reach the point where we are able to grasp this phenomenon consciously, or raise it as an image within us, we are approaching one of the greatest problems which the devout soul has to confront every year, namely the problem of resurrection. St. Paul expresses it in the First Letter to the Corinthians by saying: 'But if there be no resurrection of the dead, then is Christ not risen; and if Christ be not risen, then is our preaching vain, and so is your faith.' (I Corinthians XV:13–14). Concerning these words Rudolf Steiner says in the sixth lecture of the cycle *From Jesus to Christ*:

> For what is it that St. Paul says? [He says] that the whole of Christianity has no justification, and the whole Christian faith no meaning, if the resurrection is not true! That is what is said by Paul, with whom Christianity as a fact of history had its starting-point. And it means that anyone who is willing to give up the resurrection must give up Christianity as Paul understood it.[1]

Taking such an indication seriously means not being content with merely believing in the resurrection of Christ, nor being content with the thought that it cannot be understood anyway, but rather to wrestle actively, especially at Easter, with the question of the meaning of Christ's resurrection. This question is more profound than words can express. It signifies that a God went through death; that He rose and was among his own for forty days. It means that He appeared to them, talked with them and taught them. He appeared not only to individuals, but to two, three, five, even five hundred, and all of them, disciples and apostles, saw him alive. He walked among them, even taking food and allowing Thomas to put his fingers into the wounds. Indeed, this is quite extraordinary.

In the fourth, fifth and sixth lectures of the cycle *From Jesus to Christ* which Rudolf Steiner held in Karlsruhe in October 1911, he tried with the greatest care and exemplary exactitude to lead his listeners step by step towards the secret of resurrection. He shows, for instance, that the Christianity of St. Paul differs from the Christianity of the disciples and the gospels. This is because the disciples only gradually became aware of the fact, without really grasping its full import, that the Lord was among them and spoke to them as the Risen One; that He really had arisen as the scripture prophesied and as He Himself had said, but which none of them had believed. Rudolf Steiner shows how at first St. Paul did not understand at all what this meant, and how only in the event on the road to Damascus did he suddenly realise: the Lord lives! After that St. Paul tried as an initiate to grasp and fully understand what had really happened. He tried to explain it through his own way of thinking by speaking of an old Adam who perishes and a new Adam who resurrects, and how the old Adam must be gradually permeated and replaced by the new Adam. As a consequence of his spiritual-scientific deductions Rudolf Steiner pointed out the fact that none of the disciples would have been able to think such thoughts, and that St. Paul was only able to think in this way because not only was he a believing Jew, he was also a Greek. As a Greek rooted in Grecianism and imbued with the Greek folk-spirit, he also experienced sorrow at the loss of the bodily organism. This feeling lived strongly in the Greek people, and they suffered profoundly from the fact that the human body, which they considered the greatest pinnacle of creation by nature and the Godhead, perished in death. In our present context we could say that 'throughout life, breath is stronger than pulse' and therefore the divine form is continually being destroyed. Rudolf Steiner pointed out that everything in our body which is matter, the material and substances of our organs, tissue etc., is not important, because they are only held together during life by that form, that *Gestalt*, which the Greeks saw perish, and which they valued above all else. Through the event on the road to Damascus, St. Paul suddenly realised as an inspiration that the old Adam, the form-body of our physical frame, must be destroyed! The new Adam has arisen and all who give themselves to the new Adam, all who confess Christ, will be able to experience the renewal of the old Adam through the new Adam.

This is the gist of the sermon St. Paul gave in Athens. What mattered was to tell the Greek people, the Greek world, that their sorrow had come to an end, for now in the joy of resurrection the old Adam can be replaced by the new Adam. This is the point at issue, but how can we understand it a little better?

May I briefly remind you how in our Christmas lectures we tried to understand the old Adam?[2] In connection with the organ of man's sense of Ego, which we described as the human form, we spoke about the spirit germ, that mighty organism which is prepared for every human being between death and a new birth. We described how both hierarchies and human beings, and the individual human being itself, work and weave in order to fashion the spirit germ which every one of us then takes with him into earthly existence. This form of the spirit germ becomes the old Adam; it fashions the embryo and its sheaths, building up the foetus so that it gradually takes on human form. With this understanding we can now see that from the day of conception the old Adam is formed and developed in the mother's womb by the human pulse. If we were to describe this fully then world images would appear before us, for in the course of embryonic development during the first days after fertilization the most diverse circulations are formed. A yolk-sack circulation appears; a placental circulation is formed; a body-circulation develops and, at the point of intersection of all these circulations on which, so to speak, shines the light of the world, the human form develops as the 'end of God's paths'. Rudolf Steiner once expressed this by saying: 'Man in his form, in his *Gestalt*, is the religion of God.' This is what develops in the mother's organism and leads us into the earthly world, giving us the organ of the sense of Ego. You will remember that we called this the archetypal phenomenon of all social existence which opens the possibility of direct and meaningful contact with all men.

However, at the very moment we are born and begin to breathe, death sets in. Death gnaws at the old Adam. This moment is heralded by the trumpets of labour, which if we think of a symphony is an exact description. Imagine a symphony by Bruckner or Mahler for instance, where suddenly all the brass and wind strike up, or the sound of the whole orchestra suddenly breaking into a mighty crescendo; this is an image for what happens when the pains of labour set in. At that moment destruction begins its work, and will continue throughout life until the moment of death. However, it is through this death process alone that Ego-consciousness is created. Ego-consciousness only began to dawn after the Fall of man, the event which induced breath into the body and which brought with it the destruction of pulse. Consciousness knocks against the physical organism in breath, through which speech awakens and the power to think is formed, and through the power of thinking the pulse must take hold of gravity and bring about uprightness.

It took many thousands of years until Ego-consciousness awakened for the first time in the Greek epoch. However, by the time this happened the old Adam had been destroyed to such an extent, had been so ruined by the power of breath, that the ancient Greek prophecy contained in the myth of Prometheus had come true. This prophecy was that Prometheus would be chained to the rock of the Caucasus and his liver gnawed at every day by an eagle. There could be no better image for what we have tried to describe. Prometheus was the Titan who stole the fire from heaven, which means he took Ego-consciousness from the Gods and brought it to men on earth. Therefore he was chained and the breath of the eagle gnaws at the source of his blood formation and the process of destruction increases. The story tells how the more the liver was restored during the night, the greater became the power of the eagle's claws, so that there was nothing but death in store for the Titan until Hercules appeared, killing the eagle and setting Prometheus free. Hercules is the symbol of the Sun-power that wanders through the twelve signs of the Zodiac; he is an image of the coming Christ. This all leads to an understanding of the old Adam.

When we approach the events in the gospels prior to the Mystery of Golgotha, we find the great heathen epic of Prometheus transformed inwardly into the descriptions of the Christian raisings of the dead. Three great, yet very simple, raisings of the dead are performed by Christ. These are the raising of the youth who is the son of a widow; of the girl who is the daughter of a ruler of the synagogue, and of the man who is the brother of two women: in other words the raising of the youth of Nain, of Jairus' daughter, and of Lazarus, the noble member of the high priests' family.

Although these raisings from the dead are a Christian form of the mighty heathen myth of Prometheus, what do they really portend? We know they are three preliminary steps to the Mystery of Golgotha. Christ indicates that it is not a real death, for when he hears about Lazarus he says: "Our friend Lazarus sleepeth; but I go that I may wake him out of sleep." He says of Jairus' daughter: "Weep not; she is not dead but sleepeth." So these are not true raisings from death—from a death which has completely destroyed the human body—but are a public repetition of what had previously only taken place within the Mysteries. Therefore, the gospel relates how Christ calls: "Lazarus come forth"; how He says to Jairus' daughter: "Maid, arise", and how He commands the youth of Nain: "Young man, I say unto thee, arise."

What really lies behind this? Christ re-enlivens the breath of these three which had stopped. He re-awakens the process which makes life conscious into the depth of consciousness, and so makes it possible for the process of dying to set in once more after 'death'. What has happened here is what always took place in the Mysteries, namely that a death-like sleep befell the neophyte who was to be initiated, and that the hierophant re-awakened the breath by certain spiritual measures which worked down into the physical body. Goethe expressed this same process later when he wrote:

> As long as you do not attain
> This dying and becoming,
> You are but a dull guest
> On the dark earth.

The decisive point for all three—the youth of Nain, Jairus' daughter, and Lazarus—was the process of 'dying and becoming'. Only in the Mystery of Golgotha, which followed as a fourth event after the three preparatory ones, is there a re-awakening not only of the breath, but also of the pulse. Now we know what is meant when it is said that the spirit-germ, the old Adam, cannot be reawakened. He has become the cross, but on this cross the roses have begun to bloom. The resurrection begins and death becomes life. Easter jubilation—which passed unheard by men, but was heard by all the Gods—resounded through the cosmos: Christ rose; the new Adam was born; the first Easter began.

This is as far as I would like to go today. We shall continue our attempts to understand the new Adam, and with the help of Rudolf Steiner's insight I hope it will be possible to achieve this to some degree.

Easter, the Festival of Resurrection

Föhrenbühl, Easter Sunday, 18th April 1965

Now Easter has finally come. This year we have tried to approach it in a special way by attempting to take the first steps towards understanding that great secret which lies hidden in the simple word 'resurrection'. Time and again the human spirit tries, although often in vain, to reach an understanding of the riddle of resurrection. But whatever contribution we try to make to advance our understanding, whether as the fruit of thinking or as a meditative effort using the sources opened for us by Rudolf Steiner, will only be a stepping stone towards the glory of resurrection which lies ahead of man, perhaps only at the end of earth evolution. Therefore we should remember that it can only ever be with hesitant, imperfect or incomplete, yet nonetheless striving steps that we endeavour to approach this secret. However, the Easter impulse, the tender dawn of the Easter jubilation, will always give us the courage to go forward, resolutely treading the path in pursuit of this mystery.

A week ago, on Palm Sunday, we approached it from a specific angle through Rudolf Steiner's *Calendar of the Soul*, trying to grasp what we called the world breath and world pulse from the point of view of the cosmos and of nature. Then, on Holy Wednesday, we proceeded a step further in trying to understand the breath and pulse in man, and we were helped in this endeavour by the mythological image of Prometheus chained to the rock, haunted day after day by the eagle, a symbol for the breath, eating into his liver and thus into his life. As an image this is an accurate analogy for what happens in the human being, for during life the breath also gnaws constantly at the power of the pulse, eating into the power of the blood. It was even expressed by saying that man's life between birth and death is in reality an unceasing battle between the gnawing breath and the continuously renewed blood, and that the breath gains the upper hand and so leads to death. Death is the inevitable end for Prometheus as a result of the eagle gnawing at his liver, as it is for every man by the breath eating into his pulse. At death the form of the human body disintegrates, and we realised that this human form is identical with that sensory-supersensory formation which we had described earlier at Christmas, and which we called to mind again in the last lecture. It is what Rudolf Steiner called the spirit germ that is created anew for every man during the time between death and new birth. It is the spirit germ into which is woven all human destiny, the work of the hierarchies and all those who were connected with us during our former life, thus bringing about a mighty spirit form which becomes smaller and smaller until the moment it unites with the physical germ of the developing human being that is forming in the mother's womb.

We described how the spirit germ is received by the pulse, the circulation of the blood, as a spiritual form, and also how breath sets in at the moment of birth, and with it the process of death which accompanies man throughout his life. If as a first outline we try to visualise the spirit germ pictorially, we must imagine it as the human form.

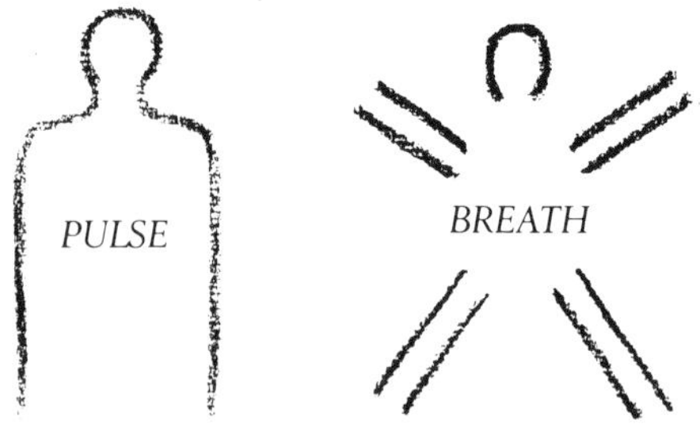

Of course, it is extremely primitive to draw it like this, nevertheless it is the human form consisting of head and body. Now the moment breath sets in, which can be observed and studied by comparative anatomy, the human form extends into the shape of the limbs, and so it is justified to write 'pulse' here and to call this 'breath'.

Here we can see immediately that the formation of the limbs represents the formation of the earth, for it is only by means of our limbs, especially our legs, but also our arms, that we become citizens of the earth. This form is still the image of man as he is born in the image of God. However, from the hour of birth the breath begins to gnaw at this form so that in the course of the first years of life the 144 (12 times 12) pulse beats per minute which the child has before birth are compressed to such an extent that they are reduced by half, and thereafter we have to be content with 72 beats. This has to be considered in a first attempt to grope towards the secret of resurrection.

This differentiation between pulse and breath, between the cosmic light and cosmic breath which permeate the world, is essential, for without it we cannot approach what St. Paul called the old and the new Adam and, two thousand years later, Rudolf Steiner called the 'phantom'. We should know that the phantom described by Rudolf Steiner is identical with what St. Paul called the old and the new Adam. Rudolf Steiner spoke extensively about the nature of the phantom in the lecture cycle *From Jesus to Christ*, and we will now try to wrestle for an understanding of what is meant by the phantom. In the sixth lecture Rudolf Steiner says:

> In our time the more clairvoyance is developed in man, the more will he gain clarity that those physical substances and powers which he lays down with the physical body are not the whole physical body, that this would not even be the whole structure (Gestalt). No, to these substances and powers there belongs something more which we must call—if we want to speak in a pertinent way—the phantom of man. This phantom is the form structure of man which as spirit-tissue works up the physical substances and forces so that they come into the form which we meet later as man on the physical plane.[1]

What is described here as the phantom is called the 'spirit germ' in Rudolf Steiner's later writings.

It is important to recognise at the outset that the phantom is the same as the old Adam; that figure which was given to man as a physical form by the Gods. In the course of those lectures, Rudolf Steiner even said that men were not in fact meant to fill this form with earthly, material substance, but that it should have remained a sensory-supersensory form, which means a physical and yet invisible one. It was only as a result of the Fall that this form no longer remained physical but became material: originally it was *only* physical. The Divine Thought did not intend man to become the physical-material bodies we are today. However, while the Fall brought about a densification of soul-spiritual substance, a deeper immersion of man's Ego-being into the minerals and substances of the earth, it also awakened something which every man experiences today as his Ego-consciousness. It is of great importance to try once again to grasp what it is that makes us conscious. The materialisation of the form of the body, of the phantom, brought about our self-consciousness, our Ego-consciousness, for in coming up against this corporeality which was becoming ever denser, in knocking against it, the Ego awoke to a consciousness of itself; to its own self-consciousness. Rudolf Steiner spoke about this in the seventh lecture of *From Jesus to Christ* in the following way:

> It is impossible to understand Christianity without realising that at the time of the events in Palestine mankind all over the earth had come to the point where the disintegration of the physical body had reached its climax and that there was consequently the danger that the Ego-consciousness, the specific achievement of earth-evolution, would be lost. If no new impulse had been added to what was there up to the events of Palestine, the process would have continued and more and more destruction would have entered the human physical corporeality, and men born after the events of Palestine would have had to live with an ever duller experience of the Ego. That which depends on the perfection of the mirroring faculties of a physical body would have become ever duller.[2]

We can now see that man was created in a form which corresponded to the rhythm of his pulse, the cosmic rhythm of 12 times 12. This form was meant to be a true microcosm, both human and divine. However, it went through the Fall and man became mature for the earth. The human breath began its gnawing work, creating powers of destruction which made consciousness possible until, within this general consciousness, self-consciousness appeared. Yet parallel with man's rising self-consciousness came those destroying powers which, working ever more strongly, caused ever greater disintegration of the first God-created human form, which resulted in the gradual dimming of his Ego-consciousness. The repercussion of this awakening thinking was the progressive destruction of the God-willed form which still held man together.

I am aware that some found difficulty in understanding why it is that pulse and blood are linked with gravity, and breath with speech and thought. It is not possible to enlarge on this fully now, other than to touch on the subject by repeating that light and sound, the two primeval powers which permeate all creation, should be understood as being active in pulse and breath. It is the light in the pulse which encounters gravity and thereby creates the power of uprightness, and it is the sound in the breath which encounters disintegration in the chemical structure. Thus the human form, which Rudolf Steiner here calls the phantom, proceeds step by step towards gravity and disintegration. I have described all this from a number of angles because I believe that these are fundamental steps to be ascended in order gradually to reach the veiled image behind which the riddle of resurrection is hidden.

You see, what is said by Rudolf Steiner in the passage we have just read, namely that the importance of Christianity can only be understood if it is realised that at the time Christ incarnated the decay of the phantom had advanced so far that people would not have been able to continue living without their experience of Ego becoming ever dimmer, or even losing it altogether, is also described in the four gospels. In the last lecture we referred to the three raisings from the dead: the raising of Jairus' daughter, of the youth of Nain, and of Lazarus, the brother of Mary and Martha. What Rudolf Steiner tried to express in the passage just quoted is revealed in these three events. We are concerned here with three persons: a girl who has just attained the age of twelve; a youth who is about sixteen or seventeen years old, and a mature man, all of whom die without apparent reason; without illness. It seems that these three are persons whose forces of life have begun to dwindle away.

Concerning these healings of the sick, the gospels do not say what kind of illness, sin or error is involved but simply describe what happened: the maiden dwindled away, the youth died, and about Lazarus of Bethany nothing is said except that after his death and burial his sisters sent messengers to Christ saying: 'Our brother has died, come and help.' If we try to read the gospels very carefully we can find signs which perhaps allow us to discover what the issue really is. The raising of Jairus' daughter is told in the three so-called synoptic gospels, and each time it is preceded quite pointedly by the story of the woman who suffered from an issue of blood for twelve years. In a rather modern way it is even noted that she spent all her money on doctors, but none could help her. Yet it is emphasised that she had suffered the illness for twelve years, which means that she had suffered the issue of blood for as many years as the daughter of Jairus is old. In this way both events are linked in the composition of the three gospels, and we may ask what this means. We are told that when Christ is called by Jairus and He sets off to go to the daughter, the woman touches the hem of His garment and He realises that at that moment a power has gone out of Him. At that same moment the woman's issue of blood ceases and she is healed. Now it is pertinent to ask what had been the matter with this woman. The simple answer is that she suffered from a continuous menstruation which would not stop. If we ask when the monthly period normally ceases in the life of any woman, the answer is plain: when pregnancy begins. However, a woman becomes pregnant only when a new spirit germ, the phantom of an incarnating child, descends and takes up its dwelling in the mother's organism. At that moment the monthly period stops. This is what happened here, because when the woman touched the border of Christ's garment the powers of the phantom streamed into her and stemmed the flow of blood. We can therefore say that having reached the age of twelve the daughter of Jairus should have started her monthly menstrual flow, but was dying because her phantom did not have the strength to hold the blood. Consequently the blood is overcome by gravity; it flows down and with it the girl's powers of life ebb away just as the powers of life of the woman flowed away. Christ touches the girl and she is healed.

The case of the youth of Nain is similar, and yet different. Rudolf Steiner once said that the youth of Nain whom Christ raised was the youth of Sais who in a former life had been unable to recognise the Being of Man in the Mysteries. He had been rejected in the Egyptian Mysteries and was now reborn as the son of a widow. The absence of a father signifies that the power to cast one's anchor into the earth is missing; the will is lacking. In a similar way to the daughter of Jairus in whom the blood is overcome by gravity, so in the youth of Nain the blood is overcome, but in his case by levity, and it becomes volatile. Therefore Christ Jesus had to come in order to touch the youth and heal his phantom, his physical body, so that he can be restored to the widow, his mother.

The secret of Lazarus' death is different, yet similar. What lies hidden in this secret is later given as an image when, after entering Jerusalem, Christ curses the fig tree which bears no fruit and next morning the tree is seen to have withered and died. For when Lazarus the rich youth approached Christ and asked "Master, what shall I do?", Christ replied "Give away all your treasures", which meant that he should give away all the treasures of wisdom which he had gained by being one of the elders of the Jews. He is asked to become like a fig tree without fruit. For a man whose phantom body is disintegrating it is impossible to do this, but Lazarus does it nevertheless. It is an immense sacrifice for him to relinquish this wisdom in the name, one could say, of all who still drew upon the old wisdom, because in doing so he withers away; he dies. The blood, the pulse, cannot hold its own against the onslaught of the new that opens up on letting go of the old.

Each of these three is raised from death. These raisings, however, are nothing else than the renewal of that figure which will hold the blood together in order that it can meet, at least for a while, the onslaught of the gnawing waves of breath. We can also say that these three are reawakened by the abounding power of Christ's love. This is indicated in the gospels when Christ tells Jairus: "Fear not, believe only". When Christ sees the widow, the gospel says: 'And when the Lord saw her, he had compassion on her, and said unto her: Weep not'; and when He comes to Lazarus' sister, it says: 'When Jesus therefore saw her weeping and the Jews also weeping which came with her, he groaned in the spirit, and was troubled.' The all-pervading love of Christ springs forth in eyes, hands and heart and from it flows the strength for the renewal of the phantom of these three.

The point at issue here is not that these three alone should have been raised, but that what happened to them should also happen for all men. In a remarkable lecture about these three raisings from the dead,[3] Rudolf Steiner once said that we should really view them in such a way that we see in them how the three great post-Atlantean cultures were healed. Christ takes up what had decayed in the Indian culture and heals it by raising Jairus' daughter. Similarly, the decaying Egyptian-Babylonian culture is healed by reviving the youth of Nain. What this means is that these were the representatives of mankind's past in whom the phantom was re-illumined. But what should happen to men of the fourth and fifth epochs, for it was also necessary to work into the future? This was the great question which at that time presented itself cosmically, so to speak, and which was to be solved by the Christ-event on Golgotha.

In order to understand this more fully we shall have to approach these immense problems from yet another side. You will remember that at Christmas we considered the two Jesus children, and how from a new aspect we tried to understand what the Nathanic and the Solomonic beings were and are. Of the Nathanic child, who was born at the turning-point of time and welcomed by the shepherds, we know that it received an earthly body for the first time. This was that Ego-being which had been preserved since the first beginnings of mankind; since the time of Adam, the Lemurian age. It did not go through the Fall with the rest of mankind but waited untouched until it descended to earth at the turning-point of time. This being then became the bearer of the Ego of the other, Solomonic, Jesus child in its twelfth year and, as Jesus of Nazareth, only in its thirtieth year did it become the vehicle for the Christ-spirit at the baptism in the river Jordan.

Let us now place this very earnestly before our spiritual eyes. Here is an untouched being that descends to earth for the first time and permeates itself with earthly substance, but brings with it an untouched, blameless, innocent Ego, into whose sheaths the Christ enters. Concerning this Rudolf Steiner says in the seventh lecture of *From Jesus to Christ*:

> It came to pass that one man, who was the bearer of the Christ, had gone through such a death that after three days the specifically mortal part of the physical body had to disappear, and out of the grave there rose the body which is the force-bearer of the physical, material parts. The body that was really intended for man by the rulers of Saturn, Sun and Moon—the pure Phantom of the physical body with all the attributes of the physical body—this it was that rose out of the grave. So was given the possibility of that spiritual genealogy of which we have spoken.
>
> Let us think of the body of Christ that rose out of the grave. Just as from the body of Adam the bodies of earth-men are descended, in so far as these men have the body that crumbles away, even so are the spiritual bodies, the Phantoms for all men, descended from that which rose out of the grave. And it is possible to establish a relationship with Christ through which the earthly human being can bring into his otherwise decaying physical body this Phantom which rose out of the grave of Golgotha. It is possible for man to receive into his organism those forces which then rose from the grave, just as through his physical organism at the beginning of the earth evolution, as a consequence of the Luciferic

> forces, he received the organism of Adam.
>
> It is this that Paul wishes to say. Just as man, through his place in the stream of physical evolution, inherits the physical body in which the destruction of the Phantom, the force-bearer, is gradually taking place, from the pure Phantom that rose out of the grave he can inherit what he has lost. He can inherit, can clothe himself with it, as he clothed himself with the first Adam; he can become one with it. Thereby he can go through a development by means of which he can climb upwards again, even as before the Mystery of Golgotha he had descended in evolution. In other words, that which had been taken from him through the Luciferic influence can be given back to him through its presence as the risen body of Christ.[4]

Here we are coming a little closer to what we are trying to understand. Out of the grave arose the new Adam, the phantom, renewed through Christ indwelling the body of Jesus of Nazareth. Can we understand this even further?

To do so we will have to add yet another aspect. This year as a preparation towards Easter we read the Gospel of St. Mark, which I believe was very important, and yesterday evening during the Bible evening and again this morning we heard the passage which relates how the three women go to the grave early on the morning of Easter Sunday. Finding that the stone has been rolled away they look into the sepulchre but cannot find the body of Christ, and instead they see a young man sitting at the right side of the grave. The question now arises: Who is this youth? Here Rudolf Steiner gives a very clear answer. In the lectures on the Gospel of St. Mark he refers to a previous chapter of the gospel which mentions this youth in the description of Maundy Thursday night and the arrest of Christ by his persecutors. He quotes the passage:

> And there followed Him [closely]* a certain young man, having a linen cloth cast about his naked body; and the

* The original Greek says 'who followed him closely.'

> young men laid hold on him: And he left the linen cloth and fled from them naked. (Mark 14: 51–52.)

and then he continues:

> Who is this young man? Who was it who escaped? Who is it who appears here, next to Christ Jesus, nearly unclothed, and then slips away unclothed? This is the youthful cosmic impulse, it is the Christ who slips away, who now has only a loose connection with the Son of Man. Much is contained in the 51st and 52nd verses. The new impulse retains nothing of what former times were able to wrap around man. It is the entirely naked, new cosmic impulse of earth evolution. It remains near Jesus of Nazareth and we find it again at the beginning of the sixteenth chapter: 'And entering into the sepulchre they saw a young man sitting on the right side, clothed in a long white garment; and they were affrighted.'
>
> This is the same youth! In the whole artistic composition of the gospels nowhere else does this youth confront us, the youth who slips away at the moment when they condemn the Son of Man, who is there again when the three days are over, and who from now onward is active as the cosmic principle of the earth.[5]

Summarising all this we can say that the spirit-being of Christ partly leaves the sheath of Jesus of Nazareth at the moment men lay hands on Him, and what is left is the sheath of the Nathanic being of Jesus of Nazareth forsaken by the cosmic impulse. So it is the Son of Man who goes through death. He is accompanied by the Son of God, but it is the Son of Man who is crucified, suffers death and is placed in the grave. What happened is described by Rudolf Steiner in the eighth lecture of *From Jesus to Christ*:

> When the body was taken down from the Cross, the parts were still coherent, but they had no connection with the Phantom; the Phantom was completely free from them. When the body became permeated with certain substances,

> which in this case worked quite differently from the way in which they affect any other body that is embalmed, it came to pass that after the burial the material parts quickly volatilized and passed over into the elements. Hence the disciples who looked into the grave found the linen clothes in which the body had been wrapped, but the Phantom, on which the evolution of the Ego depends, had risen from the grave.[6]

So you see, the resurrection—and I beg you to take these words in full earnesness—the resurrection is the salvation and renewal of the phantom. However, the Risen One himself is connected with the Christ-impulse. These belong together just as breath and pulse belong together in man, and yet they are twofold. The phantom is saved through the fact that the untouched being of Jesus of Nazareth, who as the Nathanic Child was born for the first time in the human form of man at the turning point of time, is permeated during the three years by the power, strength and light of the Christ-spirit. Christ has risen and is the Risen One: the phantom is saved and is the resurrection. We must gradually come to realise this if we wish to approach these questions with a certain degree of clarity.

You see, the Mystery of Golgotha was really a further step continuing on from three preliminary steps that we already know.[7] Once during the Lemurian age and twice during the later Atlantean age—at its beginning and again at its end—powers of love streamed down to men as healing for all mankind through the Nathanic being which had received the Christ-spirit like a cup. During Lemuria the senses were soothed in the first act of healing; the organs harmonised in the second act of healing, and ordered thinking, feeling and willing within the human soul were brought about in the third act of healing. Then a further step followed when this being took on earthly shape and sacrificed itself once more in being permeated by the Christ-spirit and thereby the human form, the spirit germ, was renewed. It is in this light that we can speak of a new Adam in the sense intended by St. Paul, or about a new phantom body as Rudolf Steiner meant it to be understood. The secret of the phantom is the secret of the fourth deed of sacrifice of the Nathanic being, for it is the Son of Man who goes through death and through whom the resurrection, the renewal of the human form created in the image of God, now takes place. We can now understand that at the time the moon left the earth, when male and female were created and the breath came into being and began to gnaw at man's pulse, already then that Ego which remained pure was retained. It accompanied all mankind and through the fact that Christ ensouled Himself in it, it became the threefold healer until it descended to earth for the fourth deed of healing.

At that moment something happened which, following on from the end of the last lecture, we can contemplate as the Cross permeated by death on which the roses have begun to bloom through the resurrection. You see, it is the purpose of true Rosicrucianism to endeavour to give those men who have dedicated themselves to it the foundations whereby they can connect themselves to the new Adam, for the new Adam is neither gained by blood or kinship, nor can it be acquired by any earthly force. The new Adam works wherever the human spirit begins to triumph over need and hardship; over gravity and levity; over every earthly power. The new Adam has a part in everyone who sets out to become a true man in the sense of the Rose Cross. What happened at the turning-point of time takes place today in every man of goodwill, for Christ walks today through the earth-sphere as the Risen One. He is here; He is risen. We men, however, have the task of taking up what is revealed in the resurrection and becoming what in truth we already are: brethren of Christ.

Tomorrow we shall try to round all this off, drawing further conclusions from a few more aspects of these facts, thoughts and ideas with which we began a week ago.

Earthly Creation, Human Form and Human Ego

Föhrenbühl, 19th April 1965

Tonight we will conclude our present efforts to understand the great mystery described by the word 'resurrection'. What we undertook this Easter was rather exceptional and at times very complicated, even confusing, especially when occasionally it contradicted our ordinary way of thinking. This was because we were attempting to relate sense-perceptible phenomena to supersensible events so as to bring out the importance of what lies behind the riddle of resurrection. Easter demands this of us because in its events we are confronted with supersensible events taking place in the realm of the senses. As an example of this we need only read in the Gospel of St. Luke how two disciples wander to Emmaus and suddenly are joined by a third, an unknown man who talks with them and explains the events which have so shaken them, accompanies them into the house, sits down at table and breaks bread with them, and then disappears. Or how on the same day the Risen One appears to the disciples in the Upper Room, and not only do they see and recognise Him but they give Him a piece of fish and some honey which He eats, and then He disappears again. This is Easter; the supersensible is so anchored in the sensory that it can be perceived.

In an Easter lecture Rudolf Steiner once said that:

> During the fifth post-Atlantean epoch a new tendency has been at work, a tendency towards a scientific knowledge that is adapted to the power of human reason and judgement; and now it is time that this should go further and develop into a knowledge of the supersensible world. For the event of Golgotha is one which falls absolutely

> within the *supersensible* world. And the event of Damascus, as Paul experienced it, is an event which can be understood only out of supersensible ideas. On the understanding of this event depends whether or not one can in very truth feel something of the Christ Impulse, or whether one cannot. The man of the present day is faced with a severe test when he asks himself: In the time that has been christened 'Easter', how do I stand in regard to supersensible knowledge? For Easter should remind man, by the very way its date is determined, to look up from the earthly to what is beyond the earth. The man of modern times has left himself no more outlook into what is beyond the earth than at worst that which is given him in mathematics and mechanics, and now in spectro-analysis. These sciences are the groundwork upon which he tries to build up his knowledge concerning all that is beyond the earth. He no longer feels that he is himself united with those worlds, and that the Christ descended thence when He entered into the personality of Jesus.[1]

In the lectures last week we tried to follow this Pauline attitude because it seems to be an essential element in our endeavours. It is an attitude in which a new attempt is made to represent the existence of supersensible phenomena in the realm of the senses. Therefore I began by considering cosmic pulse and breath, and trying to understand human pulse and breath. We also tried to reach beyond the perception of purely sensory phenomena to an understanding of the phantom, that physical yet supersensible form which holds together the material and substance of our mineral body so that it becomes visible, and because of which we can speak of a physical-material corporeality. Now, if we wish to understand a further aspect of the phantom, which despite being the physical form is invisible to human eyes, is it beyond the bounds of possibility to develop imaginative thought in order to do so? Perhaps the following approach may prove helpful.

The alchemists (by which I do not mean the charlatans but the genuine alchemists) spoke truthfully about the philosopher's stone some four, five or six hundred years ago. They themselves did not search for a stone (only the charlatans did that) for the true alchemists knew very well what the philosopher's stone really was. If they had been asked, as was customary among initiated alchemists, they would have said that it is nothing other than that element which every man carries in himself, which permeates everything living, everything organic. The philosopher's stone is simply carbon, one of the most essential building stones of all organic and inorganic substance. If one were to have asked an alchemist about the form of the human body, the structure of the old and new Adam (which he would have well understood), he would have said: 'Observe carbon and understand that diamond, graphite and black coal are one and the same. Know, however, that to really understand the nature of diamond you have to imagine it still more transparent than it appears, for in truth it consists of nothing other than geometrically formed light. If you can imagine and grasp this, then you will realise that a crystal is an archetypal image of salt, and that it is a form of light. Then you will also see how during the course of the earth's development this light form darkened, becoming tangible, visible graphite, and later changing to become coal.'

In the path from diamond via graphite to coal we can see the transformation from what the alchemist calls salt into what he calls ash. Diamond is still the purest, almost intangible, almost invisible salt, because it is formed out of pure light. Yet the denser carbon becomes, the more substance is deposited in it, the more it becomes ash. In the same way the old Adam evolved out of what was once the pure Adam, the untouched human form, and it breaks up because ash components are mixed into its form. Rudolf Steiner expressed this in the lectures from which I quoted last time:

> We said yesterday that that which we call the human Phantom—the actual primal form which takes up into itself, absorbs, the mineral elements and then yields them up at death—this Phantom had degenerated in the course of human evolution up to the time of the Mystery of

> Golgotha. In a certain way, we may grasp the idea of this degeneration as follows: At the beginning of human evolution it was actually pre-ordained that this Phantom should remain untouched by the material parts which are taken up by man as nutrition from the animal, plant and mineral kingdoms. The Phantom was intended to remain untouched by these, but it did not remain so, because, through the Luciferic influence, there came about a close union between the Phantom and the forces which man takes into him through earthly development, especially with the mineral ash constituents. Therefore, it was a result of the Luciferic influence that the Phantom, while accompanying humanity in its further evolution, developed a strong attraction for the ash-constituents and instead of accompanying the etheric body of man, it went with what were the products of disintegration.[2]

We will now take a further step and try to understand the phantom which had become a centre of attraction for the particles of ash. We have learned that the breath gnaws continuously at man's phantom, just as the eagle gnaws at Prometheus' liver. Through this continual erosion of the pulse which carries man's phantom, the phantom was doomed to perish at the time of the Mystery of Golgotha. In an entirely different context Rudolf Steiner spoke about the seven life-processes. He described how in the course of earth evolution, through Ahrimanic and Luciferic influences, these seven life-processes became something different from what the Gods had intended. In describing the first three processes of breathing, warming and nourishing he said that breathing became consumption, warming became burning, and nourishing became depositing. Then he went on to say:

> Concerning breathing, one can say that we do not actually breathe as we would if the regular divine-spiritual impulses were solely active in breathing, those impulses spoken of at the beginning of the Old Testament. We do not breathe as if the power of Jahwe only was working in

> our breath. Our way of breathing is a result of the transformation of our breathing system through Ahrimanic power which interfered with human life in the Atlantic period. In fact, we do not just breathe, we consume our organism by breathing and in this consumption a certain feeling of pleasure in life is created. Indeed, it is fundamental for our life betweeen birth and death that we put more energy into the breathing process than should be necessary. The consumption of our life powers is very much connected with this Ahrimanic influence. In a crude fashion one could say we would inhale less oxygen if the Ahrimanic influence was not there. At the same time the process of ageing—the consumption of our organism as it expresses itself in ageing—would not take place in such an intensive way but would happen in such a way that one could see that ageing is not just a completion of years. All this is connected in many ways with this Ahrimanic influence on the breathing process.
>
> Warming is connected through the Ahrimanic influence with a much stronger process of burning in our organism than would be the case in the course of regular evolution. Consumption—burning. In fact we burn ourselves.
>
> And nourishing is connected through the Ahrimanic influence with depositing whereby what we take in as food is not just digested but is, so to speak, deposited more or less as foreign matter in the organism.[3]

What the breathing process does within man is clearly described here: it consumes. This means that our powers of life are continually consumed by the breathing process. Warming changes from warmth into fire and, as Rudolf Steiner expresses it, man 'consumes' himself. As a further consequence of this consuming and burning, nourishing becomes depositing. You see, if we consider this and gradually learn to comprehend it, then we will realize that what was once the 'diamond' of the phantom had to change into 'graphite' and become black coal through consuming, burning and depositing.

Taking this new aspect we are now able to grasp what we tried to understand yesterday concerning the blood, namely the three raisings from the dead described in the New Testament: that of Jairus' daughter, of the youth of Nain and Lazarus of Bethany. I have already pointed out that these three passed away without illness, without apparent cause, and that by their deaths they were each representative of earlier epochs of mankind's history in which the phantom had disintegrated. Through laying His hand on them and calling them back from death, Christ caused the power of the renewed phantom in Him to be transferred to these three, and in them arose a first inkling of what St. Paul called the new Adam.

From what has just been said about consuming, burning and depositing we can take a further step, a physiological one, to discover what really happened in these three cases. In Jairus' daughter it was as if the power of the blood dwindled away when she entered puberty. The power of the blood was extinguished because the breath was so strong that it had consumed the body after only twelve years. When considering the youth of Nain we said that he had been a widow's son and so lacked a father, and therefore he did not have the will for earth existence. Consequently he was burned up after sixteen or seventeen years, and died as a result. For Lazarus, who had sacrificed all the treasures of wisdom he had gathered, life could not continue because everything that had become deposit in him carried him into the grave. We could say that all the healings and raisings from the dead in the New Testament are in fact endeavours by Christ to give new life to the seven life-processes in their archetypal form. These things offer potential for a new recognition which we shall have to acquire in order to understand the realities, right down to physical details.

This has brought us closer to an understanding of human pulse and human breath. Let us now recollect the first lecture in which, with the help of the *Calendar of the Soul*, we tried to understand the processes of cosmic breathing and cosmic pulse. You may remember that we asked ourselves many questions. What, for example, is meant by *Werdelust*, the 'rapture of becoming' in the two verses immediately prior to Passiontide? And what is it in the cosmos that comes to meet the exhaled breath of the earth? What is the light of the sun that ascends and descends four times in the course of the year, permeating the great inhaling and exhaling breath of the year with light? What is this cosmic 'breath', and whence did it originate? Is it still in the same state as on the first day of creation, or has it perhaps become something quite new and different, perhaps even akin to another cloak or sheath of the earth? Rudolf Steiner spoke about this on many occasions, but in one lecture he said:

> When the earth emerged and lifted itself, so to speak, out of the darkness of cosmic space, it was a space glowing with inner warmth, and living within it were the first forms of mankind as warmth-beings. When, with clairvoyant sight, you look back at what actually existed of man at that time you find at first these original human rudiments as if the whole warmth sphere has many, many currents in it.[4]

This is a description of the earth before the preceding stages of Old Moon, Old Sun and Old Saturn. The earth was then a mighty body of warmth which reached the present orbit of Saturn, and it was nothing but Man—Man formed out of warmth, the human form fashioned from currents of warmth, which looked approximately like this. *(see diagram)*

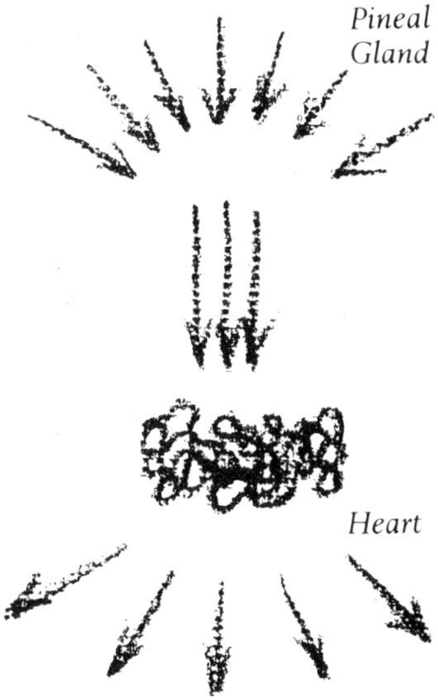

Currents of warmth streamed in from the periphery to a certain point from which they flowed down, forming a vortex of warmth, and then radiated outwards. Here we see a process which is also found in the development of the human embryo.* Rudolf Steiner tells us that here *(see diagram)* is the archetypal organ of what later became the pineal gland, while below it is the archetypal form of what later became the heart. The earth evolved from millions and millions of such human forms. It is the archetypal form. It is the seed of the phantom which was formed here and which later developed between the heart and the great warmth organ, the pineal gland.

Warmth became denser, and from it came both air and radiating light. Then air condensed and gave rise to water, and just as light came from air, so sound or tone evolved from the watery element. Thus step by step the entire organism of the earth evolved through a process of condensing and separating. Animals, plants, minerals and mountains all evolved in this way until finally–although always present from the beginning–Man appeared. Everything that condensed too early became plant, mineral and animal.

In the Ephesian mysteries where above all else earth evolution was taught as a manifestation of the power of the Word, pupils were given an image of this development. They were taught that during the early Lemurian period the earth was not yet solid. What had begun to condense was still surrounded by a vast fluid atmosphere of albuminous vapour which was not yet liquid but gaseous, and permeated with a little moisture. However, it was living matter, living organic albumen, which extended outwards a long way; so far, in fact, that it reached the moon. In this albuminous atmosphere something lit up from time to time which became green and then disappeared, became green again and then vanished once more. It was the first coming and going of spring and autumn.

Within this process of greening, plants sprouted and withered away again. These were not plants which grew on the earth but floated in a gleaming, fluorescent sphere. Into this plant realm worked what today is the silica process, and in this atmosphere

* For a fuller discussion of this subject, the reader is recommended to Karl König's essays entitled *Embryology and World Evolution*[5].

were also denser parts which could be seen as ascending and descending clouds. These clouds contained lime which condensed, formed animal shapes, and then disolved again. In this floating sphere of albumen many shapes were formed so that fluorescent plant life and solidifying animal life developed. Processes of breathing and nutrition were still one and the same at that time, because animal, plant and man inhaled and exhaled albumen. But step by step as the process of condensation unfolded, forms became permanent, plants took root, animals were born and died, until gradually everything took on organic form.

Nothing now remains of this creative power, except rhythm. What we call cosmic pulse today is just a remnant of what was once cosmic plant existence, and what we call cosmic breath is what remains of those traces of creation which are closely associated with the substances of lime and silica, out of which the limestone, granite and sandstone mountains arose, as well as all the animals of the earth. Plants became organs of the earth's surface. And amidst all this is Man.

What happened to the cosmic breathing process which had run down? When the cosmic breath approaches the earth in spring, it calls the beings which had formerly lived in it to awaken: plants begin to sprout and animals are born. A memory is evoked and revitalised by the cosmic breath so that the elemental beings, the Sylphs, Undines and Salamanders, emerge out of the earth. These exhale so as to meet what had once been their mother sheath. With their help plants become green, animals awaken, and light rises and fades away. Thus development continues because the memory of creation can still be called up and enlivened.

Just as we can look back to our youth, so in spring the earth remembers its former creative power and strength, but as a memory picture. A remnant of this is the mysterious interplay of breathing, continually weaving between plants and animals by virtue of the fact that animals exhale carbon dioxide and plants take it in and transform it through light to provide oxygen. Animal and man then inhale the oxygen, transforming it into carbon dioxide again. So all organic existence can still be maintained by this giving and taking; through the decaying which emanates from animals, and the enlivening which reappears in plants. This is further mirrored in man in what we called the 'breath that gnaws at the pulse of our existence', for while the gnawing breath induces decay, the radiating blood enlivens. Just as everything that flowers outside in nature is connected with chlorophyll, so everything that is enlivened within us is connected with almost the same substance: red haemoglobin.

Just as creation slowly evolved externally, so ash—which we have now come to see as an image of carbon—gradually developed within man. Now we face a great question: Why is it that ash develops in man through the fact that breathing changes into consuming, warming into burning and nourishing into depositing? Rudolf Steiner gave an important indication as to this in the lecture from which we quoted earlier:

> What pressed ash into human bodies was henceforth thought, which made sound—tone—into word. Even in Atlantean times, when everything was immersed in mist, what the human being spoke was not the only articulated language, but man understood the speech of the rustling trees, the rippling springs and fountains. The meaning, the significance of the world pressed into this living substance the ash that was formed out of the combustion process. Man was penetrated by thoughts—by self-consciousness—to the degree in which the osseous (bony) system gradually condensed towards the end of the Atlantean age. His intellect lit up and he became increasingly a self-conscious being.[6]

We may understand this indication better if we realize that thoughts enter man from without. Man does not form his own thoughts, but they first enter him from the world of archetypal thought. These thoughts change sound into word within him, thereby giving him self-consciousness. However, owing to this continuous and ever deeper entry of thinking into man, the phantom begins to disintegrate under its onslaught.

We now face the primal question with which we started, the posing of which is indeed a daring venture: What is the relation of the phantom to the human I? This is the true Easter question. What is the connection between the Ego—which we are somewhat conscious of and which runs like a golden thread throughout life from the moment memory begins in the third year—what is the relation of this Ego to the human form?

If we look back beyond the present stage of earth evolution, about which we have just spoken, to the earlier stages of Old Moon, Old Sun and Old Saturn and allow images of those stages to rise within us, then we can say that first the physical body was created by the gods in the primeval conditions of Old Saturn. Then during the course of the following stage of earth evolution, that of Old Sun, the forces of life, the ether body, were woven into the primal conditions of the physical body. During Old Moon, feelings and sensations entered into this physical-etheric body, whose nature had by now become one of warmth, light and air. In the developing human form the first inklings of outside and inside awoke, of being related to the divine surrounding and of a dawning, dreamlike consciousness of self, and thereby what became the astral body was incorporated. All this was human form—physical, etheric and astral form—created and evolved over aeons from the Old Saturn, Old Sun and Old Moon to the present Earth when the three earlier evolutionary stages were recapitulated once again and shaped into the form of the physical, the living and the sentient that we now know. Only after this form had been created did what we call the human Ego begin to descend into it.

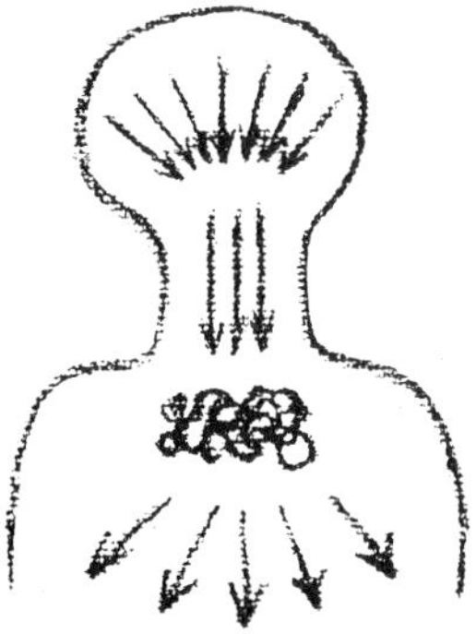

We can divine that the human form developed in the way we tried to outline earlier. The form of a head evolved into the form of a body. You will remember the form which we drew yesterday—it was this which was created. But the human Ego remained above it until all was completed.

Then the human Ego entered in and the Divine Thought which created the Word out of sound became Man. We could perhaps say that the human Ego remained above, waiting throughout the whole of creation until the moment during the Atlantean age when the mid-point of earth evolution had been reached and it could enter into its own; for only because it was itself form could it take up dwelling in its own form, that is, in the human form which had been shaped three times.

Perhaps we could advance a step further and say that in a similar way in which the human Ego waited above from the beginning of creation until its form had developed, so also from the beginning of earth evolution a part of that Ego which took its dwelling in the form of man, had waited above. It remained above as the new Adam in order not to go through the Fall, through earthly temptation and destiny. Just as the great Ego of mankind waited from the beginning of creation, so the higher brother of the Adam-soul waited from the beginning of earth evolution, and only at the turning point of time became that child whom the shepherds came and adored.

Following carefully what Rudolf Steiner repeatedly tried to say about this Nathanic being, we can note that he described it as the Ego, and yet also says that it consisted of only three sheaths—the physical, etheric and astral sheaths into which the other Jesus entered in the twelfth year. From this we might divine that human form, phantom and Ego are one and the same but in different guises. The I is created; it is the Word, and it lives as form in the pulse, as word and thought in the breath, and can only realise itself by seeing, by recognising itself in its own mirror and knowing: this is I.

Perhaps this can be a fitting conclusion to our journey along the many paths which we have walked this past week. It is something which Novalis expressed in a similar way when he said that the youth of Sais can only behold the image by tearing away the curtain, but that he then sees—'greatest of wonders'—himself! This is, perhaps, a first understanding of what St. Paul called the old and the new Adam. Rudolf Steiner called it the phantom, the consumed and the renewed form, and he described how out of that part of the Ego which became the Nathan being, which in turn was enlightened and irradiated by the Logos, can arise what is now renewed for every human being. This is what I wanted to say, but perhaps it is justified to quote one more passage from the Easter lecture of the 2nd April 1920 in order that Rudolf Steiner has the last word at the end of these considerations:

> The only possible way in these days for man to unite a right feeling with Easter is for him to direct his thought in this connection to the world-catastrophe of his own time. For in very deed a world-catastrophe is upon us. I do not mean merely the catastrophe that happened in the recent years of the war, but I refer to that world-catastrophe which consists in the fact that men have lost all idea of the connection of the earthly with that which is beyond the earth. *The time has come when man must realise with full and clear consciousness that supersensible knowledge has now to arise out of the grave of the materialistic outlook.* For together with supersensible knowledge will arise the knowledge of Christ Jesus. In point of fact, man has no other symbol that fits the Easter festival than this—that mankind has brought upon itself the doom of being crucified upon the cross of its own materialism. But man must do something himself before there arises from the grave of human materialism all that can come from supersensible knowledge.[7]

The Social Organism is Threefold

Undated Essay

(probably late 1940's)

The Social Organism is Threefold

The social organism has three members; it is threefold. Each of these three members is an independent formation, connected with the others and joined to them in manifold ways. And yet we have to study the social-biological structure of each of these three members separately and according to their own laws.

In studying an organism, we first have to ask what are the units that build it up. The nerve system consists of neurons, the liver of hexagonal liver cells, and the muscles of fibres. What are the units of the social organism? Are they the same for all members, or are there different units for each member?

As everything living consists of cells, so everything social consists of mankind. The cell of the social organism, of the body social, is the single human being who, as a physical-spiritual being, has passed through the Fall, bearing the human bodily form and human individuality.

However, this human cell is never a single independent being able to live in isolation, except in rare cases such as mental illness. Through the mere fact of being human it forms connections to other human beings, other human cells. As far as can be seen, these connections created by the unit for its corresponding social sphere are different for each of the three spheres.

The units which form these members of the social organism are:

—the human personality in the free spiritual life,
—the family in the life of rights,
—the congregation in the economic life.

Each of these members is more than just one human being, more than one human cell. Each of these units is also more than the human cell, for they each have a different ancestry.

The *human personality* goes back to its own ancestor, its Ego which, created once upon a time, moves from one incarnation to the next carrying its own stream of destiny and the development its own karma.

The *family* goes back to the ancestral parents Adam and Eve. It is the family which, especially and specifically bears the bondage of the Fall and takes care of the flowing-on of the blood stream (lineage) and of the powers of heredity.

The *congregation* is a community of single human beings who, out of freedom, confess more and more that neither their own karma, nor their sin-laden body, but something *new* has to work in the social organism. Their ancestor is not their own Self, nor Adam and Eve, but Christ chosen in freedom.

In the *free spiritual life*, and only here, the single human individuality comes to expression. Here, in learning and teaching in schools and universities, in the give and take of art, in religious contemplation, each individual finds the expression of his or her own personal path.

Karma will bring it about that some or many people have the same common endeavour within this framework. They will combine in associations so that they may give expression to this striving. Thus, for example, an anthroposophical society, an association of free artists, a group of people in pursuit of a scientific problem, will form their own associations. But man is free in these associations; he serves himself and his destiny, for he is the successsor of his own ancestor, the Ego once created for him.

In the *life of rights* it is the family which is the determining member. Here father, mother and children form the unit. In the family, sin and the hereditary blood line still prevail. The family ensures the continuance of the human species and gives the single human being the possibility of receiving a body for his earthly existence. The life of rights governs the rights of the family: it orders the rights and duties of each member to the others, the connections between the families, and those of the families and single members to the institutions of both the spiritual and the economic life. The life of rights regulates the income of the breadwinner of the family; it regulates and guards the right of each member of the family to free exercise of religious, scientific and artistic opinions and activities. The family is the guardian of the people and their language, for the building of the Tower of Babel, like the Fall, is preserved through the bond of the family.

In the *economic life* it is the congregation which permeates it more and more. But here one must differentiate between two things: the organisations of the economic life and the church 'parishes', the congregations themselves. The former act so that the latter can ever more unfold their being. The members of the economic organisations are such entities as workshop, factory, shop, farm, mines, fishing boat, means of transport for freight, money (banks) and many others. These form an interlocking organisation which serves not the single human being, but all mankind; not the single nation, but all nations. There are no state boundaries, only the earth as a whole. The earth, as the body of Christ, gives its products—ore, oil, corn, fruit—to the economic life, and man tends, trades and distributes these goods all over the earth. In order that this is done in the right way, a common consciousness is needed. But this consciousness can only be created by the congregation. However, the processes involved in a growing consciousness can only arise when as equals everyone can partake of the most precious goods of the earth—bread and wine—as the true body of Christ; that is, when the congregation gathers round the sacrament and becomes the brotherhood of Christ.

Each single human being should grow more and more into a member of these three units. As a representative of the economic life he is a member of the congregation of the parish. As a member of the family he is a helper in the life of rights. As a bearer of destiny, united with others, he forms the spiritual life.

Man's free individuality, his Ego, forms the substance of the spiritual life. Here *freedom* must prevail. For the created Ego this means: *Ex Deo nascimur*.

The family, as bearer of the body of sin and handing down the heritage, forms the harmonies which live between human spirit and world spirit, between earth matter and spirit substance. Man, as a single individual, must here experience *equality*. For those working in this sphere this means: *In Christo morimur*, for only thus, only through offering their life to Christ, can sin be transformed.

The congregation must become the consciousness of the organism as a whole and the foundation of this consciousness is created by the economic life. Here *fraternity*, brotherliness, prevails. As this is a consciousness in process of evolving, *Per Spiritum Sanctum reviviscimus* resounds through this sphere.

The social organism thereby receives its substance through the individual Egos of human beings living on earth. This is a process similar to that which takes place in the human organism in the marrow of the bones. Here, on earth, red blood corpuscles are created; there, in the spirit, all human Egos were once created by the Godhead.

Human Egos grow into their earthly bodies in the same way as erythrocytes become cells lacking nuclei, in definite stages. Just as the erythrocytes stream into the lung after having completed the physical process of maturing in the bones, so too the human being is born into a family after having completed a process of soul development before birth. As the erythrocyte takes in oxygen, so the newborn child takes in air. From then on the erythrocytes become servants of the metabolism in man's lower organism, while man himself becomes a bearer of the spiritual life. The erythrocytes become carriers of material precipitation; man becomes the bearer of the economic life. The process of maturing in the erythrocytes corresponds to the process of development of the individual Ego in its existence between death and a new birth. The mature red blood corpuscle is without a nucleus; the human individual soul has become ripe for earth life. In the streaming of erythrocytes from marrow to lung, the embryonic process comes into existence; in the breath of the lung birth is fulfilled. As the erythrocyte moves to and fro through the heart, so the child enters and leaves the family.

As the blood streams into each single organ, man can likewise be active in each area of spiritual life. In the kidneys, liver, spleen, etc. he forms the schools, societies and institutions of learning of the free spiritual life.

Man is born into the family. Here right and equality prevail which are the rhythms of our organism.

We are born out of the spirit. Our skull is the image of the earth onto which we descend. The brain within the skull is the fully-developed economic life and in the centre of the brain is the pineal gland which is kept alive by 'the specially delicate substances of our food'. This is a picture of how the congregation is placed within the economic life: like the pineal gland in our brain. The pineal gland is not outwardly active, but creates consciousness. Thus the congregation surrounding the altar should not be outwardly active, but create consciousness within the economic life.

Today the head is the only part in man which carries an awake consciousness. Therefore the congregations of the Christian church on earth should become the bearers of an awake consciousness and thereby the regulators of the social organism. That is their task.

The human Ego enters the world through the human body. Thus the red blood corpuscle enters the bloodstream from the bone marrow.

The Ego is born into the family, receiving the burden of sin through race and family. Thus the erythrocyte receives its task as bearer of the exchange of oxygen and carbon dioxide in the realm of the lung.

In the sphere of the free spiritual life man meets his own creative faculties. Here he works as an eternal, individual being. In like manner the blood flows in each single organ, there meeting two streams; the ordinary, earthly nutrition stream and the cosmic nutrition stream.

Bibliography

The Threefold Structure of the Social Organism

First Lecture:

1: Denkwart Alexander Rüstow. *Freedom and Domination. A historical critique of civilization.* Princeton University Press, Princeton, New York 1980.

2: Rudolf Steiner. *The Threefold Social Order.* GA 23. Anthroposophic Press, New York 1966.

Second Lecture:

1: Rudolf Steiner. *Von Seelenrätseln.* 1917. GA 21. Extract contained in *The Case for Anthroposophy.* Rudolf Steiner Press, London 1970.

Third Lecture:

1: Rudolf Steiner. *Cosmic Memory.* Harper and Row, New York, 1959. (See 3rd essay.)

Fourth Lecture.

1: Karl Jaspers. *The Origin and Goal of History.* Routledge & Keegan Paul, London 1953.

2: Rudolf Steiner. *Ancient Wisdom and the Heralding of the Christ Impulse.* 8 May 1912, Cologne. GA 143. In: *Anthroposophical Quarterly* Vol. 18: no.1, 1973.

3: Rudolf Steiner. *The Foundation Stone*. 25 December 1923–1 January 1924, Dornach. GA 260. Rudolf Steiner Press, London 1979.

Fifth Lecture:

1: Rudolf Steiner. *The Philoosophy of Freedom*. Rudolf Steiner Press, London 1964. GA 4. (Also published under the original title *The Philosophy of Spiritual Activity*. Anthroposophic Press, New York 1984.)

2: Rudolf Steiner. *The Inner Aspect of the Social Question*. 3 lectures, 4 February–9 March 1919, Zurich. GA 193. Rudolf Steiner Press, London 1974. (All quotations from 2nd lecture, 11 February 1919.)

3: ibid.

4: ibid.

5: ibid.

6: ibid.

7: ibid.

8: ibid.

On Community Building.

First Lecture:

1: Johann Valentin Andreae. *The Chymical Wedding of Christian Rosenkreutz Anno 1459*. Trans. E. Cockcroft. Minerva Books, London.

2: Rudolf Steiner. *Rosicrucianism and Modern Initiation*. 6 lectures, 4–13 January 1924, Dornach. GA 233. Rudolf Steiner Press, London, 1982. (See 3rd lecture, 5 January 1924.)

3: ibid.

Second Lecture:

1: Rudolf Steiner. *The Last Address*. 28 September 1924, Dornach. GA 238. Rudolf Steiner Press, London 1967.

2: Rudolf Steiner. *Christianity as Mystical Fact and the Mysteries of Antiquity*. GA 8. 2nd edition. Rudolf Steiner Press, London 1972.

3: Rudolf Steiner. *The Last Address*. 28 September 1924, Dornach. GA 238. Rudolf Steiner Press, London 1967.

4: Rudolf Steiner. *The Creation of a Michael Festival out of the Spirit*. 23 May 1923, Berlin. GA 224. In: *The Festivals and their Meaning*. Rudolf Steiner Press, London 1981.

5: ibid.

6: ibid.

7: ibid.

8: ibid.

9: Rudolf Steiner. *The Michael Impulse and the Mystery of Golgotha*. 2 lectures, 18 and 20 May 1913, Stuttgart. GA 152. Incomplete extract in: *The Festivals and their Meaning*. Rudolf Steiner Press, London 1981.

10: Rudolf Steiner. *The Michael Meditation*. In: *Verses and Meditations*. Rudolf Steiner Press, London 1979.

Third Lecture:

1: Rudolf Steiner. *The Creation of a Michael Festival out of the Spirit*. 23 May 1923, Berlin. GA 224. In: *The Festivals and their Meaning*. Rudolf Steiner Press, London 1981.

2: Rudolf Steiner. *Vom Menschenrätsel* 1916. GA 20. Not available in English.

3: Rudolf Steiner. *Von Seelenrätseln* 1917. GA 21. Extract contained in *The Case for Anthroposophy*. Rudolf Steiner Press, London 1970.

4: Rudolf Steiner. A *Michael Lecture*. 13 January 1924, Dornach. GA 233. In: *The Festivals and their Meaning*. Rudolf Steiner Press, London 1981.

5: Rudolf Steiner. *Knowledge of the Higher Worlds and its Attainment*. GA 10. Rudolf Steiner Press, London 1969.

6: Haeckel. *The Evolution of Man*. 2 vols. 5th Edition. Watts & Co., London 1910.

7: Rudolf Steiner. *Occult Science*. GA 13. Rudolf Steiner Press, London 1969.

8: Rudolf Steiner. A *Michael Lecture*. 13 January 1924, Dornach. GA 233. In: *The Festivals and their Meaning*. Rudolf Steiner Press, London 1981.

9: Rudolf Steiner. *Esoterisches Präludium zu einer exoterischen Behandlung der sozialen Frage*. 2 lectures in: *Geisteswissenschaftliche Behandlung sozialer und Pädagogischer Fragen*. GA 192. Not available in English.

10: König refers here to the new organ for spiritual perception in the human brain formed by the forces of Gabriel. (See 5th lecture, 1 June 1913 in: Rudolf Steiner, *The Occult Significance of the Bhagavad Gita*. 9 lectures, 28 May–5 June 1913, Helsingfors. GA 146. Anthroposophic Press, New York 1984.)

11: Rudolf Steiner. *The Michael Meditation*. In: *Verses and Meditations*. Rudolf Steiner Press, London, 1979. (See also: *The Last Address*. 28 September 1924, Dornach. GA 238. Rudolf Steiner Press, London 1967.)

12: Rudolf Steiner. A *Michael Lecture*. 13 January 1924, Dornach. GA 233. In: *The Festivals and their Meaning*. Rudolf Steiner Press, London 1981.

Man as a Social Being and the Mission of Conscience.

First Lecture:

1: Karl König. *On Community Building.* 3 lectures, 20–30 September 1964 Föhrenbühl.

2: Rudolf Steiner. *The Calendar of the Soul.* 1912. GA 40. *(Various English translations exist, and the reader is advised to examine more than one version.)*

3: Karl König. *Rudolf Steiner's Calendar of the Soul—A Commentary.* 2nd edition, Rudolf Steiner Press, London 1989.

4: Rudolf Steiner. *Social and Antisocial Forces in the Human Being.* 12 December 1918, Bern. GA 186. In: *Anthroposophical Review* Vol.1, Nos. 2 & 3, 1979.

5: ibid.

6: ibid.

7: ibid.

8: Rudolf Steiner. *Study of Man.* 14 lectures, 21 August–5 September 1919, Stuttgart. GA 293. Rudolf Steiner Press, London 1966. (See 8th lecture, 29 August 1919.)

9: Karl König. *The Threefold Structure of the Social Organism.* 5 lectures, 2–30 March 1964, Föhrenbühl and Brachenreuthe. (See 3rd lecture, 22 March 1964.)

10: Rudolf Steiner. *Study of Man.* 14 lectures, 21 August–5 September 1919, Stuttgart. GA 293. Rudolf Steiner Press, London 1966. (See 8th lecture, 29 August 1919.)

11: ibid.

12: Rudolf Steiner. *Das Rätsel des Menschen. Die geistigen Hintergründe der menschlichen Geschichte.* 15 lectures, 29 July–3 September 1916, Dornach. GA 170. Not available in English. (See 14th lecture, 2 September 1916.)

13: Rudolf Steiner. *Anthroposophy and the Social Question*. 1905. GA 34. Mercury Press, New York 1982. (See 2nd essay.)

14: Rudolf Steiner. *Social and Antisocial Forces in the Human Being*. 12 December 1918, Bern. GA 186. In: *Anthroposophical Review* Vol.1, Nos. 2 & 3, 1979.

Second Lecture.

1: Rudolf Steiner. *Man's Being, his Destiny and World Evolution*. 6 lectures, 16–21 May 1923, Christiania (Oslo). GA 226. Anthroposophic Press, New York 1984. (See 2nd lecture, 17 May 1923.)

2: ibid.

3: Rudolf Steiner. *Good Fortune, its Reality and Semblance*. 7 December 1911, Berlin. GA 61. Anthroposophical Publishing Co., London 1956.

4: Rudolf Steiner. *The Course of My Life*. Anthroposophic Press, New York 1986.

Third Lecture:

1: Rudolf Steiner. *Die Mission der neuen Geistesoffenbarung*. 14 June 1911, Vienna. GA 127. Not available in English. (See also: Rudolf Steiner. *Faith, Love, Hope*. 2 lectures, 2–3 December 1911, Nuremberg. GA 130. Steiner Book Centre, Vancouver.)

2: ibid.

3: ibid.

4: ibid.

5: ibid.

6: ibid.

7: Karl König. *The Threefold Structure of the Social Organism*. 5 lectures, 2–30 March 1964, Föhrenbühl and Brachenreuthe. (See 4th lecture, 29 March 1964.)

8: Rudolf Steiner. *Man's Being, his Destiny and World Evolution*. 6 lectures, 16–21 May 1923, Christiania (Oslo). GA 226. Anthroposophic Press, New York 1984. (See 2nd lecture, 17 May 1923.)

9: Rudolf Steiner. *The Foundation Stone*. 25 December 1923–1 January 1924 , Dornach. GA 260. Rudolf Steiner Press, London 1979.

Fourth Lecture:

1: Rudolf Steiner. *The Fifth Gospel*. 7 lectures, 1–6 October 1913, Christiania (Oslo). GA 148. Rudolf Steiner Press, London 1968.

2: ibid.

3: Novalis. *Henry von Ofterdingen*. Frederick Ungar Publishing Co., New York 1964.

Fifth Lecture:

1: Traditional. *The Dream Song of Olaf Åsteson*. Trans. Eleanor C. Merry. Rudolf Steiner Press, London 1988.

2: Rudolf Steiner. *The Gospel of St. Matthew*. 12 lectures, 1–12 September 1910, Berne. GA 123. Rudolf Steiner Press, London 1985. (See 4th lecture, 4 September 1910.)

3: Rudolf Steiner. *The Gospel of St. Luke*. 10 lectures, 15–26 September 1909, Basle. GA 114. Rudolf Steiner Press, London 1975.

4: Rudolf Steiner. *The Occult Significance of the Bhagavad Gita*. 9 lectures, 28 May–5 June 1913, Helsingfors. GA 146. Anthroposophic Press, New York, 1984. (See 5th lecture, 1 June 1913.)

5: Rudolf Steiner. *The Gospel of St. Luke*. 10 lectures, 15–26 September 1909, Basle. GA 114. Rudolf Steiner Press, London 1975. (See 7th lecture, 21 September 1909.)

6: Rudolf Steiner. *The Occult Significance of the Bhagavad Gita*. 9 lectures, 28 May–5 June 1913, Helsingfors. GA 146. Anthroposophic Press, New York, 1984. (See 5th lecture, 1 June 1913.)

7: Rudolf Steiner. *The Christ Impulse and the Development of Ego-Consciousness*. 7 lectures, 25 October 1909–8 May 1910, Berlin. GA 116. Anthroposophic Press, New York 1976. (See 7th lecture, 8 May 1910.)

Reawakening and Resurrection.

First Lecture:

1: Rudolf Steiner. *The Calendar of the Soul*. 1912. GA 40. *(Various English translations exist, and the reader is advised to examine more than one version.)*

Second Lecture:

1: Rudolf Steiner. *From Jesus to Christ*. 10 lectures, 5–14 October 1911, Karlsruhe. GA 131. Rudolf Steiner Press, London 1973. (See 6th lecture, 10 October 1911.)

2: Karl König. *Man as a Social Being and the Mission of Conscience*. 5 lectures, 13 December 1964–6 January 1965, Föhrenbühl. (See 4th and 5th lectures, 27th December 1964 and 3rd January 1965.)

Third Lecture:

1: Rudolf Steiner. *From Jesus to Christ*. 10 lectures, 5–14 October 1911, Karlsruhe. GA 131. Rudolf Steiner Press, London 1973. (See 6th lecture, 10 October 1911.)

2: ibid.

3: Rudolf Steiner. *The Four Sacrifices of Christ.* 1 June 1914, Basle. GA 152. Anthroposophic Press, New York 1981.

4: Rudolf Steiner. *From Jesus to Christ.* 10 lectures, 5–14 October 1911, Karlsruhe. GA 131. Rudolf Steiner Press, London 1973. (See 7th lecture, 11 October 1911.)

5: Rudolf Steiner. *The Gospel of St. Mark.* 10 lectures, 15–24 September 1912, Basle. GA 139. Anthroposophic Press, New York 1986. (See 9th lecture, 13 October 1911.)

6: Rudolf Steiner. *From Jesus to Christ.* 10 lectures, 5–14 October 1911, Karlsruhe. GA 131. Rudolf Steiner Press, London 1973. (See 8th lecture, 12 October 1911.)

7: Rudolf Steiner. *The Four Sacrifices of Christ.* 1 June 1914, Basle. GA 152. Anthroposophic Press, New York 1981. (See also: *The Three Pre-earthly Deeds of Christ.* 7 March 1914, Pforzheim. GA 152. Steiner Book Centre, Vancouver 1976.)

Fourth Lecture:

1: Rudolf Steiner. *Easter: The Festival of Warning. The Event of Damascus and the new Knowledge of the Spirit.* 2nd April 1920, Dornach. GA 198. In: *The Festivals and their Meaning*, Rudolf Steiner Press, London 1981.

2: Rudolf Steiner. *From Jesus to Christ.* 10 lectures, 5–14 October 1911, Karlsruhe. GA 131. Rudolf Steiner Press, London 1973. (See 8th lecture, 12 October 1911.)

3: Rudolf Steiner. *Die geistigen Hintergründe der menschlichen Geschichte. Das Verhältnis des Menschen zum ganzen Universum.* 7 lectures, 21 August–3rd September 1916, Dornach. GA 170. Not available in English.

4: Rudolf Steiner. *The Influence of Spiritual Beings upon Man.* 11 lectures, 6 January–11 June 1908, Berlin. GA 102. Anthroposophic Press, New York 1982. (See 5th lecture, 16 March 1908.)

5: Karl König. *Embryology and World Evolution*. In: *British Homoeopathic Journal* Vol. 57: nos. 1, 2, 3 & 4, 1968 and Vol. 58: nos. 1 & 2, 1969.

6: Rudolf Steiner. *The Influence of Spiritual Beings upon Man*. 11 lectures, 6 January–11 June 1908, Berlin. GA 102. Anthroposophic Press, New York 1982. (See 5th lecture, 16 March 1908.)

7: Rudolf Steiner. *Easter: The Festival of Warning. The Event of Damascus and the new Knowledge of the Spirit*. 2nd April 1920, Dornach. GA 198. In: *The Festivals and their Meaning*, Rudolf Steiner Press, London 1981.